THE LIGHTS OF

A Century of Latin American Writers in Paris

Jason Weiss

Routledge
Taylor & Francis Group
New York London

Published in 2003 by
Routledge
711 Third Avenue
New York, NY 10017

Published in Great Britain by
Routledge
2 Park Square, Milton Park
Abingdon, Oxon OX14 4RN

Copyright © 2003 by Taylor & Francis Books, Inc.
Routledge is an imprint of the Taylor & Francis Group, an informa business

All rights reserved. No part of this book may be reprinted or reproduced or utilized in any form or by any electronic, mechanical or other means, now known or hereafter invented, including photocopying and recording or in any information storage or retrieval system, without permission in writing from the publisher.

Library of Congress Cataloguing-in-Publication Data
Weiss, Jason, 1955–
   The lights of home : a century of Latin American writers in Paris / Jason Weiss.
   p. cm.
   Includes bibliographical references and index.
   ISBN 0-415-94012-5 (alk. paper)—ISBN 0-415-94013-3 (pbk. : alk. paper)
   1. Authors, Spanish American—20th century—Homes and haunts—France—Paris. 2. Spanish American literature—20th century—History and criticism. 3. Spanish American literature—Appreciation—France. 4. Paris (France)—Intellectual life—20th century. I. Title.
PQ7081.3 .w45 2002
840.9'868044361—dc21   2002021337

Contents

LIST OF ILLUSTRATIONS • VII

PREFACE • IX

Introduction: The Lure of Paris • 1

1. The Voyage Out (1893–1939) • 15

The French Reception • 41

2. Writers' Beginnings
   *(Gabriel García Márquez, Mario Vargas Llosa,
   Alfredo Bryce Echenique)* • 47

3. Clarifying Sojourns
   (Octavio Paz, Alejandra Pizarnik) • 59

4. Diplomatic Pastures
   (Miguel Angel Asturias, Pablo Neruda, Alejo Carpentier) • 67

Tradition of Pilgrimage: The Dream City • 75

5. Interstitial Spaces
   (Julio Cortázar) • 81

6. Transgressive Gestures
   (Severo Sarduy, Copi) • 95

Outside Looking In: Paris, City of Exiles • 121

7. The Privileged Eye: Writing from Distance
   (Julio Ramón Ribeyro, Juan José Saer) • 137

8. Tsuris of the Margins
   (Luisa Futoransky) • 163

*Living in Another Language:
The Problem of Audience, Community* • 177

9. The Translated Self
    (Edgardo Cozarinsky) • 183

10. New World Transplants: Foreigners in French
    (Eduardo Manet, Silvia Baron Supervielle) • 191

11. Académicien
    (Hector Bianciotti) • 221

Conclusion: The Lights of Home • 235

NOTES • 237

BIBLIOGRAPHY • 267

INDEX • 273

Illustrations

Gallery appears following page 127.

1. Julio Cortázar, Saint-Germain-des-Prés, 1961
2. Alejandra Pizarnik
3. Octavio Paz, early 1960s
4. Mario Vargas Llosa, 1960s
5. Nivaria Tejera, 1971
6. Miguel Angel Asturias
7. Pablo Neruda, Chilean Embassy library, Paris, 1972
8. Severo Sarduy, 1972
9. Alejo Carpentier, Cuban Embassy library, Paris, 1968
10. Gabriel García Márquez, 1970s
11. Julio Ramón Ribeyro, Alfredo Bryce Echenique, 1974
12. Copi, 1980s
13. Juan José Saer
14. Luisa Futoransky
15. Rubén Bareiro Saguier
16. Edgardo Cozarinsky, 1991
17. Hector Bianciotti, 1990s
18. Eduardo Manet
19. Silvia Baron Supervielle

Preface

A few questions about terms must be dealt with at the outset. To begin with, Latin American. On the purely academic front, it might be more accurate to say Spanish American throughout, since the phenomenon of going to live in Paris pertains especially to Spanish-American writers and not so much to Brazilians. There have indeed been some Brazilian writers who spent time in Paris: Jorge Amado, a lifelong visitor, first lived there in the late 1940s when the Communist Party was outlawed in Brazil, and again during the last decade of his life, in the 1990s, he resided in the Marais district with his wife (to escape his fame at home, it was said). But Brazil has tended to be more self-contained throughout its history, and most artists who went abroad or into exile did not stay away long. To say Latin American, however, is to speak with a continental perspective and that is usually my intention. Moreover, Spanish Americans refer to themselves collectively as *latinoamericanos*, which serves to remind people that they come from a quite different culture, or set of cultures, than the Anglo-Americans up north. Where it is appropriate to make national or linguistic distinctions, I do not hesitate, but it is the spirit I wish to track in this work, the spirit of Latin Americans who went off to Paris.

Does Latin America, therefore, include the Caribbean? If only such terms were that easy. As with so much else in the Americas—culture, race, religion, language—these terms overlap. The Spanish-speaking islands have long been considered part of the Caribbean and Latin America, but the coastal areas of the mainland also share that dual quality, partaking of both histories that are at any rate intimately connected. Many Cubans have gone to live in Paris, and inevitably their affinities have shown that they fit comfortably into both groups, while remaining distinct unto themselves. The present study seeks not so much to explore specific national communities in Paris, nor to disentangle allegiances among Caribbeans or Latin Americans, but rather to see how such forces play out in individual writers' experiences.

A final note: Throughout, book titles are in English when the work has been translated, and in their original language, Spanish or French, if not.

x • Preface

I would like to thank the following individuals who have helped with their suggestions, assistance, interest, and overall support: Timothy J. Reiss, Maarten Van Delden, Anne Husson, Jacques Leenhardt, Claude Couffon, Claude Fell, Claude Cymmerman, Tomás Guido Lavalle (who first spoke to me of his time in Paris as a young man in the early 1960s), Irene Devlin-Weiss, Miriam Ayres, Robert Myers, Isaac Artenstein, Mark Weiss, Christian Bourgois, China Botana, Richard Sieburth, Sylvia Molloy, Fernando Aínsa, Orlando Jimeno-Grendi, Ana Becciu, Julio Olaciregui, Gregorio Manzur, Saúl Yurkievich, Alejandro Jodorowsky, Antonio Seguí, and editors at the following journals where some portions of this work originally appeared in different form —Clayton Eshleman (*Sulfur*), Saúl Sosnowski (*Hispamérica*), Lee Smith (*Voice Literary Supplement*), Belkis Cuza Malé (*Linden Lane Magazine*), Ana Nuño (*Quimera*), Eliane DalMolin (*Sites*), Ilan Stavans (*Hopscotch*). I would also like to thank the photographers who were kind enough to allow me to use their portraits of the writers: Jerry Bauer, Baldomero Pestana, Angela Mejias, Antonio Gálvez, John Foley, Jorge Damonte, Tamara Pinco, Denis Roche, Pepe Fernández, Jean François Bonhomme, Ignacio Gómez-Pulido, Daniela Haman.

Introduction
The Lure of Paris

Over the past two centuries Paris has held a unique importance for Latin American writers. At first, like a star on the horizon, it served to guide and inspire the emerging nations of the New World. Later, as Paris grew into the international capital of arts and letters, it became like a second home to successive generations of Latin Americans who made the voyage and took up residence there.

After the colonial era, which ended in the early decades of the nineteenth century for most of the countries, Latin America was naturally drawn toward France. The ideals of the French Revolution, the efforts to establish a democratic republic, as well as its rich intellectual tradition, ensured that France represented the best of modern Europe—in contrast to the closed medieval society of Spain that Latin America had rejected through its struggles for independence. And France was more familiar than the rest of northern Europe, due to the Latin connection through language, education, and religion.

To some degree, the affair was mutual. Despite numerous instances of neglect or misunderstanding, the French were the first foreign culture to appreciate Latin America and its literature; in effect, the French helped bring that literature out into the world. The quality of interest among the French may have been fickle or even facile at times, too eager to find a certain notion of the exotic, but over the long run that interest proved constant enough that gradually Latin American literary activity became more or less integrated into the overall intellectual and artistic scene in Paris.

Of course, Paris has long been an exile's city, and Spanish-American literature in particular was made possible by exile. Most of its important writers spent some significant time living in foreign lands. Whether as a voyage abroad that lasted far longer than anticipated, or as a determined response to untenable political and social circumstances at home, exile enabled the forging of an identity that was at once individual, national, even continental. So that if literature and landscape partly reflect each other, then the Latin American landscape is composed not just of its lands and seas but also of many *distant* mirrors in the hands of its writers. As Luis Harss and Barbara Dohmann noted in the mid-1960s, the Latin American continent "always needed distance and detachment to gain an adequate perspective on itself. Europe was the vantage point. The road to insight . . . led through displacement and uprootedness."[1]

Until recent decades, most Spanish-speaking countries in the Americas lacked the conditions that might sustain writers domestically: sufficient opportunities to publish, an informed readership, and a sophisticated level of critical discourse. As well, the recurring instability of the state, which could be life-threatening, hardly offered a favorable environment. Writers had to go abroad to discover new ideas and gain a sense of the world, but also to meet others from their own continent. Due to the history of colonial dependence, the countries of Latin America communicated less with each other than with the capitals of Europe. Even into the 1960s, as José Donoso observed, writers were often quite unaware of what was being written in neighboring countries, because the books simply were not available.[2] The means of distribution, the lines of contact, still had not been adequately set up whereby writers and readers could really know about each other across the length and breadth of Latin America.[3]

But why did the foreign journeys of so many Spanish-American writers converge in Paris? For one thing, Paris was the only place where such a tradition might develop, due to its singular position culturally and politically. Throughout the nineteenth century, French culture, literature especially, stimulated the discovery of a native culture within Latin America; the twentieth century saw the flourishing of that culture whose very identity was changing—amid increased immigration from Europe and beyond—even as it was being articulated. Given the hybrid or *mestizo* nature of Latin America—and *mestizaje* was an Iberian trait well before the Spanish Conquest, considering seven centuries of Moorish dominion on the Iberian Peninsula—any understanding of the national quickly became an intuition for the international. Writers were thus poised with one foot heading out, as it were, and instinctively they turned toward Europe.

However, the relationship with Europe was complex. It involved a desire for *fraternité* and therefore recognition. But it provoked a mutual questioning, as well. To what degree was the New World like the Old World that engendered it? How were the people different? What was to be learned from Europe's experiment and transformation in the Americas? Those Latin Americans who set out, in what might be called a return voyage of discovery, were embarked on a sort of grappling with history, with both the past and the future. At the same time, the voyage could also be a way to situate oneself in that ongoing encounter between the New World and the Old.

As the countries of Latin America evolved, so did their views of Europe. In the mid-nineteenth century, Argentine educator and later president Domingo F. Sarmiento saw the central challenge for his country as a contest between civilization and barbarism. In Argentina this meant the unifying force of its capital, the port city of Buenos Aires, which alone communicated with Europe, versus the regional fiefdoms of various strongmen in the country's untamed interior. At the time, in the 1830s and 1840s, barbarism had gained the upper hand through the provincial backwardness of Juan Manuel de Rosas's dictatorship, which quickly suppressed the early flourishing of Buenos Aires with its European ways. In the same spirit, Sarmiento lamented the failure of Argentina to capitalize on its abundant rivers, starting with the Río de la Plata, as an ideal means for developing the country by way of commerce, bringing culture and civilization to the inland provinces. Navigable rivers or canals, he wrote, were the "fountain of national growth, the origin of the early celebrity of Egypt, the cause of Holland's greatness, and of the rapid development of North America."[4] Against that legacy he posed the stubborn Spaniard and by extension the land-bound gaucho, who shunned the opportunity of such waterways.

Some three decades after independence, Sarmiento and others of his generation such as Juan Bautista Alberdi and Esteban Echeverría believed that Spanish America must take the next step in its civilization: to progress from the outmoded education it had received from Spain and look instead toward France and England, the most advanced countries in Europe. But some went further in their admiration of Europe, to the point of making the argument a matter of race. The tragic flaw of Spanish Americans, according to Sarmiento, owed to their Spanish heritage and to miscegenation, since the continuum that included the gaucho led to indigenous peoples as well, whom he perceived as obstacles to the civilizing mission. He advocated more immigration from Europe to correct the balance, citing North Americans as a model for keeping the European race pure and having, therefore, a more advanced society. In a like manner, Alberdi maintained that everything that was civilized in the Americas came from Europe; Americans, he insisted, were but transplanted Europeans.[5]

Throughout this period, North American society was often regarded in a way similar to Europe, held up as a model for its industry and progress. Indeed, when the French forces of Napoleon III invaded Mexico in 1863, Europe was eclipsed for a while, even dismissed, in favor of the United States. Yet, by the end of the nineteenth century with the rise of the Latin American bourgeoisie, Europe seemed to have lost none of its glow. On the contrary, as heir to the Greco-Latin classical tradition Europe was elevated to a higher realm, especially when compared to the rampant utilitarianism of the United States.[6] If the barbaric hordes were no longer attacking civilization, wrote the Uruguayan philosopher José Enrique Rodó in 1900, in his influential essay *Ariel*, high culture had to be vigilant nonetheless against a new threat from the north, "the inescapable hordes of vulgarity."[7] At a time when Latin America had started to grow wary of the United States for many reasons—political, economic, and cultural—Rodó was making an aesthetic argument. He invoked Shakespeare's Ariel, from *The Tempest*, to stand for "noble sentiment" and "the sublime instinct for perfectibility," the "spiritual flame." European values of beauty were the lofty ideal to which Latin America should aspire, and most intellectuals agreed that the French had refined these values the most. He derided North American arrogance in imagining it could replace Europe: in the United States, despite all its success and material satisfaction, the spirit of vulgarity knew no bounds. The idealism of beauty, he suggested, did not inspire North Americans, and so his call to Latin American youth was to look elsewhere, to take cues from Europe. "Conquered a thousand times over by the indomitable rebellion of Caliban, inhibited by victorious barbarism . . . Ariel rebounds, immortal."[8]

It was not until after World War I that the earthier, self-taught Caliban began to get his due. In the same decades that Latin American writers and artists were joining the ranks of international modernism, many were also finding ways to give voice to the distinctly non-European, the submerged elements in New World culture. Later, in the 1960s and after, Caribbean writers like Aimé Césaire, Roberto Fernández Retamar, and George Lamming directly invoked Caliban as a revolutionary hero for the postcolonial world, thus redefining him by his eloquent and defiant response to the European aesthetic of Ariel. Clearly, the old ethereal ideals of beauty were no longer enough, not when they ignored the historical dimension. After all, the twentieth century with its two world wars gave ample reminder that barbarism existed at the very heart of Europe.

Mestizaje, then, came to be seen as a harbinger of the future, where all the damage left by colonialism might eventually be redeemed in the formation of new paradigms for humankind. But along the way, the past had to be confronted and assimilated, so that the present could be fully understood. Although Latin America had achieved its political independence in the early nineteenth century, its intellectual emancipation was a more elaborate process that lasted well into the twentieth, as the Mexican philosopher Leopoldo Zea has shown. By the 1960s, therefore, when colonialism came to an end for much of the rest of the world as well as the Caribbean, Latin America was able to find common cause with many countries. What was needed now, wrote Zea, was "a just sharing of sacrifices and benefits" in the world, and a readjustment of foreign interests so that "they will be adapted to the new circumstances that the actions of the West have created." In short, he was calling for a new attitude from Europe and North America, ready or not, because Latin America along with a host of other nations was marching "toward the realization of the kind of world that the most eminent nations pioneered."[9]

But what of the journey to Paris? Speaking in particular about Argentina, David Viñas has sketched out the changing perspective of Paris since the nineteenth century. In the colonial era as for those who fought for independence (declared in 1810), going to Europe was but a continuation of other class privileges. By the next generation, however, the journey was seen from a more practical angle: one went to look and learn, to do one's apprenticeship, to seek models, for the greater benefit of society. In mid-century, Juan Bautista Alberdi, whose writings inspired the Argentine Constitution, went to Europe to study the lessons of civilization; he spent the last half of his life mostly in Paris. Another aspect of the voyage took precedence by the 1880s, when a new generation began to enjoy Europe on a more personal level "as museum, brothel, and boulevard." Thus the *gentleman*, typified by Lucio V. Mansilla after his earlier military adventures at the Argentine frontier, came to Paris as an aesthetic consumer, to contemplate its wonders; in his writings he sought not so much to inform as to impress with his acquired knowledge.[10]

At this point, according to Viñas, "the European journey becomes institutionalized . . . the itinerary turns into a rite. One travels to Europe to be sanctified there and to return *consecrated*." The experience served, in effect, to distance such visitors from their native realm, and on their return they tended to view their country through European values.[11] But to what degree did the situation extend beyond Argentina, that most European of Latin American countries? Julio Ramón Ribeyro has observed that at least fifteen Peruvian writers came to live in Paris in the nineteenth century.[12] In fact, the bias toward Europe was endemic to the upper classes throughout the continent. In Mexico, late in the century, French styles were all the rage among the high society, with the large-scale development of the capital modeled directly after Paris—and that under the dictator Porfirio Díaz, who began his career with Benito Juárez defeating the French occupation, only to end up in Paris, overthrown by the Mexican Revolution. At the same time, France excelled in maintaining its own interests: publishing in Latin America was dominated by French firms up until World War I.[13]

By the onset of the war, notes Viñas, the aesthetic voyage had been followed by its antithesis, a return to the land, to one's cultural roots. The Latin American writers, in their departure from an Old World that was tearing itself apart, sought a kind of purification in precisely New World elements.[14] The new writers who went in the 1920s and 1930s, therefore, were able to deepen the exchange with their European peers to the point that Latin American literature began to gain some respect in Paris. This relation was further developed during the World War II years as many European intellectuals fled to Latin America seeking refuge. Besides, the French had long been aware that some of their great poets were born in Latin America: José Maria de Heredia in Cuba, and Lautréamont, Jules Laforgue, and Jules Supervielle, all in Uruguay.[15] So, when another generation of Latin Americans went there after World War II, the myth of Paris as that distant place where one became a writer was well implanted. The capital of literature was on its way to becoming the capital of Latin American literature, as some dubbed Paris even as recently as 1984.[16]

Still, Paris was always more than a myth for such writers: it was a workshop for experiment, a safe haven that was not without its own perils. In Spanish America the first generation of writers after independence sought to articulate their new identities as separate from their former rulers. The task was fraught with problems. If their language and education were European, they themselves were American: it would take a full century before the implications of that difference were really understood. These writers had no models by which to know themselves; no situation existed that was quite analogous to their own. The United States came the closest perhaps, but its history of settlement and expansion, and its relation to Europe, were too divergent to draw a parallel. There was also the problem of developing an audience at home, not according to the old European tastes prevalent in their societies, but to new, as yet undefined values where this American writing could be appreciated and nurtured.

European romanticism provided the first cue. Pedro Henríquez Ureña described romanticism as "a spiritual revolution that opened to every national or regional group the road to self-expression, to the full revelation of its soul, in contrast with the cold ultrarational universality of academic classicism" that was a colonial remnant from the previous generation.[17] In 1825, the young Argentine writer Esteban Echeverría spent five years in Paris where he became a fervent adherent of romanticism. Back home his first narrative poem in that vein (*Elvira*, 1832) preceded the first recognized product of the Spanish romantic school by a year. His subsequent work celebrated nature and life in Argentina, and soon a whole generation of writers was focusing on national themes; they in turn carried the romantic movement to Uruguay and Chile. In other countries it began independently, though later, often under the influence of Victor Hugo. "As a rule the movement came from France," wrote Henríquez Ureña, which "had become for us the main source or else the channel of modern culture . . . German and English ideas came to us mainly through France."[18]

However, conditions were hardly propitious for the steady development of an artistic tradition in the countries of Spanish America. Political turmoil in the decades following independence prevented the new societies from reaching any immediate stability. Further, the general public had not yet learned to value the efforts of a national culture in the process of creating itself. By the latter part of the nineteenth century, the prosperity of the upper classes enabled many families to spend entire seasons or longer in Paris. They adopted French values as the ultimate barometer of elegance, and imported prestige art products from there. Through this same period the rise of the Parnassian poets (Théophile Gautier, Leconte de Lisle, Charles Baudelaire, Heredia, Paul Verlaine, Stéphane Mallarmé)—partly a response to the romantic movement—shaped a new aesthetic whose influence spread rapidly. Their search for a pure enduring art, elevated beyond the constraints of the quotidian world, struck a sympathetic chord in the writers who came to form the first genuine artistic movement in Spanish America, *modernismo*.

Whereas the writers who preceded them worked in other professions—as lawyers, politicians, educators—the *modernistas* were the first generation of professional writers, dedicated predominantly to their art. The effect of this shift was to be felt for generations, such that sometimes there was a sort of nostalgia for the writer's former influence in society. Many made their living as journalists, which reinforced their mobility, while some filled a series of diplomatic posts: these, and academic appointments in more recent decades, have remained the principal livelihoods for most Spanish-American writers who left their homes. Travel played a greater role in establishing artistic alliances for the *modernistas*, but even with those who didn't move around as much, the focus was away from engagement with the business of their own societies and out toward the poetic distances where a true correspondence of sensibilities might be found. If the impetus came from France, the movement took on a distinct resonance in Spanish America, appearing there more than a decade before its counterpart in Spain arose with the Generation of '98. Even the term itself, *modernismo*, as a concept and a practice, predated its use in Europe.

Modernismo began as a movement of poets, launched by the publication of José Martí's *Ismaelillo* (1882) and Rubén Darío's *Azul* (1888).[19] After years of imbibing French culture at home the new writers felt it imperative to go out and experience these forces by direct encounters—to walk the fabled streets, to meet in person some of the famous names. Paris was the center of the world for them, superseding even its classical origins. The "Paris complex" drew a large proportion of the *modernistas* to at least attempt the journey, as though to be anointed by the true spirit of poetry, and once there many decided to stay. Thus, by the turn of the century, they constituted the first real colony of Spanish-American writers in Paris.[20]

Henríquez Ureña has remarked that there were two periods in *modernismo*. The first lasted until 1896, by which point most of the original proponents had died, while the second eventually merged with other tendencies after 1920. Darío was the sole figure whose career spanned the entire life of the movement.[21] His extensive travels throughout Latin America, in addition to his literary stature, assured the continued focus on Paris among the newer writers. By the first decade of the twentieth century, besides Darío from Nicaragua, those who settled more or less permanently in Paris included: Enrique Gómez Carrillo from Guatemala, Amado Nervo from Mexico, the García Calderón brothers (Ventura, Francisco, José) from Peru, Rufino Blanco Fombona from Venezuela, Enrique Larreta from Argentina, and Francisco Contreras from Chile.[22] Nearly all of them, at one point or another, held diplomatic positions.

Though many moved in predominantly Spanish-speaking circles, some did manage to cultivate a more extensive contact with the French: the now-forgotten Gómez Carrillo became a literary celebrity in Paris, Contreras wrote a regular column "Lettres hispano-américaines" in the *Mercure de France* for over twenty years, Larreta was a frequent visitor to the Comtesse Anna de Noailles' salons.[23]

In addition to journalism and diplomatic assignments, some writers—then as now—found work in French publishing houses, as advisers for the publishers' nascent Spanish-American collections. A few even ended up editing literary or general interest magazines for a while. Sylvia Molloy has cited several examples: Gómez Carrillo was in charge of *El Nuevo Mercurio*, Darío worked on *Mundial Magazine*, and the Argentine writer Leopoldo Lugones, who also spent some time in Paris, was the editor of the politically oriented *La Revue sud-américaine*; after the war, Ventura García Calderón was one of the main editors of *Hispania* and its successor in 1922, *La Revue de l'Amérique latine*.[24]

Paris was valuable to these writers in that it galvanized them, by assimilation and contrast, to find what was truly theirs and to imagine what was yet to be done. Falling under the sway of French styles at that time helped *modernismo* "revitalize the Spanish poetic idiom," as Gwen Kirkpatrick describes the process, through "innovations in meter, rhyme, and syntax, an expansion of subject matter, and a change in the perception of the poetic function."[25] The *modernistas*' rebellion opened up new modes of expression, and in doing so the movement transcended its derivative aspects by setting forth a pattern of change that responded less to Europe than to conditions inherent in their own traditions.

Never, after *modernismo*, did Spanish-American writing draw its inspiration so much from abroad. World War I hastened a tendency already under way—in response to the lofty pretensions of *modernismo*, but also as a result of popular uprisings in Mexico and elsewhere—since the writers began to cast their attention back upon their own resources. With the war, many writers returned to their native lands (Lugones, Darío), although some did stay, even to fight and die for France.[26]

The war, and thus the "failure of Europe as an ideal," gave the newer writers no choice but to forge their values at home, yet after 1918, Paris was more attractive than ever for many of them.[27] Not only did the rate of exchange make it cheaper to live, but Paris was clearly one of the most exciting places for the arts. Besides, after exhausting itself with the war, in the 1920s and 1930s Europe needed an infusion of cultural sparks from beyond its borders. Paris during this period eagerly embraced a whole range of New World styles of music: tango, beguine, Cuban and Brazilian forms, and of course, jazz. Meanwhile, most writers at the time did not come to stay but rather to study and soak in new ideas, to make friendships otherwise unattainable.

It was also a time when the avant-garde, the surrealists in particular, showed a special interest in the genius of indigenous cultures. Many Spanish-American writers there in those years were beginning to explore an integrated aesthetic in their work, honoring the Indian or African component of their national identities. The future Nobel laureate Miguel Angel Asturias, besides frequenting surrealist circles in Paris, studied Maya religion and society at the Sorbonne; he co-translated the Maya sacred book, the *Popol Vuh*, from the French translation into Spanish, while writing his first books there. During the years she was in Paris, as her interest in native folklore began to grow, Lydia Cabrera wrote her first collection of Afro-Cuban stories. Alejo Carpentier, as well, composed a number of Afro-Cuban texts, in the decade he spent there, for musical and theatrical collaborations. Another resident for several stretches of his life was Ricardo Güiraldes, who wrote several books in Paris, including his classic novel *Don Segundo Sombra* (1926), about the last gauchos and life on the pampas. Alfonso Reyes also lived there, on the eve of the war and again in the 1920s. As a Mexican diplomat and one of the foremost intellectuals, he evoked the inherently international vision of Latin American culture and was a pivotal figure in the ongoing dialogues between Spanish-American and European writers—as was Victoria Ocampo in Buenos Aires, also a frequent visitor to Paris—counting among his friends Valery Larbaud and Jules Romains.[28]

The poets in Paris during the 1920s and 1930s were equally diverse. The Chilean Gabriela Mistral, another future Nobel laureate, highlighted indigenous values in her work while widening her concerns to more populist sympathies; in Paris on a diplomatic assignment in 1926–27, she knew Reyes and collaborated with others to make Spanish-American writing better known in France. Another Chilean, Vicente Huidobro, moved in mostly avant-garde circles; cofounder with Pierre Reverdy of the literary journal *Nord-Sud*, Huidobro wrote several books in French and collaborated with Juan Gris, Edgar Varèse, and Hans Arp. Perhaps the only poet of his generation to live out his life there was César Vallejo, who spent most of the 1920s and 1930s in Paris and died young; he eked out a living as a journalist and wrote much of his best verse in that period. Like Darío, he gained little attention from the French while he was there.

Up until World War II the pattern of migrations remained fairly constant.

Most Latin American writers who went to Paris—Ocampo, Huidobro, Teresa de la Parra, among them—were from the upper classes and so could afford the journey. Despite their numbers between the wars, the writers overall were regarded by the French cultural establishment as exotic specimens. Only gradually, due to the interest of Larbaud and others, did the French take to translating their work; still, this recognition came well in advance of that from other countries like the United States. At the same time, an active network evolved —organizations, publishing houses, literary journals—that kept the Latin American literary community more or less thriving in Paris. However, after a certain stretch of time abroad, nearly all the writers returned to Latin America. Paris might be important for a writer's itinerary, but it was better not to stay too long. Indeed, the few elder figures who spent their whole adult lives in Paris, like Gómez Carrillo, who had arrived at the turn of the century, were seen by younger Latin American writers as passé, out of touch with their origins, at best a curiosity.

In the half-century since the war, the Latin American writers' experience of Paris has altered and grown more complex. It was during the postwar period that Latin American literature fully achieved world status, in no small part by way of its reception in Paris (aided by Roger Caillois's Croix du Sud series at Gallimard, starting with the publication of Jorge Luis Borges' *Fictions* in 1951). But while the lure of Paris remained strong—due to the tradition of previous generations who went there, as well as the continuing influence of French literature—by the 1980s, this route of pilgrimage had lost its primacy. Other cities such as Barcelona, New York, and Mexico City attracted writers with new opportunities for work and publishing. Also, with the return of democratic government throughout Latin America, fewer writers felt compelled to go abroad. Nonetheless, many Latin American writers who arrived in the 1950s or 1960s, and even more recently, continued to stay in Paris as long-term residents. These writers had learned to use their edge as foreigners to develop a critical engagement with both their adopted home and the New World cultures from which they came.

This book is concerned primarily with such writers, the long-term residents over the past half-century, who spent most of their adult lives in Paris. For each writer, the journey was anything but predictable and it played out in their work in numerous ways. One could say that politics hovered always in the background of their experience; yet few, when they left, were personally threatened by events in their native lands. Rather, the political and social atmosphere tended to make living there hazardous to one's health. In Argentina, Peru, Cuba, and other countries, whether or not a dictatorship was currently in power, many artists felt the need to go look elsewhere, far away. At any rate, the choice of exile—in an era when there were both more independent nations in the world and also more exiles—was barely the beginning of their trajectory. And some writers did not even choose: they came to Paris to stay awhile and then kept on staying.

What mattered was that Paris was familiar terrain, either as cultural habit or as concrete reference to specific people and ideas, specific places. In addition, since the 1960s, Paris was growing more interested in Latin America. This was due to two factors at least: the new Latin American literature (including much more than the famous Boom of the big novelists), and the Cuban Revolution. The Cuban cause and the prospect of revolution elsewhere in Latin America rallied French intellectuals for a decade, and primed them for later popular movements in Chile and Nicaragua. Indeed, sometimes literature and revolution got mixed together too much, by French and Latin Americans alike. But most writers, even as exiles, were not overtly political.

Perhaps most striking about the Latin American writers who settled in Paris during the postwar decades is the high degree of individuality they achieved. Collectively they belonged to no school or movement or theoretical tendency. Exile was a way of carving out one's own space in the world, beyond the usual markers of belonging. In the end, it made little difference what discomforts the writers might have left behind or what they thought they were going to in Paris: the transformation of experience into literature, through memory and imagination, remained a personal process. Certainly there were shared conditions among some writers—national origin, sexual orientation, political or aesthetic outlook—but these had limited influence in determining the kind of writing that resulted.

The present study, which does not pretend to be exhaustive, proceeds first by a series of preludes. An overview of the earlier half of the twentieth century focuses on ten writers and the years they spent in Paris. Their specific works produced during that time are of less concern than the general scope of their activities, but for those who were working journalists—Vallejo, Asturias, Carpentier—attention is paid to their choice of subjects, how they regarded their various encounters and how such work fed into their writing. Shifting toward the latter half of the century, consideration is then given to the French reception of Latin American literature, above all as reflected in Caillois's efforts. What follows, after, are three short chapters that recount the experiences of some major literary figures at the time they lived in Paris, early or late in their careers.

The various investigations into the writers who have been long-term residents are grouped into three particular angles or stages of the voyage that is exile. Such angles are not meant to be mutually exclusive; instead, they highlight different aspects of the experience, as seen in the work, even if they inevitably overlap. The first perspective traces what could be called the thrust outward, the impulse to explore a space *in between* (Julio Cortázar) or else *beyond* cultures, borders, limits (Severo Sarduy, Copi). Location, even identity, are thus fluid, hard to pin down, and the creative consciousness thrives in the absence of strict definitions. The second grouping concerns the outsider's standpoint, both those who turn the distance to advantage by writing of the place from which they came (Julio Ramón Ribeyro, Juan José Saer) and those, conversely, who suffer the discomforts of the margins regarding the place where they have settled (Luisa Futoransky). The third angle comes closest to assimilation, which is impossible in France, as the writer Julia Kristeva and others have observed. Still, the foreign artist, even working in an adopted tongue, occupies a role unto himself, with unique powers of access (Edgardo Cozarinsky). All the same, those who have made the transition from Spanish to write in French ultimately reveal and even celebrate their foreign origins, whether by the very subjects chosen (Eduardo Manet), a fascination with the process of the voyage (Silvia Baron Supervielle), or a fervent devotion to French literary style which, no matter the success achieved, ends up leading back to one's sources as a Latin American (Hector Bianciotti). Whether or not writing in French can make a foreigner into a French writer, the writers themselves never forget where they started out.

1

The Voyage Out (1893–1939)

The young Nicaraguan poet **Rubén Darío** (1867–1916) had long been a partisan of Paris by the time he visited in 1893. "I had dreamed of Paris ever since I was a boy, to the point that, when I said my prayers, I prayed to God that he wouldn't let me die without seeing Paris."[1] Already a celebrated writer, veteran traveler, and experienced journalist, Darío was on his way to Buenos Aires to take up a post as consul general for Colombia, via New York and Paris, where he stayed for several months.

When he landed at the Saint-Lazare station in Paris, he wrote, "I thought I was treading on sacred ground."[2] Right away he set out on his "conquest" of the city, first looking up Enrique Gómez Carrillo, whom he had encouraged earlier in Guatemala to go to Paris. By now, Gómez Carrillo had been living there for a year and knew his way around literary circles—he spent the rest of his life in Paris, for more than thirty years writing his *crónicas*, which were read throughout Spanish America.

Among Darío's greatest desires was to meet Paul Verlaine. One night he found Verlaine, a heavy drinker, at the Café d'Harcourt surrounded by his acolytes. A friend introduced him. "In bad French I mumbled all my devotion and concluded with the word glory. . . . Who knows what might have happened that afternoon to the unfortunate maestro; the fact is that, turning to me, and without ceasing to strike the table, he said in a low resonant voice: '*La gloire! La gloire! Merde, merde encore!*'" Darío thought best to withdraw from the table, hoping to find him in better shape another night, but Verlaine was only worse.[3]

Much of the innovation in Darío's writing derived from his reading of French authors. He made use of the French metrical influence to freshen Spanish-language verse and admired the work of Victor Hugo as well as Catulle Mendès, whom he glimpsed often in Paris later. Among other writers he was friendly with on his initial visit was Jean Moréas, one of the symbolist poets; the two would go wandering about all night talking and drinking, to end up at dawn for a last round at Les Halles.

Darío always remained nostalgic for the bohemian Paris he first encountered. He returned in 1900, to cover the Exposition Universelle in a series of articles for the Argentine newspaper *La Nación*, with the intention of settling there for good. Once again he was dazzled by Paris, and the full-blown fantasy of the exposition elicits all "the violins and trumpets of [his] lyricism." Every style of architecture from the world over seems contained there, visited by multitudes of people equally diverse, and though Yankees and barbarians invade the city with their dollars, "the atmosphere of Paris, the light of Paris, the spirit of Paris are inconquerable, and the ambition of [every man] who comes to Paris is to be conquered."[4] At the start of his long residency there, nearly fifteen years, Darío was learning to view the city with more reserve. And in case he never did achieve the prominence he hoped for there, it was still a beautiful place to live out one's life, like Oscar Wilde in his final days, whom Darío met in a bar on the Rue de Rivoli soon after his arrival.[5]

In fact, Darío was far less successful in France than he was in Spanish America and Spain. Though he did have friends among French writers, his work was slow to attract the notice of French critics. "I have always been a foreigner among these people," he concluded in a piece from 1911, going so far as to suggest that Parisians have never really been interested in foreigners and that every writer arrives with the same youthful illusions, only to be disappointed. "I wrote things that were more 'Parisian' before coming to Paris than during the time I've been living in Paris."[6]

The longer he dwelled there, the more his verse looked toward American references and tones. Notwithstanding his pessimism about intellectual life in his own continent, he came to feel doubtful about his spiritual home, whose "society is wasting away, albeit beautifully, but wasting away in an exquisite moment of the world."[7] Yet he knew how difficult it was to leave. As he wrote in 1912, "Away from Paris one suffers the Paris sickness.... There is a sort of witchcraft in the divine and infernal city that takes hold of you and never lets go."[8]

Mostly, Darío worked as a journalist in Paris, and held occasional diplomatic assignments for the Nicaraguan government. He wrote abundantly for

La Nación—travel pieces, social sketches, cultural commentary—while continuing to develop as a poet (notably *Cantos de vida y esperanza*, 1905). His generation was the first to denounce imperialism as it affected Latin America, notes Octavio Paz, and though Darío was mostly apolitical, living in Paris where his own culture almost didn't count made him more conscious of the continent he'd left behind.[9]

Despite all his activity, Darío had a difficult time making ends meet. In 1911, he agreed to edit *Mundial Magazine*—a new monthly journal in Spanish for a largely Spanish American audience—financed by two businessmen brothers from Uruguay, who hoped to capitalize on the fame of the great poet to make their venture work. His friendships among the *modernistas* and modern Spanish writers stood him well, for Darío assembled a solid and consistent journal that lasted forty issues, until the middle of 1914. Among his contributors, Gómez Carrillo wrote a theater column, Amado Nervo contributed stories and poems, Ventura García Calderón wrote a number of Paris chronicles, José Enrique Rodó sent in several essays from Montevideo, and even the Mexican painter and precursor to the muralists, Doctor Atl, wrote a few pieces on Mexico. Darío himself often published several of his own pieces in each issue.[10]

Mundial was a success, though Darío knew he was being exploited for his efforts. Still, in 1912, he went on a tour to promote the magazine, through Spain, Portugal, and South America. The strain of the journey and Darío's failing health caused him to end the tour in Buenos Aires. On his return to Paris late in the year, a banquet was given in his honor. Besides the Latin American writers attending, at the Café Voltaire in the Place de l'Odéon, the French writers included: Catulle Mendès, Jean Moréas, Remy de Gourmont, Paul Fort, André Gide, and Guillaume Apollinaire. In any case, Darío had become quite disillusioned in his dealings with the magazine's owners and in his position as a writer there, and the banquet couldn't change that. He struggled on for nearly two years more with the magazine, and late in 1914 he embarked on another trip to Latin America, at a friend's behest who wanted him to go on a peace mission, lecturing about the war at each stop. He died early in 1916 back in Nicaragua. Later that year a monument was built to honor him in Paris, where it still stands in the Square de l'Amérique Latine, out toward the edge of the city in the 17th arrondissement: Mallarmé, Mendès, and Moréas have their own small streets named after them nearby.

• •

The Argentine writer **Ricardo Güiraldes** (1886–1927) made five trips to Paris in his life and although none of the visits lasted more than a few years, each was crucial to his career as an artist. He was born in Buenos Aires to a wealthy landowning family that settled in the outskirts of Paris the following year—as for many such families, it was important to expose the children to French culture. His earliest memories were of Paris, and from the time he could speak he was equally fluent in French.

Returning to Argentina in 1890, he grew up mostly on the family's *estancia*, their cattle-raising estate about seventy miles from the capital. He later found his mission as a writer in that terrain, to speak for the gaucho who "is by nature the son of the pampa."[11] Güiraldes came of age during the second wave of *modernismo*, in the wake of Darío's residency in Buenos Aires in the 1890s. By his mid-teens, most of his favorite authors were French. Finally, in 1910, attracted by all he had read, he set sail for Europe.

That year he stated his objectives as a writer: literature "must be as pure as possible—get rid of all artifices that are foreign to it and let it stand on its own merits."[12] In his desire to write concisely on specifically Argentine material, he was moving beyond his *modernista* predecessors. Before he reached Paris, during a brief stay in Granada, he sketched out a story that would develop into his first novel, *Raucho* (1917). The title character is an Argentine prodigal son who goes to Paris where he makes the rounds of the city's nightlife, falls for one woman and then another, only to dissipate in a downward spiral of drugs and drinking until he is rescued by his brother and brought home to Argentina. Güiraldes was eager to confront the reality of Paris after writing this sketch, to see how it differed.[13]

He himself ended up making the rounds of Parisian high society on that trip, where he was apparently quite popular. But he did settle down and for about a year he concentrated on writing, living in a sculptor friend's atelier and beginning three books that he would subsequently complete in Argentina. However, toward the end of 1912, longing for his native pampa, he decided to return home.

When his first books appeared in 1915, despite the Argentine subjects of his poems, his formal innovations shocked the few critics who bothered to comment. After the war, Güiraldes sought a more favorable environment for his writing, so he and his wife departed for Paris in the middle of 1919. Prior to leaving, he read *A. O. Barnabooth*, by Valery Larbaud, whom he recognized as a kindred spirit, inhabiting the difficult but fruitful space between America and Europe, though coming from the French side. He considered Barnabooth "the synthesis of the man of our time, with its ideology, its lyricism, its sensuality, its atmosphere." Larbaud's techniques to contain all this were a welcome discovery and became his introduction to contemporary writing in France.[14]

The two writers became friends, and through Larbaud he was introduced to the writers who often met at the Maison des Amis des Livres, Adrienne Monnier's bookshop on the Rue de l'Odéon in the Latin Quarter. These included Léon-Paul Fargue, Jules Romains, Philippe Soupault, and Francis de Miomandre, who was to translate many Spanish-American writers. Larbaud encouraged him to seek what was most authentic in himself, his own Argentine identity, and he was the first to recognize the importance of Güiraldes' work in an article for the *Nouvelle Revue Française* in July 1920.

That year, beset by a wave of nostalgia for Argentina, Güiraldes embarked on a book that had long tempted him, *Don Segundo Sombra*. The title character was based on an old gaucho who had settled to work on his family's estate when he was a boy, and who still lived there; the boy who follows the gaucho, learning the life of the pampa, was drawn from Güiraldes' own persistent dreams for himself. After writing the first ten chapters, he set it aside and resumed an earlier project, but by the end of the year he returned home to work on his novel.

He intended to return to Paris the following spring, but instead went traveling into the interior of Argentina to do research. He saw that here was the material for a new literary output that need not imitate Europe, though he knew of no one yet producing such work. At last, in the spring of 1922, he departed for Paris again, remaining in Europe only until December while he finished another book. Güiraldes was celebrated by Larbaud and other friends, and frequented by younger writers, as well. Sylvia Molloy points out that his presence in Paris effectively contributed to the awareness of Latin American literature in France; certainly he helped deepen Larbaud's knowledge.[15]

Back home, frustrated by the unfriendly literary environment of Buenos Aires, he was eventually sought out by a group of younger writers, including Jorge Luis Borges, who championed modern innovations in the arts and a truly Argentine sensibility in writing. Güiraldes eagerly supported their cause, and it was through his friendship with this new generation that he became recognized in Argentina as an important literary figure.

Early in 1925, he picked up *Don Segundo Sombra* again and worked on it through the rest of the year. During that time, though, he was struck down with Hodgkin's disease. In his race against death he managed to finish the book in the spring of 1926, and when it was published some months later he knew his first great success, in Argentina as in Europe, starting with Leopoldo Lugones' laudatory review in *La Nación*.

The following spring, in 1927, he embarked on his final trip to Paris, to see old friends and to consult the best doctors for his illness. He looked forward to this other homecoming, knowing it might be the last, as he wrote to Larbaud in January: "It moves me to think of it. I shall arrive as always ... with new hopes and a whole field of undefined possibilities regarding my soul ... this soul that keeps taking up more space each time ... I think of the roads of sweet France and of the little restaurants and the special form of the sidewalks in Paris and of the smell of a certain neighborhood and of that intelligence that seems to reside in everything in the city, millions of times reflected upon by those who came before us. I am going to lose myself there among everyone."[16] In Paris, and during a summer visit to the French Pyrenees, Güiraldes worked on his last books, though the doctors could not help him. That October he died in Paris. Many friends attended the funeral, including Jules Supervielle—another literary confidant—and Henri Michaux. The following month his remains were shipped back to Argentina.

• •

Alfonso Reyes (1889–1959) first arrived in Paris in late August of 1913, at a crucial moment in his life: personal tragedy and the tumult of the revolution had made it difficult for him to remain in Mexico. He chose to remove himself awhile and accepted an appointment as second secretary to the Mexican legation in Paris. At the start of a long diplomatic career, he did not live again in his native land for another quarter-century.

At first Reyes felt lonely in Paris, convinced that the French wouldn't open up to foreigners. Occasionally he saw Diego Rivera, whom he had known in Mexico, though he did not share the painter's current excitement for futurism. Pedro Henríquez Ureña, his most consistent correspondent, urged Reyes to stop worrying about Mexico and fill himself with Europe.[17] Still, Paris enchanted him even in its simple pleasures.

He was thorough in getting to know the city, taking long walks each morning, book in hand—consulting Balzac or Hugo, or else a tourist guide. Sometimes he also went to study the Mexican collections in the big libraries. He found Paris a dirtier, dustier city than those he knew in the New World, with fewer creature comforts like heat and running water in many apartments. He complained in letters of the drudgery and stupidity of his job, hoping to be spared a diplomatic career after all. Confusion reigned at the office, reflecting the situation in Mexico between Victoriano Huerta's supporters and those who preferred Venustiano Carranza's rebellion. Reyes was loyal to Huerta, but without enthusiasm. The large French investment in Mexico, built up over decades, was now at risk: much of the legation's work consisted of reassuring the French that their interests were safe.

Reyes was surprised to discover the degree of ignorance concerning Mexican and Latin American culture in Paris. It wasn't for lack of exposure: the roster of diplomats there included an impressive array of writers—Enrique Larreta from Argentina, Alcides Arguedas from Bolivia, Luis de Souza Dantas from Brazil. The Argentine poet Leopoldo Lugones was also in Paris that year, at the height of his fame, to launch his *Revue sud-américaine* with the support of Georges Clemenceau and Jean Jaurès.

Soon Reyes began to frequent the weekly gatherings at the García Calderón home. Ventura García Calderón introduced him to the two publishing houses specializing in Latin American writers, Veuve Bouret and Garnier, where Gómez Carrillo first worked when he arrived.[18] He became friendly with Supervielle, and also Jean Aubry who brought him to Chez Fast, a bar and bookstore favored by Latin Americans. He met Apollinaire as well, and in the company of Rivera and another Mexican painter, Ángel Zárraga, he visited artists in Montmartre and Montparnasse—André Lhote, Amedeo Modigliani, and the Japanese painter Fujita. Reyes became an enthusiast of the cinema and often went to the theater, especially the Vieux Colombiers with Jacques Copeau's adventurous work. Somehow, in the midst of all this, he even managed to write: poems, stories, essays, and correspondence.

Around the time that war broke out in August 1914, Carranza took power in Mexico and fired all diplomatic personnel. The only recourse for Reyes was to go south with his family to Spain. He remained in Madrid for a decade, translating and writing, and eventually regained the post he had held at the Mexican legation there. In 1923, he visited Paris to give a talk on the evolution of Mexico, and saw a rehearsal of Igor Stravinsky's *Noce*. Through Jules Romains he became friends with Adrienne Monnier and frequented her shop, where he first got to know Saint-John Perse and Paul Valéry. He also began a long correspondence with Valery Larbaud at that time. The same year he wrote *Ifigenia cruel*, "his most perfect poetic work," according to Octavio Paz, "the symbol of a personal drama and the poet's response to it"—the death of his father and his own refusal to seek revenge, achieving the freedom to say no to destiny, to the laws of blood and family.[19]

Early in 1924 he left Madrid, anticipating a ministerial post in Buenos Aires, only to end up being named minister to Paris under the new government of Plutarco Elías Calles. Since his previous stay Reyes had matured as a writer and won many distinguished friends. To celebrate his appointment, the *Revue de l'Amérique latine* organized a banquet for 200 people honoring Reyes in March 1925. Larbaud had just published in the same review an article praising Reyes and commending him in his role as cultural liaison between the two countries.[20]

Larbaud well knew the difficulties facing Latin American writers in their encounters with Europe. His friend Gonzalo Zaldumbide, Ecuadoran minister to Paris at the time, had written a decade earlier of the "vicissitudes of uprootedness," regarding Rubén Darío, and the tragedy lived by such writers who develop European tastes—they suffer from a "double bind," becoming foreigners not only in Europe but in their own countries as well, where the literary tradition can no longer accomodate them.[21]

Reyes was lucky this time in Paris with his first lodging, which happened to be the very apartment on the Rue Hamelin where Marcel Proust had lived the last three years of his life. He moved in temporarily, on November 18, 1924, two years to the day after Proust's death. He often questioned the concierge about Proust, which helped inform his second essay on *A la recherche du temps perdu* in 1927; now published in its entirety, Reyes found the work disturbing "because it puts in doubt the very notion of moral progress."[22] Through Proust he grew curious about what remained of the aristocracy in the postwar era. He became friendly with a few people who had known Proust, such as Madame de Clermont-Tonnerre and Boni de Castellane. Castellane's insensitivity to other cultures, his "French indifference," contributed to Reyes' disillusionment about the supposed superiority of that aristocracy.[23]

Eventually settling in a *hôtel particulier* in the Passy district, Reyes and his wife entertained often. They soon made a habit of receiving friends for Sunday tea, where they listened to music and recitations. Frequent visitors included Supervielle, Romains, Miomandre, Adrienne Monnier, French writer/translator Jean Cassou, Salvadoran caricaturist Toño Salazar, Uruguayan painter Pedro Figarí, and Cuban writer Mariano Brull. His diplomatic activities brought him new friendships and strengthened old ones. He was also among the few Latin American diplomats to frequent the new Soviet embassy. As an extension of his professional duties, Reyes maintained his connections to the academic milieu, attending receptions and conferences at the French university. In this regard, he helped found the Collège Mexicain at the new Cité Universitaire in the south of Paris.

Reyes did not have much time to write, although he did publish three books of poems and essays during his few years in Paris. But time and again Reyes proved himself in his official role. He worked hard to encourage French investment, and fostered many cultural and commercial exchanges. When at last the French responded with new money, Mexico was able to resume payment of its foreign debt in 1926. The previous summer Reyes also reestablished diplomatic relations with England, which had withdrawn its ambassador after an incident where bandits seized and pillaged English property in Mexico. His grand objective, however, was to engineer Mexico's entry into the League of Nations. Despite many complications, he had nearly accomplished the task by the time he was named ambassador to Argentina in 1927. In March of that year he was named a commander of the Legion of Honor, as his father had been, and a week later he and his family left France.

• •

Like many of their peers, **Teresa de la Parra** (1889–1936) and **Lydia Cabrera** (1900–1991) drew closer to their native lands by going to Europe. Both produced important work there that brought them back to their first home: Parra with her novel, *Mama Blanca's Memoirs* (1929), and Cabrera with *Cuentos Negros* (1936). But it was among the French that they first found recognition.

The two women first met in 1924, when Parra's ship—coming from France and bound for Caracas—docked in Havana; her first novel, *Ifigenia*, had been published in Paris earlier that year. Cabrera told her how she was working to go to Paris to paint and study art. Parra encouraged her and said to look her up when she got there. In the spring of 1927 they met again by chance, shortly after Cabrera's arrival in Paris, when she spotted Parra in a hotel restaurant. They resumed their friendship from then on, as Parra became her mentor and companion.[24]

Teresa de la Parra was born in Paris, to an upper-class Venezuelan family distantly related to Simón Bolívar; at the time, her father briefly held the post of consul general to Paris. Her early childhood was spent on an old sugarcane estate outside of Caracas—that experience became the basis for *Mama Blanca's Memoirs*, written in Paris thirty years later. As a young woman in the strict Catholic society of Caracas that was still semicolonial, she felt the social and cultural restraints common to her era. She soon understood that she wanted to write, and fended off notions of marriage and other conventional choices for women. Paris was not just the measure of the culture she aspired to, but also a place to be whatever she would be, outside of all that Caracas was for her. Only she had to write *Ifigenia*—about an independent woman educated in Paris—to get there, which was a culminating gesture for her before breaking away at last.

In the summer of 1923, the same year that César Vallejo and Miguel Angel Asturias set sail, she boarded the ship for Paris with the manuscript in hand. Two of her sisters already lived there with their husbands, and her mother, as well, came for long visits. Parra intended to submit her novel to the annual competition for Spanish-American novels offered by the prestigious publishing house Franco-Ibero Americana. Out of 300 entries, hers was chosen; by then, a year after she arrived, an extract was due to appear in French translation. Her book was eagerly supported by prominent Latin American writers in Paris, such as Gonzalo Zaldumbide, with whom she kept up a close friendship, and Ventura García Calderón. Among the French, her biggest supporter was Francis de Miomandre, who eventually translated both her novels as well as Cabrera's *Cuentos negros* and Asturias's *Leyendas de Guatemala*. Despite the praise and as if to confirm her departure, the press in Venezuela and Colombia attacked her for writing a protagonist who was too independent and who set a bad example for properly brought up young ladies.

By the time she ran into Cabrera again, Parra was a more seasoned woman who had grown ambivalent to her success. Besides, the book she was writing just then took her back, past the mixed press in her native land, to the time when she lived on a country estate unmoved by the world outside. Cabrera, in turn, was eager to know Paris, and she arrived with plans for a museum of reproductions in Cuba. The project, inspired by the Trocadero, was sanctioned by President Gerardo Machado, who was a neighbor and friend of her family. To the end of her days she maintained that Machado was the best president Cuba ever had, despite the popular resistance against him; because of his mounting political troubles, the museum was never built.[25] Similarly, through ties of class, Parra's family was friendly with Venezuelan dictator General Juan Vicente Gómez. Both women were basically apolitical, preferring the tyranny of such men in power, if need be, to the disorder that would likely follow. They continued to reassure each other about their views, but Parra especially found it more and more difficult to accept the violent news she was hearing.

Cabrera, who first visited Paris at the age of five, studied at the Ecole du Louvre and specialized in Oriental cultures. For two years she was an active painter, but in 1929, deciding they were really quite bad, she burned all her canvases except two that her concierge had requested. She rented an atelier in the middle of Montmartre with a sweeping view of the city, and her old neighborhood still retained its village charm; many artists lived nearby, such as the painter Maurice Utrillo across the street.[26] She made many friends in Paris: Asturias used to visit her, and she knew the poets O. V. de L. Milosz and Léon-Paul Fargue, and the Caribbean scholar Alfred Métraux. Moreover, she and Parra saw each other often. Paris was certainly the right place for Cabrera, as she recalled in Miami fifty years later: "Nowhere have I felt better, happier, than in Paris, which is a unique place but has the drawback that when you've lived there and you have to leave, you feel an exile even in your own country and you long for it. . . . Teresa loved Paris like I did, she told me she wouldn't have lived anywhere else."[27]

It was through her studies of Buddhist art that Cabrera "discovered Cuba by the shores of the Seine," as she often described it. She was studying the iconography of Borobudur, the temple in Java, when she chanced upon a bas-relief that showed a woman with some tropical fruit on her head. "I thought: But isn't this Cuba! And of course, with the distance that illusive memory had grown inside of me, that sort of nostalgia, unconscious at the time, that one feels away from one's own country. I kept discovering or better, rediscovering, what can never be seen from up close. Teresa as well experienced this process, her letters speak of it, a nostalgic memory that makes you see with a new light what was already there, what you were familiar with from before, but it had gone unnoticed."[28] For Cabrera, however, the journey entailed a further turn in that it also propelled her toward writing. The bas-relief made her think precisely of an image from the African presence in Cuba, and this combined with tendencies that were in the air—Asturias working on the Mayan tales of his *Leyendas*, even the French vogue for black culture—to remind Cabrera what she'd been hearing since childhood. She recalled the Afro-Cuban tales that servants at home used to tell, and this rediscovery opened a world for her.

But it was several years before she began to write. Parra encouraged her to do so, even after going off to live at a sanatorium in Leysin, Switzerland. Cabrera sought to entertain her friend with these Afro-Cuban tales and passed them on to her as she wrote them; Parra responded with continued enthusiasm and interest. *Cuentos negros* did not appear as a book until 1936, a month before Parra's death from tuberculosis—as if her passing had released them into the air. The book was dedicated to Parra. The French translation came out first (the Spanish-language edition appeared only in 1940 in Havana), and its publication occurred quite by chance: Cabrera ran into Miomandre one day, they got to talking about black culture, and she mentioned that she had a series of stories she wrote for Parra; he asked to see them, liked them, passed them on to Paul Morand, who bought the book for Gallimard. From there, a point that traced all the way back to her ties to Parra, a full career of books came forth, both fiction and folklore, practically pioneering—along with her brother-in-law Fernando Ortiz—the field of Afro-Cuban study.

Cabrera believed in the enduring friendship she shared with Parra. "I think now," she remarked toward the end of her life, "that my friendship with Teresa was a blessing from heaven for me. In her I felt I had a friend, for her understanding, and at the same time a mother, for her kindness."[29] But the younger woman showed her own kindness. In 1932, Parra checked into the sanatorium and for the next four years Cabrera spent most of that time living next door to her. She did make periodic trips back to Paris, but gave up her atelier in 1934 when she understood that Parra would not get better. They spent the final year in Madrid, even as Cabrera worried and planned for the approaching civil war. She returned to Paris afterward, but left for Cuba in 1938.

• •

Like Güiraldes, her compatriot, **Victoria Ocampo** (1890–1979) traveled to Paris many times. She too came from a rich Argentine family, the oldest of six sisters; they grew up surrounded by servants and tutors and, above all, a steady ambience of European culture. In every decade she visited France, never staying for more than a year or two, but during the long intervals between visits her devotion to French literature remained constant.

Each trip marked a significant turn in her life, starting in 1896 when she was six years old. Her family went to tour Europe for a year, departing in grand style aboard a German steamer with her great aunt, servants, many trunks, and —so the children could have fresh eggs and milk—live chickens and two cows. They spent the longest part of their trip in Paris, where a French governess was hired who spoke only French to the children.[30]

Thus, when the family departed for another long stay in Paris late in 1908, she felt quite at home there. What she hoped to do most on this trip was to meet famous writers. Given her age and the protectiveness of her parents, she only managed to reach the fringes of literary society. With Anatole France's secretary she visited the Louvre. She sat for several dry point etchings by the artist Paul César Helleu, a friend of Proust. But the closest she came was in the very hotel where the Ocampos were staying: Edmond Rostand and his family were also guests there. She only glimpsed the author of *Cyrano* once. However, she became friends with his oldest son, Maurice, who, like her, was beginning to write.[31]

Back in Buenos Aires, in 1912, Ocampo got married and in that way gained her freedom to leave home, but for a price. The couple left for a long honeymoon in Europe, and right off she saw it wouldn't work: her husband was jealous of her independence. In Paris she was free from the watchful eye of her parents to go out to nightclubs and elegant soirées, and even to catch the premiere of Igor Stravinsky's *Le Sacre du Printemps*, but she was miserable in her marriage. On their return to Argentina in 1914, she and her husband led separate lives, until she finally moved out in 1922.

Her next visit to Paris, at the end of 1928, signaled a new era for her. It was the first time she made the journey alone, free of husband and family, and she was now a writer herself. She was also at the threshold of an enterprise that would last the rest of her life, with the founding in 1931 of *Sur*, the literary journal and publishing house dedicated to presenting current European and North American authors alongside their Latin American peers. The friendships she made during this stay provided ample momentum for launching her project.

Ocampo moved in the highest circles that winter in Paris. She met Paul Valéry, whose conversation dazzled her at a luncheon one day. Another time, with Jean and Valentine Hugo, she drove to the outskirts of the city to have lunch with Maurice Ravel: as in a dream they talked all afternoon, yet she found herself utterly unable to tell him how much she loved his music.[32] With José Ortega y Gasset she visited the Russian philosopher Lev Chestov, where she befriended the Rumanian emigré poet and filmmaker Benjamin Fondane, who came to Buenos Aires the next summer to lecture on avant-garde film. That spring she also met Pierre Drieu La Rochelle, with whom she traveled to London and had a brief affair. Though she respected his work as a writer, she deplored his later avowal of fascism even as she remained his friend.

One place Ocampo made sure to visit was Adrienne Monnier's bookshop, La Maison des Amis des Livres. She also frequented Shakespeare and Company across the street. Sylvia Beach introduced her to the work of Virginia Woolf, especially *A Room of One's Own*, and Ocampo was delighted to discover a kindred spirit. She first became friendly with Woolf in 1934, and later, after her trip to Paris in 1939, she brought to London the photographer Gisèle Freund, who took several famous photographs of Woolf. In 1929, though, Man Ray took Ocampo's own portrait, in a photo that captured her renowned beauty. On this trip, besides an unfortunate episode with Count Hermann

Keyserling in which the German philosopher mistook intellectual interest for romantic fervor, one other meeting proved disappointing, with the Comtesse Anna de Noailles. Ocampo had admired her poetry since adolescence, but she found a woman who was a complete antifeminist.

Her trip to Europe had convinced her, as it had so many writers from the New World, that her only possible home was America, and that she could never really belong in Europe. In a letter to Rabindranath Tagore in 1930, she expressed the dilemma after her discussions with American writer Waldo Frank, who had spoken of a pan-American vision: "When we found that we shared this orphan-feeling, we also thought that it could be stopped some day or other through the whole continent . . . because so many people shared it. We miss Europe terribly, both of us, and yet when we reach Europe and live in it, we both feel she cannot give us the kind of nourishment we need. We feel, in a word, that we *belong* to America, crude, uncultured, unformed, chaotic America."[33]

Her visit to Paris in 1930 could be seen as her first professional trip. Her friends Ortega y Gasset, Drieu La Rochelle, Keyserling, Tagore, Supervielle, and the Swiss musician Ernest Ansermet, offered their support, as did new friends such as Jean Cocteau, Stravinsky, and German architect Walter Gropius. Through the following years *Sur* took up nearly all her energies. The critical response was not immediately favorable—she was accused of being an aristocrat in her tastes and of catering too much to foreign writers—but gradually the review found its public. What she wrote of Güiraldes many years later could have been said of herself: "You were what they would call a 'foreignizer,' *afrancesado* (frenchified) . . . you were delighted and at peace being that way, without hiding it. Avid for beauty, whatever its origin, you were not afraid of becoming less Argentine in making that beauty your own. With it you enriched your soul and that of your country."[34] It was true that as a result of her education she wrote almost entirely in French, but in 1937, she made a concerted effort to change that and began writing in Spanish.

Due to her work as a publisher, Ocampo began to travel to Europe more often, to see her collaborators, to meet new ones, and to give talks as well. In 1935, Drieu introduced her to André Malraux and the three met regularly during her several months in Paris. She returned at the end of 1938, where her most important encounter turned out to be with the young writer Roger Caillois. On the suggestion of Jean Paulhan, editor of the *Nouvelle Revue Française*, she attended some of the conferences at the Collège de Sociologie, which Caillois and Georges Bataille had recently founded. She met Caillois at

Supervielle's house, and some time after he came to dinner at her place with Freund and the essayist Denis de Rougemont. That winter she went south to Cannes—her friend Gabriela Mistral was staying nearby in Nice—and Caillois came to spend a few days there on vacation. She introduced him to Mistral, whom he later translated. She was impressed by the range of his knowledge and interests and invited him to Argentina to give a series of lectures. Little did he know that what started as a visit was to lead to a lifelong engagement with Latin American literature, thanks to a woman whose own engagement with Paris would continue after the war for many years more.

• •

When **César Vallejo** (1892–1938) left Peru for Paris in 1923, he had two books of poetry to his name. *Trilce* (1922) discomfited critics with its stark innovations and the raw force of its language, but only gradually did other poets, notably in Spain, recognize its importance. Vallejo spent fifteen years in Paris, where he died, yet he never published another book of poems in his lifetime.

What he did publish was mostly journalism. He began as a correspondent for newspapers in Peru, and contributed to more than thirty journals in Latin America and Europe, predominantly through the 1920s. In some 300 articles he took on many issues of his day; topics ranged from the Salon d'Automne and profiles of artists to fashion (its inherent folly), sports (tennis), spiritism (Krishnamurti), and curiosities from the European newspapers, reflecting the habits of both Europeans and Latin Americans.[35] Eventually, his longstanding preoccupation with social injustice became his primary subject.

Vallejo was always ready to challenge what he saw. Describing a new production of Maurice Maeterlinck's celebrated play, *L'Oiseau bleu*, he tells how both critics and public raved, then tears it apart as garish and ridiculous. With a certain irony he comments on the new inductions at the Académie Française, an institution that repeatedly provoked his amusement. But he makes his first serious charge late in 1923, where he writes of a Peruvian evening at a Paris theater, with a lecture on the Incas, poetry readings (himself and José Santos Chocano, of the previous generation), a concert, and a talk by the Peruvian minister to France. The entire Peruvian colony attends, to share their culture with the French, and Vallejo laments: "Solidarity? Understanding? Nothing of the sort exists in Europe with respect to Latin America. We offer our hearts to Europe . . . and Europe responds with silence and a premeditated deafness."[36]

Journalism was Vallejo's main source of income in Paris, but the newspapers did not pay promptly and sometimes he was in quite desperate straits. From the start he came to know other artists in Paris. The Spanish poet Juan Larrea was one of his most constant friends, who introduced him to the Chilean poet Vicente Huidobro; through Huidobro he met Pablo Picasso, Jacques Lipschitz, Erik Satie, and Juan Gris, with whom he was close. Only in 1925 did Vallejo begin to find enough work, with more outlets for his articles. He also became secretary at a new press agency set up to facilitate contacts between Latin America and Europe, Les Grands Journaux Ibéro-Américains, but the job was less steady than he hoped. He began receiving a small monthly stipend as well for a few years from the Spanish government. Ostensibly the grant was to finish his law studies in Madrid, abandoned earlier in Peru: all he did was take the train there every month or two to pick up his check.

In his columns, Vallejo showed an ongoing concern with theater from his perspective as a writer. "Brilliant and cruel city" he calls Paris, for it fails to appreciate George Bernard Shaw, who in turn is quoted on the city's provincialism.[37] Later he returns to his defense of Shaw: French critics find Luigi Pirandello the better playwright, yet Vallejo judges him more a technical innovator while Shaw clearly "possesses a humanism lacking in the other writer".[38] He chides the French for producing mostly mediocre work, and for knowing nothing of new Russian or German theater. He considers Cocteau a fake essentially, and when his *Orphée* opens in 1926, he writes: "At heart Cocteau is a conservative, in spite of his efforts and modernist poses. His attitudes are based on makeup; his acrobatics are clownish, that is, false. Inside, sleep the old spirit and substance . . . in truth, he is, will be, and has been a Catholic."[39] Three years later, he dismisses the realism of boulevard theater, and in praising the Russians is especially excited by the plasticity of their work; among the French, he only cares about the more innovative directors such as Charles Dullin, Jacques Copeau, and Georges Pitoëff. He himself wrote several plays at the end of the decade, trying to merge his creative concerns with social and political material, to reach a broader audience. Dullin was interested, and García Lorca tried to get him a production in Madrid, but he never saw his plays produced.[40]

His critiques notwithstanding, Vallejo appreciated the unique quality of Paris, especially where foreigners were concerned. In effect, Paris contains all the other great Western cities, he writes late in 1926, but where others, such as Buenos Aires, may be a "cosmopolis," Paris is really a "cosmic city": there the colonies of foreigners don't remain simply what they are, rather "they lose their social physiognomy and become Parisian. That is, they adopt the social rhythm of Paris . . . they come not to get rich or amuse themselves a while, but to live more fully and nobly."[41]

Despite his internationalism, Vallejo did not lose track of his own cultural origins, nor did he believe that the ultimate goal was to be taken for a European. He proposes "works that are rigorously indo-American and pre-Columbian," insisting that American folklore, Aztec and Inca particularly, holds revelations for European culture.[42] Like the people of the Orient, "we too have lost our soul and we've lost it for Europe. Because in Latin America the Europeans have ruined everything for us, philosophies, religions, industries, arts . . . since Columbus's arrival there is a terrible emptiness in our life."[43]

On the other hand, he suggests that most Latin Americans who come to Europe don't stay long enough to see the changes in the postwar era, or they remain too much within their own communities to notice. He remarks that Latin Americans are often disappointed when they arrive: "We South Americans seem more Parisian [in our ways] than the French themselves who come from the provinces. . . . To such a degree has Latin America been culturally and socially colonized by Paris."[44] By the end of 1928, after the first of his three trips to the Soviet Union, he feels more than ever the need for a new decolonized consciousness. "When young American intellectuals come to Europe, they don't come to honestly study foreign life and culture, but to 'triumph.' In their suitcases they carry books or canvases made in America, and barely do they arrive in Paris, no other desire moves them than to 'triumph.'"[45]

Increasingly, Vallejo wondered how to reconcile his political preoccupations with his work as an artist. He began to address the social responsibility of the artist, whose neutrality seems to prove "human mediocrity and aesthetic inferiority. But in what sphere should the artist act politically? . . . Above all, he must awaken a new political sensitivity in man . . . and engender new concerns and civic emotions." Contrary to Diego Rivera, who at the time favored an art more closely tied to ideology, Vallejo emphasizes that an artist is a free being who works independently of political programs.[46]

Although his journalistic work dwindled nearly to a halt by the 1930s, he did publish a series of articles on the Soviet Union and then a book, *Rusia en 1931*. It was among his only published books since living in Europe, along with *Tungsten*, his proletarian novel set in the mines of Peru, which came out in 1931 and also enjoyed some success. Of the remaining articles that he produced until his death in 1938, most were devoted to Peru, especially to Inca art and culture. The Marxist tone of his language has largely subsided in these pieces, in favor of more aesthetic and historical terms. The few articles of his last year, by contrast, arose out of his anti-imperialist and antifascist stance, and were devoted to the Spanish Civil War.

When the war broke out in 1936, Vallejo's activism grew particularly focused: he collected funds for the republican cause, attended meetings, denounced nonintervention in his articles, and even went to Spain for a few weeks to help firsthand. In spite of his difficult circumstances, he went back the following year to represent Peru at the International Congress of Antifascist Writers. But more than writing journalism now, this was the time for his last outpouring of poetry. In the final six months of his life, he wrote nearly seventy-five poems, more than he had through all his years in Paris.

• •

Ever the precocious artist, **Vicente Huidobro** (1893–1948) seemed fully formed when he arrived in Paris in 1916. In his native Chile he had published four volumes of poetry and two of prose, in which he began to experiment with new ideas like *calligrammes*, the shaped poems devised by Guillaume Apollinaire, who encouraged all artists to free themselves of a subservience to nature. He had arrived by his own route at what the European vanguard was producing, and others soon acknowledged the kinship: Pierre Reverdy remarked that "our parallel efforts have met," and Max Jacob likewise noted Huidobro's rightful place among them.[47]

He lost no time immersing himself in a wider realm of action beyond his native language. Early in 1917, along with Reverdy and Jacob, he cofounded the journal *Nord-Sud*. Named for the métro line that linked Montmartre to Montparnasse, the review promoted the development of literary Cubism, a writing full of startling juxtapositions to create its own reality. His Creationism espoused similar ideas, which he had begun to elaborate the previous summer in Buenos Aires. Reverdy helped translate his first poem to appear in *Nord-Sud*, and later, Juan Gris took on the same task. By the middle of the year, Huidobro began writing directly in French and he continued to switch back and forth until settling back into Spanish in the late 1920s.

This was a time rich in collaborations among poets, painters, and musicians, as in *Parade* by Cocteau, Picasso, and Satie, whose premiere Huidobro attended that year. He himself wrote poems together with Gris, Jacob, and others, predating surrealist techniques like the *cadavre exquis*, where each person contributes lines to a poem or drawing without seeing what the others have done. The following year in Madrid, where he went that summer for his daughter's sake to escape the noise of the war, he worked with Robert Delaunay on an illustrated edition of his poem "Tour Eiffel," first published in *Nord-Sud*. Later, in Paris, in 1922, he explored ways to get the poem off of the page, to make it perform more in other media. He worked with the composer Edgar Varèse to create "Chanson de là-haut," adapting a portion of "Tour Eiffel" for music. He also collaborated with Sonia Delaunay in a fashion show with their *poème-robe*, a four-line poem ("Corsage") printed across the torso of a dress.

Huidobro socialized a great deal in Paris, and often entertained his many illustrious friends at home. Besides those mentioned, they included Apollinaire, Blaise Cendrars, Jacques Lipschitz, and various Chilean visitors. Amid all this traffic his wife Manuela kept everything in order at their flat near Place Pigalle, at 41 Rue Victor Massé. Their children thrived in this atmosphere, although a few years later they had some trouble at school due to their father's friends: Gris and Picasso liked to fill the children's exercise books with playful drawings; however, the teachers demanded the notebooks be immaculate and so the "sullied" pages had to be torn out. When they were older the children regretted that no one thought to keep those pages.[48]

After a stay in Madrid and then Chile, in 1920, the Huidobros returned to the same flat in Paris, where they remained until 1925. During their absence Apollinaire had died and Huidobro subsequently fell out with Reverdy, who contested his claim as the founder of Creationism. Throughout this period his activity grew more diverse, and his poetry began to move beyond Cubism. He asserted his independence as a leader of the vanguard and came out against the use of chance operations in writing, while remaining friendly with Dadaist poet Tristan Tzara.

Two other abiding interests came into focus at this time. In 1923, he wrote the script for a film that led to other work later. And at the end of that year his political activism first found form, inspired partly by his contacts with Irish Republicans. He published a long political essay against British imperialism, *Finis Britannia*, in which a fictional protagonist calls for a general uprising of all the colonies against England; a footnote, citing the example of Santo Domingo, even draws the lesson as a warning to the United States. The work was praised publicly by Mahatma Gandhi, and Ireland ended up nominating Huidobro for the Nobel prize for literature.

In 1925, he returned to Chile and an abortive political career, when he ran as a long-shot candidate for the presidency. He also fell in love with a young woman from a prominent family, who was still a minor, and publicly announced his passion in a newspaper confession on Good Friday. He then separated from his wife and went off to Paris to close the family home before heading on to New York, where, in 1927, he won a film prize worth $10,000 for his script of a few years earlier, *Cagliostro*.

Settling in Paris again, in 1928, and encouraged by Douglas Fairbanks to write about El Cid, Huidobro began his first novel, *Mío Cid Campeador* (1929), as the basis for a film. The book was a big success in Spain, and so was its translation in England. In it he employed a high degree of literary inventiveness, portending the experiments of later Latin American novelists. As a follow-up, Huidobro produced a novel even more defined by film techniques, for a public with "the cinema habit," when he adapted his old script to write *Cagliostro* (1934), which appeared first in English translation in 1931. During this time Huidobro also completed his greatest work as a poet, the book-length poem *Altazor* (1931). First conceived in 1919, as a discourse on the limits of poetry, which it proceeds to demonstrate and then transcend, *Altazor* was written alternately in French and Spanish, each language generating further ideas in the other.

Huidobro returned to Chile in 1932, continuing his literary activities with the support of numerous followers. In 1937, he went to Spain to join in the defense of Madrid against Francisco Franco's forces, only to return disillusioned by events at home and abroad. He visited Europe one last time in 1944 when he went to France as a war correspondent, moving with the troops into Germany and occasionally broadcasting from Paris for Voice of America.

• •

Miguel Angel Asturias (1899–1974) lived most of his adult years in exile. His trajectory abroad ended as it began, in Paris, where he retired after serving as Guatemalan ambassador to France. When he first departed in 1923, supposedly for a six-month visit to Europe, his parents hoped to shield him from political troubles at home after he and fellow students strongly opposed the long dictatorship of Manuel Estrada Cabrera.

In Paris, he met many Latin American students and decided to stay. Among those he knew were Carlos Quijano, who later started the weekly magazine *Marcha* in Montevideo, and Víctor Raúl Haya de la Torre, soon the founder of the APRA (Alianza Popular Revolucionaria Americana) party in Peru. They helped form the Asociación General de Estudiantes Latinoamericanos; perhaps the biggest event they organized was the tribute in 1925 to Augusto Sandino, admired for his resistance to North American imperialism. The participants included Henri Barbusse, Miguel de Unamuno, José Ingenieros, and a letter from Romain Rolland.

Before long Asturias enrolled at the Sorbonne in a course taught by Professor Georges Raynaud, an expert on the Mayas. Both Asturias's parents were *mestizos*, and his own face bore distinctly Indian features, which led to a curious experience at the first class. Raynaud, as he lectured, couldn't stop looking at him, and when the class was over he came up and said, "Vous êtes maya." The professor eagerly asked the student to come with him. "Entering his apartment, he opened the door and took me by the arm to the kitchen, where his wife was cooking, and he said to her: 'Here is a Maya. And you say the Mayas don't exist!'"[49]

After four decades Raynaud was finishing his translation of the *Popol Vuh*, the sacred book of the Quiché Mayas. Subsequently, in 1927, under his guidance, Asturias co-translated the French version into Spanish, checking every word against the original Quiché text. They teamed up again the next year to translate the *Anales de los Xahil* of the Cakchiquel Indians, also by way of the French. The task entailed extensive research to precisely render native concepts, which led Asturias to find a more creative outlet. Inspired by this material, he began to recompose the legends, plus accounts of everyday events and stories his mother told him as a child, in what became his first book, *Leyendas de Guatemala* (1930). "When Raynaud discovered I had written it he looked at me with a certain commiseration, because he was a scientist and this creativity formed no part of his science."[50]

Asturias recognized that living in Paris during the 1920s was crucial to his growth as a writer and helped to direct his indigenist perspective. From the start he ventured to the famous cafés along the boulevard Montparnasse, to glimpse famous artists holding forth and to make new friends. When La Coupole opened in 1927, he met Vallejo there, "who always had frozen hands. He was extremely quiet but very polite. When he took his first drinks he would change. That silent man would start to sing, to tell us things about his country and, suddenly, he would go out to the street singing and disappear from our sight."[51] Asturias became friendly with Tristan Tzara in Montparnasse and some of the surrealists—especially the poet Robert Desnos, who traveled with him to Havana for the Prensa Latina congress. He also knew Huidobro and his experiments, and they would gather for elaborate meals at a friend's atelier with the Cuban writer Alejo Carpentier and others, Huidobro bringing cases of imported Chilean wine.

Throughout the decade he lived in Paris, Asturias made his living as a journalist, mostly for *El Imparcial*, the most influential paper in Guatemala. From his first piece in 1924—an interview with Unamuno, shortly after the exiled Spaniard reached Paris—to his last brief pieces in 1933, when he returned to Guatemala, he wrote 440 articles. Contrary to Vallejo and Carpentier, who focused more on Paris, Asturias devoted half his pieces to the social and political realities of Guatemala.

Asturias had high hopes for the possible changes his generation could bring to Guatemala, from reforming government and the management of a more equitable economy to recognizing the rich indigenous heritage that lay nearly in ruins. In his articles he constantly reflected on these matters from his distant orientation, and eventually proposed solutions. He attacked the institutions responsible for such problems, but he also sought to challenge his readers' thinking and the rigid society that bred stagnation. As he traveled more—mostly to the annual congresses of the Prensa Latina—and was able to contrast different national experiences, these articles took on a certain militancy: Asturias begins to question the very notion of Guatemalan nationality ("Hacia una patria mejor"), especially to the degree that it shuts out indigenous culture, and concludes that only by embracing the principle of *mestizaje* (crossbreeding) can the converging cultures be reconciled in America. This attitude was to become a major theme in his novels.

By 1930, the glow of his youthful optimism seemed to be fading with regard to Guatemala's future. Lamenting the lack of continuity in his own generation with its high ideals and the slim results achieved, he takes solace in Waldo Frank's advice not to despair, for theirs is a transitional generation where a new nation is being born. But disappointment has set in and through his last few years in Paris his journalism seeks a more global perspective. In *"Las lanzas coloradas"* from 1931—about the novel by Venezuelan writer Arturo Uslar Pietri, who was also living in Paris—he takes heart in books like Ricardo Güiraldes' *Don Segundo Sombra*, Mariano Azuela's *The Underdogs*, and Rómulo Gallegos's *Doña Bárbara*, which do not imitate Europe but rather create something new, a "universal Americanism," although the public for such works must still be created.

Questions of identity—both personal and national—were foremost in his mind through those years. A shift in attitude is reflected by his involvement with Prensa Latina, the organization led by Maurice de Waleffe to bring together journalists from the Latin countries of Europe and America. Waleffe had the bright idea to plan an annual congress for participating members, with all expenses paid by the country hosting the event as a form of publicity; the guests were then invited to see the principal cities and sights, and they in turn would write a series of articles on the trip. At first Asturias was pleased to belong to this great Latin family, traveling to cities he couldn't have afforded himself—starting with Florence in 1925—and entertained in grand style. Liège and Bucharest hosted in subsequent years, as did Madrid under the dictator Miguel Primo de Rivera, which Asturias refused to visit. By the time he traveled to Havana in 1928, however, he was writing *Leyendas de Guatemala*: this trip, including a visit back to Guatemala, served to reinforce his commitment to *mestizo* cultures as he moved away from the ideal of a united Latinity. Still, he remained interested enough in Prensa Latina to attend later congresses in Athens and Cairo.

Through his last years in Paris, amid his frustration at trying to influence events in his homeland, Asturias repeatedly questioned the artist's place in society, if there was a place. In the meantime, he was finding more creative channels for his political thinking, since he also wrote *El Señor Presidente*—based on the dictator Estrada Cabrera—during his years in Paris. Before leaving in 1932, he gave a copy to Georges Pillement, who translated it into French but could not send the translation to Guatemala, for it was too dangerous under the new dictatorship. Not until a decade later, when democracy was restored and Asturias went to Mexico as a cultural attaché, could he get it published.

• •

When the Prensa Latina caravan landed in Havana in March 1928, **Alejo Carpentier** (1904–1980) was not much interested in their activities. But he did know of Robert Desnos and admired his poetry. As it happened, Desnos called on him within hours of arriving, carrying letters from friends. It was thanks to the young French poet that Carpentier went to Paris, where he stayed for more than a decade. He was eager to leave Cuba at that time. His protests against the Machado dictatorship had earned him a month and a half in jail the previous year, and since then he was persecuted by the police and forbidden to leave the city.

It was due to the Dreyfus affair that his family came to Cuba. His father, a Breton architect from an old family, took Dreyfus's side in a bitter dispute with them, causing him to leave France and emigrate to newly independent Cuba with his wife, a language teacher of Russian origin. They returned to visit Europe in 1912, when Carpentier studied at a Parisian lycée for three months. By 1922, after another brief visit to Paris, he began to make his living as a journalist in Havana.

In those years he published many pieces on artistic currents in Paris. He was particularly interested in surrealism by the time he met Desnos, who encouraged him to come to France and proposed a way of getting there. The government had denied Carpentier a passport, and since Desnos held various cards and credentials from the Prensa Latina congress, Desnos gave him his own papers.

Carpentier arrived in Paris with the advantage of a job—as the correspondent for two journals he had written for since the mid-1920s. He sent in most of his columns, more than 100 pieces, during the first several years until 1933, when he began to work in radio. Right away he plunged into the cultural life of Paris, finding new friends among the more innovative European and Latin American artists. Desnos introduced him to a number of the young writers who frequented the surrealists—Michel Leiris, Georges Ribemont-Dessaignes, Roger Vitrac, Georges Bataille, Jacques Prévert, Raymond Queneau—many of whom revolted against André Breton two years later. He also published in Ribemont-Dessaignes' journal *Bifur* (on Afro-Cuban culture), which included Huidobro and Asturias, as well as Bataille's *Documents* (on Cuban music).

His experience of surrealism came at a crucial moment for Carpentier. "It made me more Latin American than ever," he said in 1975. "What *they* were looking for, *we* had (it's the eternal *here, there* of my novels). In Paris one had to milk reality with great effort in order to extract the marvelous," whereas in Latin America "the marvelous was around every corner." It was to be found there "in a raw state, within reach of our hands, ready to be used in art, in literature."[52] By the 1940s, after returning to Cuba, he articulated this notion as the *real maravilloso* (marvelous real), which became central to his Latin American aesthetic and the writing of his novels starting with *The Kingdom of This World* (1949).

The Paris years marked a long apprenticeship for Carpentier before he fully understood what lay beyond the regionalism of Güiraldes' generation, writers who "fulfilled Adam's task by naming things in Latin America." For those like Carpentier, it was now "a matter of finding out to what extent they can be universal," by way of a regional or native perspective.[53]

Living in Paris sharpened his vision of things Cuban. He found Cuban people everywhere he went. In 1933, he marvels how "a country with a small population like ours has given birth to so many impenitent travelers, so many people capable of living in the most dissimilar environments." All over Europe he has chanced upon Cubans in the street: "In the way they walk, their general aspect, Cubans carry an indefinable *something* that reveals their nationality right off to the eyes of a compatriot."[54]

Around that time, Cuban music was taking Paris by storm. He devoted numerous articles to Cuban music in Paris—composer Amadeo Roldán, songwriter Moisés Simons, bandleader Don Azpiazu, whose orchestra filled the prestigious Empire music hall—and to the cabarets and dance halls where it was being heard. From the Palermo on the Rue Fontaine, to the Palace near the Bourse, to the Bateau Ivre in the Latin Quarter, Cuban music was making a big splash during the late 1920s. In 1932, he writes that the Rue Fontaine—where Breton, who was so insensitive to music, lived—"is already on the way to being transformed into a Cuban street," with all the bars and cabarets that have opened there.[55] In the fall of that year "the most beautiful dance hall in Paris" was inaugurated, the Plantation, on the Champs-Elysées near the Arc de Triomphe, all for the glory of Cuban music: featuring Don Azpiazu and his orchestra with the dancer Mariana for the first six months, the place was packed every night.[56]

Most of Carpentier's articles were devoted to individual artists, often European, but written with a determinedly Latin American perspective. He finds that the New World has at last conquered Europe and that the experience of America—especially Latin America, with *mestizaje*—will revitalize Western culture. In 1929, he describes Heitor Villa-Lobos and Edgar Varèse as the "new invaders" of the European artistic scene, whose "singular aesthetic habits" derived from their American formation—Varèse, though French, had spent important years in New York where he wrote scores that "sounded of metal, electricity, and skyscrapers." Villa-Lobos, as a Brazilian, composes with "black and Indian saps" running through his works that contain the "vital effervescence of a virgin forest."[57]

Though journalism constituted the bulk of his writing during this time, Carpentier also wrote poetry, librettos, texts for ballet, radio texts, stories, plus he revised his first novel—written in the Havana jail—which he later disowned, *¡Ecue-Yamba-O!* (1933). In 1928–29, he supplied the scenarios for two ballets, "La Rebambaramba" and "El milagro de Anaquillé," by Amadeo Roldán. Soon after, for Marius-François Gaillard, a disciple of Claude Debussy, he contributed the nine *Poèmes des Antilles* in French; they collaborated on other work, too, including "La pasión negra" in 1932, a long dramatic poem. In 1930, another Cuban composer, Alejandro García Caturla, asked him for texts that became *Dos poemas afro-cubanos*. He worked with Villa-Lobos as well, on four "cinematic poems," and in 1931, he joined with Ribemont-Dessaignes and Desnos to write a libretto for Varèse, *The One All Alone*.

A new career opened up for him in 1933 when he was named program director for the Poste Parisien radio, thanks to Desnos. They worked with actors like Marcel Herrand, the young Jean-Louis Barrault, and Antonin Artaud, whose play, "Moctezuma," greatly impressed him when he heard it read. Among other projects, they staged Walt Whitman's poem "Salut au Monde!" In addition to straightforward broadcasts, they tried more experimental approaches —to the point that one series, "Le coq-à-l'âne," was almost entirely improvised, based on spontaneous wordplay with Desnos and Jacques Prévert, somewhat the comic equivalent of automatic writing. They also built a library of poets reading their poems: Paul Éluard, Langston Hughes, Miguel Hernández, Rafael Alberti, Nicolás Guillén. In another series, they covered the whole Fantômas story (the criminal hero of the long-running serial thriller) in brief episodes, with an original score by Kurt Weill, Artaud directing, and Desnos preparing the text. Unfortunately, none of this work has been preserved, due to decay of the materials used at the time.[58]

In 1937, when the Spanish Civil War broke out, Carpentier gathered regularly with other republican sympathizers at the Café Flore, where Vallejo and even Picasso showed up nightly to exchange news about the war. That year he traveled to the Congress of Antifascist Writers in Madrid, and wrote several moving articles about Spain under the bombs.[59] It wasn't until the beginning of 1939 that he thought to leave Paris—he was feeling the urgent need to make contact with Latin America again. But the return marked a significant point in his life: Carpentier was in effect reborn returning to Cuban soil, which led to his mature work as a writer beginning in the 1940s.

The French Reception

Upon his return to Paris in 1945 after a six-year exile in Argentina, Roger Caillois found himself uniquely qualified to become a sort of godfather to Latin American literature in France. At the time, Victoria Ocampo wrote to Paul Valéry of her protégé: "I see no other Frenchman who knows us better and . . . who has been so intelligent and generous with his interest in us."[1] Despite the increased awareness among the French before the war, typified by the writing of Valery Larbaud and the literary translations of scholars like Francis de Miomandre and Georges Pillement, Latin American culture remained largely unknown in Paris at mid-century.

Before accepting Ocampo's invitation to embark on what he thought was to be a month's tour of conferences, Caillois knew almost nothing about Latin America. And yet, he had had a remarkably precocious youth as an intellectual. Before he was twenty, in the early 1930s, he had shared some of the experiments in altered states pursued by his older friends Roger Gilbert-Lecomte and René Daumal of the Grand Jeu movement (a sort of literary offshoot of surrealism), and he had begun to frequent André Breton and the surrealists; he was particularly close to Salvador Dalí and Paul Eluard. While studying at the École Normale Supérieure, he also audited classes at the École Pratique des Hautes Études, notably the history of religions with Georges Dumézil and ethnology with Marcel Mauss. It was there that he met Georges Bataille, with whom he founded the Collège de Sociologie in 1937. During the same period he was also starting to write for numerous journals, especially the *Cahiers du*

Sud and the *Nouvelle Revue Française* under Jean Paulhan. By the mid-1930s, he had turned his back on the uncertainties of literature in favor of the stricter and more orderly realm of the social sciences. It was only through his voyage to the New World, and the revelation of Latin America, that he became reconciled with literature.

During his years in Buenos Aires he often wrote for Ocampo's journal *Sur*, but additionally, under her patronage, he began to edit a smaller journal in French, *Lettres françaises*, to help perpetuate French literature by reuniting the writers exiled throughout the Americas alongside those still living in France. By way of this enterprise, where he first published Jorge Luis Borges in translation, and thanks to Ocampo's many contacts among the elite of Latin American writers, as well as through his own travels, Caillois soon developed a commanding grasp of what he discovered to be an entire continent of new literature. Back in France at the end of the war, he sought to make use of his expertise and to further his activities as an editor: within a few months of his return, he signed a contract with Gallimard to be the director of a new collection, La Croix du Sud, devoted to Latin American literature in French translation.

The first book Caillois published in the collection was Borges' *Ficciones*, but it did not appear until 1951. In the meantime, amid other work, he continued to pursue his latest passion. In journals and small editions, he published his translations of poems by Gabriela Mistral, Antonio Porchia (who was hardly known by his fellow Argentines), and extracts from Pablo Neruda's long poem, *The Heights of Machu Picchu*. He wrote essays on Latin America and coedited the three issues of the literary journal *La Licorne*, founded by the Uruguayan poet Susana Soca. In the same year his project with Gallimard got under way, he also began a career with UNESCO as the director of an ambitious program of translations, the Collection des Oeuvres Représentatives. There he created a special section for Latin American works to be translated into French, which still exists. In its first years the UNESCO series concentrated on classic works mostly from the nineteenth century, including such writers as Domingo Sarmiento, José Martí, Joaquim Maria Machado de Assis, and José Hernández's *Martín Fierro* (translated by Paul Verdevoye, later one of the foremost Hispanists in France). Two anthologies were sponsored by UNESCO as well, one devoted to a wide range of Latin American poetry, edited by Federico de Onís, the other focusing on Mexican poetry and edited by Octavio Paz (its English edition was translated by Samuel Beckett).

The Croix du Sud collection lasted till 1970 and published fifty-two books: a quarter of the titles came from Argentina, with the rest drawn mostly from Brazil, Mexico, Cuba, Peru, and Guatemala. Nearly all were works of fiction, apart from two modern classics by Brazilian sociologist Gilberto Freyre, an essay by Mexican historian Fernando Benítez, and the last in the series, Luis Harss and Barbara Dohmann's *Into the Mainstream*, portrait/ interviews of the foremost Latin American writers. The two writers most frequently published, as noted by Claude Fell, represented the two main poles of contemporary Latin American writing: Borges, with his rigorous economy of style, his intertextual wizardry, his playful defiance of time and history; and Alejo Carpentier, a pioneer of both magical realism and the baroque in Latin America, whose work drew deeply on history.[2]

In a way, Caillois's collection at Gallimard was another sort of consecration. Such was its prestige, along with the general enthusiasm of its reception among readers and critics, that it encouraged other European publishers to translate these writers. Miguel Angel Asturias, who in 1967 became the first Latin American novelist to receive the Nobel prize, confirmed as much to Sylvia Molloy: after a new edition of his first book, *Leyendas de Guatemala*, his banana trilogy—*Strong Wind, The Green Pope, The Eyes of the Interred*—was also published in La Croix du Sud.[3] Similarly, Borges, with six books in the series, credits his renown throughout Europe, including Spain, to Caillois's efforts on his behalf.

Overall, Caillois tended to publish writers who were roughly his contemporaries, with the earliest work being a new edition of Güiraldes' *Don Segundo Sombra*. Thus, the collection saw the first books in French translation of such important figures as Jorge Amado, José María Arguedas, Juan José Arreola, Julio Cortázar, Graciliano Ramos, Augusto Roa Bastos, Juan Rulfo, and Ernesto Sábato. At the time, Caillois's inclusion of Brazilians was well in advance of their appreciation in the Spanish-American literary world, as Fell has pointed out.[4] In his selections from the next generation of writers, he proved astute as well, introducing Rosario Castellanos, Guillermo Cabrera Infante, Julio Ramón Ribeyro, and Mario Vargas Llosa.

But while the Croix du Sud collection represented the first substantial commitment by any foreign publisher to promoting Latin American literature, it also helped perpetuate certain assumptions among the French reading public. Ribeyro is a case in point; his first book of stories and his first novel were published by Caillois in the 1960s. He attributed the lukewarm critical reception of his work to the fact that he was atypical in the European view of Latin American writers. His gray urban realism did not fit in with the expectations of the time, for a certain exoticism, where the exuberance of magical realism or grand events like revolutions seemed to be the norm.[5] Though Ribeyro was optimistic about a growing sophistication among more recent European readers, an editor at the publisher Seuil, by contrast, has been less hopeful. Annie Morvan, who has a long experience with Latin American literature, considers that it has somewhat passed out of vogue in France and that interest has declined among the general public.[6]

From the start of the Gallimard collection, according to Fell, "the wild and grandiose character" of the Latin American landscape as reflected in its literature was a primary area of fascination for Caillois: among the earliest titles published figured two of the great "telluric" novels of the 1920s, Güiraldes' book and Rómulo Gallegos's *Doña Bárbara*.[7] It seemed an especially strange and hostile world from a European perspective. Thus, the exotic qualities of the Croix du Sud books (reinforced by the very name of the series) were emphasized in the back cover texts describing them; gaining particular currency in these descriptions, as Jean-Claude Villegas has remarked, were the violence and perversion found in the stories, as in the societies that produced them. It was therefore these aspects that French reviewers and critics associated most with the literature.[8]

In retrospect, what may be more surprising about Caillois's selections is the absence of some of the most prominent names in Latin American literature: João Guimarães Rosa, Juan Carlos Onetti, Carlos Fuentes, Gabriel García Márquez, José Donoso, José Lezama Lima, and Clarice Lispector. Interviewed in 1966, Caillois explained that the books published in the collection were supposed to give "an idea of [Latin America's] essence."[9] Debatable as this might be as a criterion, or even whether such writers fit the bill, a larger issue was at stake for the newer writers. Increasingly, the collection was viewed as a sort of ghetto; many, like Fuentes, wanted to be considered directly on the level of world literature and not to be marginalized in this way. For the same reason, others—Cortázar, Vargas Llosa, Asturias—moved on after first publishing there. Caillois himself was aware of these limitations and recognized the literature's new status when he terminated the series in 1970. Nonetheless, it is widely acknowledged that La Croix du Sud served, in Fell's words, as "a springboard for Latin American literature in France."[10]

Certainly, the Gallimard collection alerted other publishers in France. Even before, since 1949, as Molloy has noted, Pierre Seghers had begun to publish many Latin American poets. By the 1960s, others followed, mostly concentrating on fiction: Albin Michel became Asturias's publisher, Laffont and Casterman launched new collections.[11] Seuil took interest in the latest writers, and by the early 1970s had published the major works of Donoso, Lezama Lima, García Márquez, and Severo Sarduy. This interest was reflected as well in the numerous literary journals, which increasingly integrated Latin America into their fields of concern.

Through the decades since Caillois's initial efforts, the Latin American presence has become ever more institutionalized on the French, and especially Parisian, landscape. Concurrent with the publishers' discovery, the universities were also devoting a growing measure of their attention to Latin America. In 1954, the Institut des Hautes Etudes de l'Amérique Latine was founded in Paris, which has since developed an extensive library. On a separate front, partly associated with the countries' embassies, various cultural centers opened around the capital. Since 1983, in a more concerted effort involving all the embassies, with most of its support coming from the French government, the Maison de l'Amérique Latine has offered a full calendar of cultural events in its stately quarters on the boulevard Saint-Germain. The Maison itself was founded in 1946 by the foreign office to help strengthen ties between France and Latin America, but it was not until the early 1980s that the Association pour la Fondation France-Amérique Latine was created, which had the building renovated. The site also serves as a meeting place for diplomats as well as people in the arts, sciences, and business.

In the domain specifically of literature, and the result of an equally ambitious plan of cooperation, the Colección Archivos was started in 1984. Based at the Nanterre branch of the University of Paris, and copublished with UNESCO, to date the Colección Archivos has brought out more than forty critical editions of twentieth-century literary classics from Latin America and the Caribbean; the original agreement between research organizations in the eight European and Latin American member countries called for 120 titles in the series. Each volume—some based on a single title, some on the collected work of an author—includes an appreciation by a well-known writer as well as a number of critical texts: a contextual analysis, a study of the work's reception, three critical readings of the style and themes in the work, plus a section of relevant documents such as the writer's notes and correspondence. The Archivos project dates back to 1967, when Asturias donated his manuscripts and archives to the Bibliothèque Nationale in Paris, which were to be the source for subsequent critical editions of his work. Many of his manuscripts, however, did not arrive where they were intended, and this pointed up the need to combine resources among scholars to safeguard such historically important papers. The initial volume in the collection, therefore, presented Asturias's collected journalism during his first stay in Paris, in the 1920s and 1930s.

2

Writers' Beginnings

(Gabriel García Márquez, Mario Vargas Llosa, Alfredo Bryce Echenique)

If Paris was the place where one went to become a writer, according to the myth, there were plenty of examples that seemed to support this. Such was the case between the wars with Miguel Angel Asturias, Alejo Carpentier, and Lydia Cabrera, while others like Rubén Darío earlier and César Vallejo, though not beginners, wrote much of their mature work there. After the war the pattern continued, even if its causes were hardly mythical. In the late 1940s, Ernesto Sábato came as a scientist, a discipline he eventually abandoned in favor of literature. In the 1950s, there were Julio Cortázar, Julio Ramón Ribeyro, Eduardo Manet, and in the 1960s more still—Severo Sarduy, Copi, Hector Bianciotti, and Rubén Bareiro Saguier—to mention only a few people. The three writers briefly discussed here also came early in their careers, remaining in Paris over quite different spans of time. While it was not the French capital that *made* them into writers, the time there enabled them to understand what was specifically theirs, as writers and as Latin Americans.

By the time he left for Europe in the summer of 1955, **Gabriel García Márquez** (b. 1928) was just starting to emerge as a writer. Earlier in the year he had published his first short novel, *Leafstorm*, which introduced Macondo as a setting in his fiction, and he had won a national prize for a short story. However, in Colombia he was known as a journalist, and it was in that capacity that he was sent abroad by the Bogotá newspaper, *El Espectador*; the trip also enabled him to get away from the virtual state of civil war then rampant in the country. His first stop was Geneva, to cover the summit meeting of Western leaders with the Soviets. Over subsequent months, he went to Rome, writing about the pope on vacation and a Jehovah's Witness convention, as well as a long series on an Italian political scandal, and briefly studying at the Experimental Film Center; to the Venice Film Festival; and to Vienna, Warsaw, and Prague, reaching Paris before Christmas. He remained in Paris for most of the next two years.

But nothing was ever straightforward for Latin Americans in Paris. Weeks after arriving, at a café with his friend Plinio Apuleyo Mendoza, they discovered from a few lines in *Le Monde* that *El Espectador* was shut down by the dictatorship of Gustavo Rojas Pinilla. The paper's owners then launched a substitute, *El Independiente*, where García Márquez published a long series on a French political scandal, before that paper, in turn, was closed in mid-April. When he was sent a return ticket, he cashed it in. Throughout 1956, his material situation was often dire. At one point he resorted to gathering and selling empty bottles. And he got further and further behind on the rent for his garret in the Latin Quarter, in the Hôtel de Flandre on the Rue Cujas. In the meantime, though, he kept busy writing.

He worked on two short novels while in Paris. Every night until dawn, according to Mendoza, he would sit with his knees up against the radiator, a picture of his future wife pinned to the wall, writing *In Evil Hour*. Soon he interrupted that book for a more pressing story, *No One Writes to the Colonel*. Like its author, who kept waiting for a check in the mail that never came, the old colonel has waited many years in vain for the military pension promised to him, having fought in his youth alongside Colonel Aureliano Buendía.[1] But beyond the personal echo, these works marked a decisive detour for García Márquez, which would help lead to the culmination of his Macondo stories a decade later in *One Hundred Years of Solitude*: what was earlier a preoccupation with the mythic dimension in his fiction became now, with the distance, a need to reflect the specific reality of present-day Colombia.[2] Thus, the reigning atmosphere of silence in the colonel's story, set in the mid–1950s, is the explicit result of martial law and censorship.

There were historical and artistic reasons why he chose to confront the social realities. Many Latin Americans were then in exile, from dictatorships in Argentina, Peru, Venezuela, Cuba, and Guatemala. In France, the Algerian war dominated politics, and on the Parisian streets García Márquez himself was often taken for an Algerian, both by the French and Algerians; he was even locked up once by French police because of the confusion.[3] As a writer, his shift in emphasis was partly due to his journalism as well as his interest in film, especially Italian neorealism, but also to his reading of Ernest Hemingway and Albert Camus, just as in the late 1940s his readings of William Faulkner affected his earlier fiction.

With respect to older writers, García Márquez did have two significant near-encounters in Paris at that time. An admirer of Cortázar's stories, late in 1956 he decided to go meet him at the Old Navy, the café on the boulevard Saint-Germain where Cortázar often went to write. Every day he waited there until after several weeks Cortázar finally appeared—but in the end, the younger man just watched, not daring to approach him.[4] Then, the following spring, walking up the boulevard Saint-Michel he recognized Hemingway across the street. "Adrift and without direction in Paris," as he described himself many years after, García Márquez didn't know whether to ask for an interview or express admiration. Rather than spoil the moment, he cupped his hands and yelled across the wide boulevard, "Maaaeeestro!" Hemingway turned, raised his hand and shouted, "Adióoos, amigo!" The man whom García Márquez credits with having "the most to do with my craft" left him with "the impression that something had happened in my life, and had happened for all time."[5]

This encounter came at a propitious point for him. By then, his intermittent journalism work had dried up, he had finished *No One Writes to the Colonel* (which would take four years to get published), and soon after he learned, again in the company of Mendoza, who was once more visiting Paris, that the Rojas Pinilla dictatorship had fallen in Colombia. The journalism itself had served as a sort of writer's workshop for García Márquez. Jacques Gilard, who has made an extensive study of his articles of this period, notes that the two long series on political scandals, Italy in 1955 and France in 1956, were good exercises in the construction of narrative: with the investigative part available from the work of other reporters, he was able to focus on the telling of the stories (sometimes adding slight elements of fiction), which helped him in the pacing of longer works. Later, in 1956, from August until March of the next year, he published pieces on a freelance basis in *Elite*, a weekly magazine from Caracas, then edited by Mendoza. There too, the real work consisted of crafting secondhand material, but it also gave him opportunities to dwell on the theme of power, which would be central to his novel *The Autumn of the Patriarch* twenty years later: for *Elite*, among other subjects, he wrote on Charles De Gaulle, the Shah of Iran, the Queen of England, Aristotle Onassis, and Anthony Eden during the Suez crisis. Finally, in the summer of 1957, he traveled with Mendoza throughout Eastern Europe and the Soviet Union, acquiring the direct experience to reflect more deeply on his socialist principles. That fall, in a maid's room in Neuilly, he wrote a ten-part reportage on his travels, "90 días en la Cortina de Hierro" (Ninety days in the Iron Curtain), which he could not get published in Colombia—where he had intended it as his part in the national dialogue—until almost two years later.[6]

Despite his difficult situation in Paris, his European sojourn—two and a half years in its entirety—proved important as a catalyst for García Márquez. Before setting foot there he was already formed in his cultural awareness, and Europe confirmed what he already knew as a Latin American. Indeed, as Gilard observes, the image he gives of Western Europe is of "a decadent world near total exhaustion," even as the Third World is rising up. In his articles he shows a talent for folklorizing the Europeans, while his American values serve as a means of both affirmation and defense. Moreover, he himself foresaw such an experience, writing several years earlier of a Colombian poet who had traveled to Europe, summed up by Gilard in this way: "contact with Europe did not at all mean the gaining of new elements, but rather it concluded a chemical sort of process that was purely American."[7]

• •

Since childhood **Mario Vargas Llosa** (b. 1936) had dreamed of going to Paris to become a writer. As it happened, the dream came true relatively soon, when he was only twenty-six, three years after moving to Paris: his first novel, *The Time of the Hero*, won the prestigious Biblioteca Breve prize from the Barcelona publisher Seix Barral in 1962. By the time he moved to London in 1966, he was embarked on his third novel and recognized as a major figure in the so-called Boom in Latin American literature.

Many factors contributed to the launching of his destiny by way of France. As Vargas Llosa himself has noted, like previous generations, he came of age when Peruvian intellectuals had to go abroad to flourish as writers. He was an avid reader of French authors—Jules Verne, Alexandre Dumas, Victor Hugo, later Gustave Flaubert—and it was not until his late teens that his friend Luis Loayza introduced him to the work of major Latin American writers such as

Jorge Luis Borges, Juan Rulfo, and Octavio Paz. He even had, unwittingly, a foretaste of the French experience as an adolescent at the Leoncio Prado military academy—he was sent there by his father to forestall his ambitions, and it became the setting for his first novel—where his French teacher turned out to be César Moro, the poet who had spent the prewar years in Paris with the surrealists. Moro, who wrote in French and was gay, had by then quietly settled into an internal exile; Vargas Llosa did not discover his teacher's achievements until several years later.[8]

His first visit to Paris only confirmed his resolve to return there. He had won a short story contest offered by a deluxe French journal *La Revue Française*, for its Peru issue, and so, early in 1958, at the age of twenty-one, he was brought to Paris for a month. He was wined and dined, put up in a fancy hotel near the Arc de Triomphe, and went often to the theater. Though he had hoped to shake hands with Jean-Paul Sartre, one of his passions at the time, he did manage to meet Albert Camus—a curious signal of his own later shift in attitude as a writer. On his return to Lima, he secured a scholarship to study in Madrid, to write a thesis on Rubén Darío, and he left for Spain that summer; his aim, however, was to get back to Paris. At the end of 1958 he visited the French capital again, and there at the house of a mutual friend he met an Argentine writer who looked to be about his own age: it was not until the end of the evening that he learned the man he'd been talking with was Julio Cortázar, whose work he knew well and who, in fact, was really twice his age.[9]

In the summer of 1959 Vargas Llosa at last came to live in Paris, accompanied by his wife, with the expectation of another scholarship that never materialized. For much of his six and a half years there he resided in the Latin Quarter, mostly on the Rue de Tournon. One of the first things he did, as he recounts in his book-length study of Flaubert, was to buy a copy of *Madame Bovary*; he began to read the novel that same afternoon and was so captivated that he read on through the night until dawn.[10] But he was soon broke and found a poorly paid job teaching Spanish at a Berlitz school, followed by a stint doing copywork in the Spanish bureau of Agence France-Presse. Eventually he landed a good job with evening hours at the French Radio-Television Network, where he helped produce shortwave broadcasts to Latin America. In the early 1960s it was often through his activity at the radio, interviewing them for shows, that he first met a number of Latin American writers: Borges, Fuentes, Carpentier, and Asturias.

During his first years in Paris, Vargas Llosa worked assiduously to finish his novel, begun in Spain. The months prior to its triumph in the fall of 1962 were among the most difficult for him, due to a family crisis and the decline of his marriage, and his initial efforts to find a publisher were unsuccessful. With the success of his novel he was more in demand as a journalist, collaborating with *Marcha* in Montevideo and later with several journals in Lima, and he used his new position to speak out on politics, an abiding interest since adolescence. Just weeks after the Biblioteca Breve announcement, he made his first trip to Cuba and reported on his experiences for *Le Monde*. Like many Latin American artists at the time, he was a fervent supporter of the Cuban Revolution and social causes elsewhere in the continent. Regarding Peru, he favored the armed guerrilla movement (a view he later abandoned), notably in a 1965 position paper co-written with Ribeyro and others; in two memorial articles, he recalled friends killed in the struggle, comparing the finality of these events with their liveliness when he knew them in Paris.[11]

Throughout his exile, Peru was his prime obsession as a writer; this was also like a response to the exile of his childhood, having grown up mostly in Bolivia. Indeed, nearly all his fiction in the first two decades of his career was sparked by the dozen years he had lived in Peru. When *The Time of the Hero* was published in 1963, as if to remind him of the necessity for such distance and despite widespread acclaim, a thousand copies of the book were burned at the military academy he had dared to criticize. By then, he was already writing his second novel, *The Green House*, set in the Amazon jungle and the Peruvian coastal city of Piura, where he lived when he was ten. He first visited the jungle in 1958 before leaving for Europe, and later did extensive reading on it, visiting once more in 1965. That work, published in 1966, won him even greater recognition for its technical mastery and the maturity of its vision. His massive third novel, *Conversation in the Cathedral*, finished after he moved to London, was set in Lima during the Odría dictatorship of the 1950s. The book was "bitterly pessimistic," according to Gerald Martin, reflecting the writer's "full awareness of his own political scepticism," partly a result of his growing disillusionment in the late 1960s with Cuban socialism.[12]

As an adolescent Vargas Llosa had taken eagerly to the work of Sartre, which he felt could "save him from provincialism," from the regionalism and local color then dominant in Latin American fiction, and open him to new narrative possibilities. Most important, Sartre's theory of commitment seemed to show him a way to combine a literary vocation with a concern for social justice, without falling into the traps of socialist realism.[13] Twenty years later, by the mid-1970s, and after his break with Cuba, Vargas Llosa's allegiance had shifted to the liberal reformism of Camus, emphasizing a moral rather than ideological commitment and a persistent defense of the artist's freedom against the control of a state or party.[14]

In a sense, his gradual change in outlook was implied from the start of his exile with the project of his first novel. "I have never been able to write about things that are near," he said many years later. "One has to be able to work with enough freedom to transform reality." It was in exile that he learned to treat writing as a discipline, a daily labor. Moreover, his separation from Peru taught him the value of nostalgia, how the memory becomes enriched through longing. After his first few years away he managed to return there almost annually for a month, but that distance shaped his perspective in that it helped him distinguish what was essential.[15]

Above all, it was the freedom to come and go that counted most for Vargas Llosa. In a 1966 memorial essay about Sebastián Salazar Bondy, he noted that "every Peruvian writer is defeated in the long run," because they were struggling against rampant illiteracy, on the one hand, and against social indifference to serious literature on the part of those who could read. In short, the writer almost didn't count. For that reason, "all our creators were or are in some way, at some moment, exiles." Even to remain in Peru and continue writing, the artist had to assume some form of inner exile in order to protect oneself "against the poverty, the ignorance, or the hostility of the environment." Thus, Salazar Bondy was a heroic figure, for he not only returned from exile early in his career; he also devoted his efforts to developing an audience and a critical discourse for serious literature to exist in Peru.[16]

Vargas Llosa did not return to live in Peru until 1974, after sixteen years in exile. When he left Paris in 1966, it was in part to escape his celebrity in a place that was then teeming with Latin Americans and also to accept a job teaching in London. Still, he loved that city where he had flourished and that often amused him with the "civilized" curiosities described in his articles: the dog cemetery in Asnières ("*Toby*, descansa en paz"; Toby, rest in peace), the new Inca-inspired religion taken up by the French ("La religión del Sol Inca"), the film projectionist and fanatical nudist who worked at the Gennevilliers studios where the writer used to dub French newsreels for export ("El nudista"). Several decades later, after his unsuccessful bid for the presidency of Peru, he would recall in his autobiography how, like Cortázar, he too had felt that

> Paris had given something profound to his life that could never be repaid: a perception of what was best in human experience; a certain tangible sense of beauty. A mysterious association of history, literary invention,

technical skill, scientific knowledge, architectonic and plastic wisdom, and also, in large doses, sheer chance had created that city where going out for a stroll along the bridges and the quays of the Seine, or observing at certain hours the volutes of the gargoyles of Notre Dame or venturing into certain little squares or the labyrinth of dark, narrow streets in the Marais, was a moving spiritual and aesthetic experience, like burying oneself in a great book.[17]

• •

With his usual self-mocking humor, **Alfredo Bryce Echenique** (b. 1939) tells a story that illustrates the continued tradition of Latin American writers in Paris around the mid–1960s: one day, to increase his luck with literature, he went to the little hotel run by Madame La Croix, a woman who had done "more than anyone for Latin American literature." By chance, she had been the manager at the two different Latin Quarter hotels where, each in their time, García Márquez and Vargas Llosa had ended up broke at the start of their careers while writing their first books; on both occasions she had let them run up their debts until they could pay. "I set down my typewriter, a pack of paper, and my passport on the reception desk," recounts Bryce Echenique, "and gazing toward the future, I asked for a room." The hotel is full, he was told. "'Not even if I pay, Madame?'" "'Not even paying double,' she replied and called for her husband."[18] By then, of course, the poor woman was a legend among Latin Americans.

Like Vargas Llosa, who was his professor back in Lima in the late 1950s though only three years older, Bryce Echenique had long wanted to go off to Paris to be a writer. Of an old upper-class Peruvian family, he too had his dreams thwarted when his father insisted he go to law school. His friends had even thrown a farewell party for him, and for seven years they kept asking when he was going to be a writer. In the meantime, while studying law, he also did a degree in literature with a thesis on Hemingway. Finally, in the fall of 1964, with the help of his mother, he took the boat for France.

Every turn in Bryce Echenique's experience, it seems, has added to the "exaggerated" quality of his life, like the fictional alter egos that have propelled his novels. He had started his journey with a grant to study at the Sorbonne, for a doctorate in literature. As a tribute, he thought to choose one of his grandfather's favorite writers—he recalled the long-lost yellow bookcovers, but couldn't quite remember the author. Later he would suffer the scorn of professors and peers for having chosen the reactionary playwright Henry de

Montherlant, and he eventually abandoned his efforts, only to revive them more than a decade later at a time when he considered moving back to Lima, completing his doctorate there in 1977. Not long after, in Paris, strolling by the *bouquinistes* along the Seine, he chanced upon those yellow volumes published by Garnier and discovered the writer he had meant to choose after all was Maurice Maeterlinck.[19]

But if his destiny as a writer was to be played out in Paris, it first had to undergo the sort of digressions and detours that became so characteristic of his writing. Partly to evade his task he traveled a lot, until in the summer of 1965 he holed up in Perugia specifically to write his first collection of stories. No sooner did he return to Paris, however, than the manuscript was stolen from his car. Vargas Llosa in particular was scandalized by the loss, even as he detailed the illustrious tradition of writers such as Hemingway who had suffered a similar setback. Bryce Echenique then rewrote the entire book, *Huerto cerrado* (Closed Garden), which borrowed the unified model of Hemingway's Nick Adams stories and transposed it to the character of Manolo in Peru. A friend submitted the book to the Cuban publisher Casa de las Américas, where it was published in 1968. Still, Bryce Echenique did not actually see his first book until much later, when he was surprised to discover it in a Latin Quarter bookstore among other titles from Cuba. The store was frequented by leftists, many of whom tended to steal books; by principle, those who got caught were only thrown out and never reported. Totaling the cost, Bryce Echenique decided to steal all seven copies of his own book and naturally was caught. When he explained the situation and that he was the writer, the store gave him the copies as a gift.[20]

By then his first novel was about to be published by Barral in Barcelona, thereby ending his "short happy life" as an unknown writer. With its narrative ease and ironic humor, *A World for Julius* (1970)—about a sympathetic boy ignored by his upper-class parents in Lima—earned its author wide critical acclaim. Uncommon as it was to write critically of the Peruvian oligarchy, Bryce Echenique disavowed any political intentions in the novel; by the time it came out, though, when a left-wing military government was in power, it was hailed as revolutionary, as he saw on his first visit back to Lima in 1972; later, it came to be seen more as the swan song of a social class.[21] But these issues aside, the novel shows the full flowering of his distinctive style, a fluency for storytelling marked by its oral quality. That orality had long obsessed Bryce Echenique as a fundamental trait of Peruvians, who in his view show a great talent for replacing reality with a new version after the fact. Likening it to the experience of soccer, he recalls how "the Peruvian team was always the most elegant... always the moral victor." And yet the team always lost. But after each game, following the crowds to the bars and cafés, he noticed "how the marvelous oral account began... every game was won afterward." That "capacity to arrange reality, even to make fun of it," he wanted to bring to his literature, along with that measure of humor that he considers crucial for putting up with life in Peru.[22]

Throughout his career, Bryce Echenique's work—like that of Vargas Llosa and Julio Ramón Ribeyro, a friend since Paris—has been a function of distance: in the often retrospective angle of his narratives, the interest in marginal characters, and in the recovery of a conflictive Peruvian reality that may perhaps be best apprehended at a physical remove. Above all, he insists, his years in Paris taught him to what degree he was a foreigner and a Peruvian. "I am rather a defrenchified Peruvian," he writes in his autobiography, "France latinamericanized me."[23] The cultural identity of his fictional antiheroes remains ever unstable, especially in the later work where most have left Peru. Reflecting on his American experience of Europe, he looks not only to predecessors like Vallejo but also to Henry James and Hemingway, whose own myth of Paris he sought to demolish in writing *La vida exagerada de Martín Romaña* (The Exaggerated Life of Martín Romaña). César Ferreira has pointed out that Bryce Echenique's fiction offers the recurring figure of "a person permanently tormented by his incapacity to situate himself in the world."[24] As a writer, he draws on all his cultural sources, employing a complex web of intertextual references that play upon not only the confrontation between New World and Old, but also within the Americas between South and North, as well as—given the literary generation to which his writing belongs—between the purposes of the Boom writers and those who came after.

Bryce Echenique came of age as a writer at a time when Latin Americans were much in fashion in Paris. Since 1968, he had been teaching at the Nanterre and Vincennes branches of the University of Paris, both jobs due to the Paraguayan writer Rubén Bareiro Saguier, but too many distractions, and eventually his own celebrity, made it impossible for him to write there. By 1980, the idealism and effervescence of that period had long faded and he moved to Montpelier to teach; in 1984, he left France and teaching altogether and settled in Spain. Only gradually, however, did the European experience really enter his writing, mostly after he left Paris. In his first collection the opening story was set in Rome, where Manolo decides after a few years in Europe to return to Peru; the rest of the stories then examine his previous life back home. Bryce Echenique's second book of stories, *La felicidad ja ja* (Happiness Ha Ha, 1974), ventured back and forth across the Atlantic, but the only Paris story portrayed a Peruvian student's misery and disillusionment there. His second novel, *Tantas veces Pedro* (The Many Lives of Pedro, 1977), further mines the problem of identity in exile with an amorous protagonist who insists wherever he goes—the United States, France, Italy—on his being Peruvian, only to come up against confusion and misunderstanding.

This led Bryce Echenique to his fiction of the 1980s, with *La vida exagerada de Martín Romaña* (1981) set mostly in Paris, around the events of May 1968. There the movable feast proves elusive, especially for a Latin American not living on dollars, and the city's image from afar hardly matches the reality. The protagonist, moreover, ends up rejected by his Latin American friends and wife as not leftist enough. By contrast, in *El hombre que hablaba de Octavia de Cádiz* (The Man Who Spoke of Octavia of Cádiz, 1985), which forms a diptych with the previous novel, Martín, convinced that he's only a "rotten oligarch," finds himself rejected by the French aristocracy as a "dangerous leftist."[25] Cultural dislocation also permeates *La última mudanza de Felipe Carrillo* (The Last Move of Felipe Carrillo, 1988), where a successful Peruvian architect finds it impossible to settle back in Peru and returns alone to Paris.

3

Clarifying Sojourns

(Octavio Paz, Alejandra Pizarnik)

In the many travels of **Octavio Paz** (1914–1998), it would seem that most roads led if not to, then at least through, Paris. He first visited in 1937, on his way to and from Spain, as the youngest of three Mexican delegates to the second International Congress of Writers in Defense of Culture. Coming and going, swept up in the Spanish republican cause, he made contact with a number of poets he had known just from books: Pablo Neruda, who had invited him, César Vallejo, Vicente Huidobro, Miguel Hernández, Antonio Machado, and Benjamin Péret. Spending the last few months of the year in Paris, he met other writers as well; Alejo Carpentier, for instance, introduced him to Robert Desnos.

Important as these early encounters were, it was only after World War II that Paz began to come into his own as a writer, a period corresponding to his longest and most important stay in Paris. Offered a diplomatic post at the Mexican embassy there, he arrived in December 1945, and remained until the end of 1951, when he was transferred to India. Despite the material deprivations experienced in the French capital after the German occupation, he found a rich cultural milieu that shaped him artistically and intellectually for the rest of his life. Through Péret, who became closer to Paz during the war years while an exile in Mexico, he got to know André Breton and soon was attending the surrealists' meetings at their regular café in the Place Blanche. At the same time, he was friendly with more independent thinkers like Roger Caillois, Henri Michaux, E. M. Cioran, and he enjoyed long discussions on poetics with María Zambrano. Above all, he was a keen follower of the intellectual debates then prevalent, especially concerning the questions of political engagement that divided Jean-Paul Sartre and Albert Camus. As with Breton, he found in Camus a lasting model of moral integrity: both had denounced the crimes and excesses of Stalinism.[1]

Paz achieved his first major work as a cultural critic, *The Labyrinth of Solitude* (1950), during this time. He saw the book as belonging to the French moralist tradition, by its analysis of certain Mexican attitudes placed within a historical and universal context. But the book takes its lead perhaps, as Enrico Mario Santí has shown, from the work of the surrealist dissidents Caillois and Georges Bataille, who sought a more scientific alternative to surrealism by studying cultural processes, in order to recuperate a sense of the sacred as a sort of antidote to modern alienation.[2] Postwar Paris also struck a certain echo that helped Paz appreciate his theme in a wider light: from the Mexican-American subculture of the *pachucos* that he had observed during a stay in Los Angeles in 1943, which provided his initial focus in the book, to the disaffected French youths whom he noticed a few years later and who dressed in a similar manner, he was able to see the forms of Mexican solitude as reflecting a larger problem found throughout the contemporary world.[3] "We Mexicans," he writes, approaching a conclusion, "have always lived on the periphery of history. Now the center or nucleus of world society has disintegrated and everyone—including the European and the North American—is a peripheral being. We are all living on the margin because there is no longer any center."[4]

Though he had been gathering his insights for over a decade, it wasn't until the summer of 1949 that he wrote *The Labyrinth of Solitude*, some of it during off-hours at the embassy. "The distance helped me," he commented some forty years later, "I was living in a world far away from Mexico, immune to its ghosts."[5] If that remove from home granted access to a deeper vision of his native culture as well as of his own identity, by the twin paths of nostalgia and dispassionate inquiry, it affected his poetry in equal measure. That same summer, what he considered to be really his first book of poetry, *Libertad bajo palabra* (1949), was published in Mexico. With its unified structure, the way it made a coherent itinerary out of fifteen years' worth of production, the book not only sketched the development of his personality as a poet, it also explored "the conditional freedom of the work," the idea of freedom in tension with the limits of language.[6] As Jason Wilson points out, many of these poems—like *Labyrinth* itself—were a kind of exorcism against the dehumanizing forces and general despair of the postwar years; Paz's mission, in effect, was to defend life.[7] However, he did not treat Mexico directly in his poetry until after writing *Labyrinth*, starting with the prose poems of *Eagle or Sun?* (1949–50), his most surrealist work and marked by a reading of Michaux, where, he says, "the pre-Columbian world appears as part of my own psychological subsoil."[8]

But beyond the specific books he wrote, this period was significant for the openings Paz found on several fronts that he would develop later. His first readings of the Marquis de Sade at the time led him to question the surrealists' interest in such a figure, regarding the nature of Sade's revolt and of the freedom he represented; Paz rejected the negative extremes of rationalism exemplified by Sade, but the subject provoked him into an ongoing consideration of love and eroticism, culminating in one of his final books, *The Double Flame* (1993). It was also in these years that he began to grapple with the legacy of the seventeenth-century Mexican poet Sor Juana Inés de la Cruz, resulting long after in his monumental study, *Sor Juana or The Traps of Faith* (1982). Three times he wrote on her between 1949 and 1950, as Santí relates: first in *Labyrinth*, in his chapter on colonial Mexico; then, in his introduction to *An Anthology of Mexican Poetry* that he edited for UNESCO. The origin of his future book, though, was an essay he devoted specifically to Sor Juana, where the emphasis was less on her work than on the intellectual crisis she endured when forced by ecclesiastical authorities to renounce the life of the mind in favor of her religious vocation. Prior to this piece, a crucial polemic flared up on the left, when the writer David Rousset published a set of documents that denounced the Stalinist penal camps or gulags; most alarming to Paz was to see intellectuals like Sartre and Maurice Merleau-Ponty defending the Soviet orthodoxy against Rousset's evidence. Paz made a selection of these documents and with his wife, the writer Elena Garro (who later remained in Paris for many years on her own), translated them into Spanish for Victoria Ocampo's journal *Sur*, in 1951, which published his essay on Sor Juana later the same year.[9] That act, in his view, presenting the dossier to Latin American readers, entailed an "open break" with some friends on the left, which was only to grow sharper in subsequent decades.[10]

Paz next lived in Paris as a diplomat between 1959 and 1962, before being named Mexican ambassador to India. Since his last stay, he had spent a year in the East (India, Japan) and returned to Mexico, where he wrote his best-known long poem, *Sun Stone*, based on the Aztec calendar. Though not quite as fertile literarily as his previous residency there, these few years in Paris were a pivotal time as he renewed old friendships and developed new ones, including with younger writers like Alejandra Pizarnik. He also revised the two big books produced a decade earlier: for the new edition of *Labyrinth* he added a final chapter on "the dialectic of solitude," emphasizing the need to awaken from the nightmare of reason that is history, to discover the liberating forces of love, poetry, and the inner life; with the new edition of *Libertad bajo palabra*, he incorporated all the poetry written in the interim, thus preparing for a new era in his work. Indeed, the poems of *Salamandra* (1962) employ a shorter line, experimenting more with the space of the page and the play of words, reflecting his readings of Stephane Mallarmé, Guillaume Apollinaire, and Japanese poets. During this period as well he wrote a long essay on Sade, chiefly a meditation on eroticism, and many of the short texts on art, politics, and contemporary themes that were collected in *Alternating Current* (1967).

Paz continued to visit Paris in later years, where nearly all his books were translated and some even appeared first in French. But it is worth noting one further stay there, in effect bracketing his time in the East. After resigning as ambassador in 1968, in protest against the massacre of students in Mexico City, he spent some months in Paris on his way home. With the French poet Jacques Roubaud he devised the project of writing a collective poem based on the Japanese form known as *renga*, so they invited the Italian Eduardo Sanguineti and the Englishman Charles Tomlinson to collaborate, each writing in their own language. Over five days in April 1969, they worked together in a basement room of the Hôtel Saint Simon, where Paz and his second wife were living. The result, *Renga* (1971), was thus a poetic crossroads, in which the four personalities and languages fed off of each other to produce a new and unexpected creation.[11]

• •

For years the poet **Alejandra Pizarnik** (1936–1972) dreamed of going to Paris. Early in 1959, well before she left Buenos Aires, she wrote to a friend: "Here I am and my heart's in Europe. . . . As for Paris, if you ask me how I'm managing to go, I don't know what to answer. But I'll take a big white boat, with my Montgomery bag and my black glasses, without a cent as always and I'll be gone. The essential thing is wanting something and I want to go. Everything else will work out. On the other hand, I don't care if it gets worked out or not. The essential thing, like you say, is to live."[12] Paris the enchanting, beacon of literary destinies, homeland to poets far and wide; it was also the place to escape from her immigrant parents, where she could develop on her own, come what may. She reached Paris in the summer of 1960, and stayed until 1964, when she returned to Argentina. If survival wasn't easy for her there she did make many friends, and by the time she left she had also matured substantially as a poet.

Her aim was, in effect, to live for poetry, even to give higher loyalty to poetry than to life. By the end of 1960, wondering whether to stay or return, ambivalent about keeping her job, she concludes in a letter, "What matters is not returning, what matters is my solitude in my little room . . . my freedom of movement and this absence of others' eyes on my acts."[13] Night became her domain—and a familiar word in her poems—and she often stayed up all night writing, reading, and talking with friends. Ivonne Bordelois used to visit Pizarnik in the apartment she rented for a while from Laure Bataillon, translator of many Argentine writers, on the rue Saint Sulpice facing the church; the place was like "the drunken boat of Rimbaud, a zone of intense tobacco and the prodigious disorder of books and papers, a nomad's shop where a samovar dominated and that special atmosphere which grows in places where silence grows like an invading honeysuckle, nocturnal, permanent; the silence and a static, vibrant concentration, where the voice of Alejandra reigned."[14]

The material difficulties of her situation were almost like a test, for she would not—and could not—get full-time work; she wasn't looking for a career anyhow, only to write. What sooner provoked her anxieties, she says at one point, was the move to Paris, "the sudden change of life; I who am so possessive find myself here with nothing: without a room, without books, without friends, without money."[15] This pared-down existence reflected a similar process in her work, as her poems grew shorter—"little fires for the woman who went about lost in the strangeness"—more condensed than her writing prior to Paris. Poetry became "the place where everything is possible," and even with the sparest of lines it stood in contrast to any feeling "of exile, of a perpetual waiting," for the poem itself was "the promised land."[16] Still, in poetry as in life she pushed at the limits, stalking death. Hence, her insomniac nights (aided by amphetamines). Above all, she feared going mad, while tiptoeing at the edges of it: a decade later she would be interned in a psychiatric hospital in Buenos Aires, the year before she took her own life. Yet despite her frequent bouts of darkness and anxiety, Pizarnik flourished in Paris, in her way.

She loved the city, its streets "that tell, that sing. I do nothing more than walk and see and learn to see." She was quick to meet young poets and painters, French as well as Latin American. Before long she met Octavio Paz and began to see him often; he wrote the preface to her first book of poems written in Paris, *Arbol de Diana* (Diana's Tree, 1962). She grew close to Julio Cortázar, too, and Aurora Bernárdez, his wife. She became friendly with Italo Calvino and also the French surrealist André Pieyre de Mandiargues. In Les Deux Magots she even conversed with Simone de Beauvoir, who especially liked Pizarnik's tale of running away from home as a teenager.[17] Her most regular job—for some two years until she quit at the end of 1962—was a half-time position as proofreader for *Cuadernos*, the journal edited by Germán Arciniegas that was later revealed to receive CIA money (its publisher, the Congress for Cultural Freedom, being a Cold War project funded by the agency). She disliked working there, even if it did present her with chances to publish, like interviewing Marguerite Duras and writing a review of Paz's new book of poems, *Salamandra*. "The fact that nearly everything I do in the office is machine-like and routine," she writes, "is precisely what I need. First because I am automatic by nature and second because as much as I'm shown the contrary I'm no good for creative tasks in an office *simply because I am not of this world*. . . . But after, it's the morning, and I wake up enamored of my life, it's eight o'clock and the bus goes along the Seine and there's fog on the river and sun in the stained-glass windows of Notre Dame . . . " At any rate, she didn't care about the cloud of suspicion over *Cuadernos* for she had no interest in politics. "To hell with ideologies. I'm not about to die of hunger in homage to leftist intellectuals."[18]

Looking back, at the end of the decade, Pizarnik would consider those four years in Paris as "the only time in my life that I knew happiness and plenitude."[19] During her stay there she began collaborating with literary journals in Latin America as well as France and achieved a certain renown for her dark, jewel-like poems, reflected in the larger publishers for her books from this time on. At the university in Paris, she read her work with Roberto Juarroz, Arnaldo Calveyra, and one of her mentors, Olga Orozco, presented by the eminent Latin Americanist Paul Verdevoye. She also contributed to the *Nouvelle Revue Française* and discussed working with Maurice Nadeau on an issue of *Les Lettres Nouvelles*, which published her poems in French translation in 1963.

In spite of the hardships, she knew all along that "at any moment I can return to Buenos Aires—my bourgeois home."[20] Though she did consider going back several times, longing for family and friends, when she did negotiate her return—describing it as a "visit"—it was with the hope of buying a round-trip ticket. "It's very important, in every sense, for me to continue in Paris," she wrote to her parents. "More than important, it's primordial and it would cause a catastrophic effect on me, abruptly cutting this slow growth that has begun inside me since I arrived."[21] Five years later, after receiving a Guggenheim fellowship and passing through New York, she managed to return briefly to Paris, in the spring of 1969, but it was not the same. Despite renewing old friendships, she was quite disenchanted with Paris, for the city had changed. In the streets and cafés where once she glimpsed any number of writers and artists, she saw now the unstoppable train of Americanization.

4

Diplomatic Pastures

(Miguel Angel Asturias, Pablo Neruda, Alejo Carpentier)

Since the nineteenth century when many Latin American writers doubled as statesmen, no other region of the world has so often, on an official level, represented itself with writers. Among the most coveted assignments, more of a reward, was a diplomatic post in Paris. This was not without its moral compromises in some cases, given the problematic history of the governments that offered these positions. But be that as it may, the past half-century has seen many notable examples in the continued tradition of the writer-diplomat from Latin America.

Besides the three figures discussed more at length here, it is worth mentioning a number of other writers who enjoyed such assignments in Paris. Octavio Paz, of course, was one of the first writer-diplomats to serve in Paris after World War II. In the 1960s, and again when Pablo Neruda was ambassador in the early 1970s, the Chilean writer Jorge Edwards held posts there; he was closely involved with many of the Latin Americans then active in Paris. From 1975 to 1977, after being a frequent visitor throughout the previous decade, Carlos Fuentes was the Mexican ambassador to France, where he kept so busy he had no time for writing fiction. At the beginning of the 1970s, already a long-term resident, Julio Ramón Ribeyro began his climb through the ranks, eventually retiring in 1990 as the Peruvian ambassador to UNESCO. In the 1980s, the Argentine novelist Abel Posse, a career diplomat, was stationed in Paris for a few years, as was the Mexican novelist Fernando del Paso. One of the more remarkable instances of the post as fitting reward may be found in the poet and writer Rubén Bareiro Saguier, who lived in Paris for most of three decades during Alfredo Stroessner's dictatorship: in 1994, with the return of democracy, he became the Paraguayan ambassador to France.

A resident there at the start of his career, from 1924 to 1933, **Miguel Angel Asturias** returned to live in Paris in the mid-1960s. By then an elder figure with his major work behind him, he retained many literary friends from before the war and had been a close friend of Roger Caillois since the 1940s. Though his books focused mostly on his native Guatemala, alternating between a recuperation of the indigenous Mayan culture and exploring the country's sociopolitical problems, he had spent most of his adult life in exile. In 1964, he settled in Paris—in the same Latin Quarter hotel he had inhabited four decades earlier—then moved to Genoa, Italy, where Amos Segala and other scholars had been supportive of his work. When a democratic government was elected in Guatemala with Julio César Méndez Montenegro as president in 1966, Asturias was named ambassador to France.

His diplomatic career had begun in 1946 and continued during the sweeping reforms of Jacobo Arbenz's government, until the U.S.-backed military coup of 1954. Throughout his life he remained devoted to the cause of a unified, integrated Latin America. Yet his acceptance of the post of ambassador to France was roundly criticized by much of the Latin American left. Gabriel García Márquez, for instance, viewed the Guatemalan government of the time as reactionary, especially for its fight against the guerrillas.[1] But Asturias considered it his duty as a Guatemalan to serve, and he had even been advised to do so by both Arbenz himself and friends from the Guatemalan Workers' Party. During his tenure at the embassy until he retired in 1970, he initiated cultural activities and obtained scholarships for his country, and most importantly, he planned a huge exhibit of Mayan art from Guatemala that was shown at the Grand Palais in 1968—André Malraux, another old friend, offered extensive French support for the event, including sending teams of underwater divers who found pottery and other objects at the bottom of Guatemalan lakes.[2]

Despite earning the utmost prestige for his books, with the Lenin prize in 1966 and the Nobel in 1967, Asturias clearly had an uneasy relationship with the younger generation of writers then gaining prominence. Though one of the first along with Alejo Carpentier to employ magical realism, his work nonetheless tended to be seen as part of the old guard, with its emphasis on regional practices and its commitment to an overriding sociopolitical reality. In contrast, Asturias may have been jealous of the commercial success of some of the Boom writers, whom he dismissed as "mere products of publicity."[3] He resented García Márquez's critique of the committed novel as granting only "a partial view of the world and life" and accused the Colombian, in turn, of substantial borrowing from Balzac in *One Hundred Years of Solitude*. Above all, he felt that all the attention given to the Boom was out of proportion, ignoring the whole development of the Latin American novel since the *modernista* writers.[4]

Paris remained his home until his death in 1974: Asturias lived on a small street off the avenue de la Grande Armée near the Porte Maillot, in a rather staid neighborhood of the 17th arrondissement. But the half-dozen books he wrote during his final years in Paris largely reflect a return through distance and time to his earliest preoccupations. The stories of *El espejo de Lida Sal* (Lida Sal's Looking Glass, 1967) fit into the line of his first book, *Leyendas de Guatemala* (Legends of Guatemala, 1930) in that both are tales drawn mostly from indigenous sources. With the novel *Maladrón* (The Bad Thief, 1969) he reached back to the period of the Spanish Conquest, in the story of five Spanish soldiers who lose their way in the Guatemalan jungle and must learn to adapt to the nature of the New World. The same year he published a book written with Neruda celebrating the pleasures of food, *Comiendo en Hungría* (Eating in Hungary). In 1971, the Geneva publisher Skira, as part of its series Les Sentiers de la Création, published *Tres de los cuatro soles* (Three Out of Four Suns), a meditation on his own creative activity as grounded in the world of Mayan legends and beliefs. Conceived together, his final two novels, *Viernes de dolores* (Friday of Sorrows, 1972) and *Dos veces bastardo* (Twice a Bastard, 1974), returned to social themes, chronicling his generation's commitment during their student years in Guatemala and how later that same professional elite betrayed the people by selling out to foreign interests.

After retiring from the embassy he also wrote some sixty essays and chronicles, mostly for the Venezuelan newspaper *El Nacional*. These are striking for their informal tone and the modernity of their subjects. Whereas in his fiction Asturias generally drew universalist implications by way of the local, in many of the newspaper pieces the local is often absent altogether. Writing of urban problems or curiosities, he usually chooses not to mention any specific city—as though in deemphasizing Paris, his daily experience has blurred into the cities of his travels. Indeed, the four pieces treating urban traffic—street congestion, accidents, the valor of pedestrians, and personality changes when one steps behind the wheel—conjure up any number of cities, although Paris remains the immediate occasion for his reflections. Similarly, in a piece on "theatrical phone calls," he dwells on the sight of people talking into public phones and the entertainment its half a dialogue may offer to the spectator.[5] In other articles he discusses do-it-yourself hobbies, the relation between publicity and pornography, and urban nuisances like noise and the decay of buildings due to pollution. Whatever the theme, this was an arena where he could relax and amuse himself. And if the occasional pieces lacked the fire of his best work, they showed that he still remained alert to the world around him, but with a new appreciation for ordinary details.

• •

By the time **Pablo Neruda** (1904–1973) left for Paris in November 1970, as the Chilean ambassador for Salvador Allende's government, he had begun to suffer the first symptoms of prostate cancer and had effectively retired to his home in Isla Negra. Despite his illness, however, he wanted to help the new government and requested the assignment by way of friends. But there was also another reason for the journey: due to domestic tensions of his own making, he sought a change of scene for the sake of his marriage.[6] At any rate, it was a natural step for Neruda, who had worked in consular posts in the Far East and Spain early in his career and was directly involved in Chilean politics in later decades.

Although he never really lived there, he had often visited since first passing through Paris in 1927. In the late 1930s, he was in Paris several times on his way to and from Spain on behalf of the Spanish republic; in 1939, based in Paris, he led a campaign to secure passage to Chile for 2,000 Spanish refugees aboard a huge ship. In the late 1940s and into the 1950s, he visited enough that he kept a small apartment for a while in Paris. Later, in the 1960s, with his annual trips to Moscow, he would return by way of Paris for an extended stay. Among the friends he saw there in this period were Jorge Edwards, then stationed in Paris, Carlos Fuentes, and the French poet Louis Aragon, whom he had known since the 1930s and who was later a regular visitor when Neruda returned as ambassador.

Edwards has observed that Neruda's behavior in his role as ambassador gradually changed over the two years he served in Paris: at first, he tended to be conciliatory, charming his adversaries, hosting unlikely (and usually unsuccessful) combinations of guests at embassy dinners; later, as Chilean politics became more heated with Allende's supporters struggling against the forces of reaction, he grew more combative. He was never particularly comfortable living at the "mausoleum," as he called the embassy, but he was well aware of the gravity of his mission. Two issues crucial to the success of Allende's reforms had to be confronted: renegotiation of the foreign debt and an embargo of Chilean copper led by one of the American companies that had been nationalized without compensation. At their first meeting with Neruda who had recently been awarded the Nobel prize in the fall of 1971, the French treasury officials could not contain their surprise, "A poet and a novelist are renegotiating Chile's foreign debt." Numbers were not his strong point, but according to Edwards he proved more lucid and nuanced in his understanding of the issues compared with the Chilean economists and lawyers, whose theoretical arguments made compromise difficult. Yet he was not against employing literature for reasons of state either. Seeking help on the embargo he met with French president Georges Pompidou, who had once been a literature professor and edited an anthology of French poetry: first Neruda discussed poetry and gave him the new French translation of *One Hundred Years of Solitude*, and then he got down to business; not long after, the embargo was lifted by a French court.[7]

In those years Cuba, a natural ally of Allende's Chile, had reached a point where it was alienating many former supporters; notably the imprisonment of the poet Heberto Padilla who, after international protest, was released in 1971 but forced to sign a self-critique, cleaved an irreparable division among Latin American artists. Neruda, a member of the Chilean Communist Party since the late 1940s, managed somehow not to take a stand. Though supportive of the Cuban Revolution, he had been wary of Fidel Castro's methods from the start. Moreover, after a trip to the United States in 1966, for a meeting in New York of the International PEN Club, Neruda had received an open letter of reproach from Cuba, signed by writers like Alejo Carpentier and Nicolás Guillén, who both held important posts. Because of that letter, which questioned Neruda's leftist commitment, he scorned those writers ever after, even when Carpentier was also stationed in Paris.[8] Edwards especially was not trusted by Cuba: hired at Neruda's insistence as the second in charge at the embassy, he had arrived fresh from four disastrous months posted in Cuba, where he ran afoul of the state security forces. Every morning before heading off to the embassy in Paris, he wrote his controversial memoir of Castro's Cuba, *Persona non grata*. Neruda encouraged him to write the book, but to wait some years before publishing, when it might be more instructive than harmful.[9]

Neruda's symptoms from the cancer steadily worsened during his time in Paris and that, combined with other ailments, made even the reduced hours he spent at his embassy labors more and more difficult. Still, he continued to write, working on several books of poetry as well as his *Memoirs*. The poems of *La espada encendida* (The Flaming Sword) spoke in nearly mythical terms of love, inspired by the young woman with whom he had an affair prior to his departure for Paris. Another book, considered one of the best of his last years, *Geografía infructuosa* (Barren Geography), was largely written while riding in cars, first in Chile and later in Normandy. With his Nobel prize money he had bought a small house in Normandy, where he went whenever he could, often with friends. He kept projecting a visit back to Chile, which he sorely missed, postponing the trip for reasons of health, until he left Paris for good in November 1972. When Neruda died shortly after the military coup of September 1973, he left eight more books of poetry that he had hoped to publish for his seventieth birthday the following year.

• •

When he returned to live in Paris in 1967, as the Cuban cultural attaché until his death in 1980, **Alejo Carpentier** had reached a position where he might enjoy the best of both worlds. In part because of his longstanding ties to France, however, accentuated by his French-pronounced r's in Spanish, he was in a sense constantly trying to prove himself loyal to revolutionary Cuba, to serve as its mouthpiece. Beyond any controversy, beyond its persecution of intellectuals, he wanted to believe in its overall infallibility as a model for Latin America's future. Right up to the end he was claiming in interviews that the revolution had never disappointed him, that it was in better shape than ever, that it had already conquered its greatest difficulties.[10] He had lived in Cuba twice since his first departure for Europe: during the war years, and then again in 1959 following the triumph of the revolution, after a decade and a half in Caracas working in advertising. The Cuban Revolution gave meaning to his life, he liked to say, it made him feel useful in the collective effort to forge a new society. Before long, he was named director of the state publishing house, which had a crucial mission in light of the massive literacy campaign undertaken by the government: over five years they published seventy million copies of a wide range of titles, including literary works by Franz Kafka, James Joyce, Marcel Proust, André Malraux, Alain Robbe-Grillet, and many Spanish-language authors. But in the mid-1960s, for reasons unknown, or even if it was by choice, he left his post and went to Paris. From there he traveled frequently throughout Europe, on behalf of Cuban cultural affairs, and returned for yearly visits to Cuba.

In Paris, Carpentier's routine was to rise early each morning and write for several hours before going off to the embassy. Asked in early 1969 if he was satisfied with his diplomatic work, he responded diplomatically that he was, reaffirming his commitment to the revolution, and that if he should ever be assigned a different task, in Cuba or elsewhere, he would be just as happy to do so.[11] In another interview around that time, for the Cuban daily *Granma*, he found himself in the curious position of defending the new regulations for serving on the jury of the Casa de las Américas prizes, which stated that writers had to come from their country of origin, not the European countries where some had settled. He maintained that not many Latin American writers of renown still lived in Europe, and at any rate those residing in their native lands would bring fresh news of their respective literatures.[12] Yet Carpentier did acknowledge the cultural benefits in living abroad: like Cortázar with Buenos Aires, never had he felt Havana so intensely as when he lived far away, and that distance, he said, granted him a more complete perspective of his country.[13] Above all, in two decades he never publicly criticized the revolutionary government. If his commitment did not convince everyone, the regime was content to share in his prestige and let him do what he did best, serve as cultural liaison to Europe.

In his art, Carpentier struggled throughout the 1960s and 1970s to write a novel reflecting the historical process that the Cuban Revolution represented. He came to believe in an epic novel of commitment as the only viable path for Latin American literature in a time of such important social changes, insisting that modern man was no longer capable of escaping politics and the issues of the day. As Edwin Williamson reminds us, he began as a writer "in the nationalist avant-garde of the 1920s" and he sought to "contribute to the creation of an authentic cultural identity for Latin America."[14] In terms of narrative thrust, Roberto González Echevarría notes that "the plot in Carpentier's stories always moves from exile and fragmentation toward return and restoration."[15] In this respect the Cuban Revolution seemed to bring a certain fulfillment, in that Latin Americans were creating new rules, new modes of being, by seizing control of their own destiny.

At any rate, ever since his first long stay in Paris, he had grown increasingly wary of the European perspective and the colonialist habits that took hold in Latin America. His novel *Explosion in a Cathedral*, finished in 1958 but not published until 1962, explored the impact of the French Revolution on the Caribbean. But the book was more than a critique of revolutions; rather, what is most significant is conveyed by the irony of its original title, *El siglo de las luces* (The Age of Enlightenment). At the close of the eighteenth century the looming presence of the guillotine, and the last waves of the Reign of Terror, were the bitter legacy brought over from the land of reason, suggesting that indeed nothing had changed since the Conquest.

In fact, Europe tended to be more present in Carpentier's later works, since his engagement with New World questions of identity inevitably put Europe itself into question. Another novel begun prior to the Cuban Revolution, and not finished until more than a decade after, *Reasons of State* (1974) managed to be a parody and subversion of European traditions. As the portrait of a dictator modeled on five real Latin American dictators in the first part of the century, the novel shows a tyrannical ruler infatuated with Paris where he eventually retires after falling from power. Here again Carpentier's original title, *El recurso de método* (The Recourse of Method), plays sharply on its European source, the *Discourse on Method* of René Descartes, whose work is ironically quoted at the start of most chapters, offering a philosophical key to the dictators's wily bag of tricks, his methods for retaining power. Moreover, in this book Carpentier performs a sort of literary cannibalism, particularly drawing on figures out of Proust to depict the outmoded cultural values to which the Head of State still clings even after he is defeated.

The novel that resulted from Carpentier's determination to place art at the service of the revolution, *La consagración de la primavera* (The Rite of Spring, 1978), attempted a different synthesis, to present the history of popular struggles in the twentieth century as culminating in the triumph of the Cuban Revolution. "A vast historical melodrama," in González Echevarría's words, it traces the complicated paths of two lovers who meet during the Spanish Civil War and follows them to Cuba where they are at last reconciled—the book ends in the early years of the revolution, after the defeat of the United States at the Bay of Pigs.[16] There were at least three other titles during the decade and a half he was known to be working on the novel, and at one point it was projected as a trilogy. The result, though, was less than satisfying, due especially to the programmatic and essayistic quality of the writing. His final short novel, *The Harp and the Shadow* (1979), returns to the ultimate source in that it centers on efforts to have Christopher Columbus canonized by the church, who is eventually rejected because, among other reasons, he set in motion the process that introduced slavery into the New World. Thus the writer, who himself straddled both shores, manages to have the final word on behalf of New World cultures in the long struggle to reclaim their own history.

Tradition of Pilgrimage: The Dream City

Whatever personally motivated writers to make the journey, be it adventure or exile or a diplomatic post, the myth of Paris was powerful for several reasons. There was the substantial history of previous writers who went there, including many of the most illustrious figures. Also, French literature remained prominent in Latin American educations. Julio Ramón Ribeyro recounts how his father, who never managed to go himself, kept a large map of Paris at home, following all the streets and landmarks each time he read a French novel.[1] For Alfredo Bryce Echenique, when he decided to go off to Paris, his mother was delighted with the idea of having a Proust in the family.[2] The writers who flocked there in the first decades after World War II were inscribing their names within a gilded tradition where the French pantheon of writers seemed to welcome their distant Latin American cousins. But there was a further element to the myth of Paris as well, and that was the somewhat parallel history of North Americans who had gone, like the "lost generation" of the 1920s, and apparently thrived: writers from the United States, by contrast, earlier in the century as well as later, were typically oblivious to the Latin American presence.

As in the classic pattern found in Henry James and others, the story of the American who goes to Europe only to encounter disappointment and a loss of innocence had its own resonance for Latin Americans. While their northern counterparts benefited from a strong dollar and the G.I. bill through the 1950s, most Latin Americans struggled desperately to make ends meet; moreover, they were hardly viewed by the French with the same indulgence. Like a number of young writers, Sebastián Salazar Bondy managed to get there on a French scholarship in 1956, to study theater for a year: "I was very much struck by the alienation of the students and the artists who went to live in Paris. Paris, according to Hemingway, was a feast, but I found no such feast."[3] The result for him was a book of stories, *Pobre gente de París* (Poor Folks in Paris, 1958), which chronicled the rise and fall of Latin American expectations about life in Paris.

The book is framed by the title story, told in eight parts, which alternate with other tangentially-related stories. Already, on the first page, the Peruvian narrator struggles with his frustration, after three months in Paris, that he may have been fooled by saving up to come there. He is lonely, poor, and at a loss about how to improve his situation. One night in his hotel, he hears a coded message through the bathroom pipes, and grows hopeful that it is meant for him; after much effort he ascertains that his secret correspondent is a young Frenchwoman from the floor below. At last they meet, and seeing his dark complexion, she takes him for a North African; when corrected, she confuses Peru with Venezuela. They become friendly, and despite the teasing of his Latin American friends at their café in the Latin Quarter, he thinks he's falling in love with her. His courtship is soon interrupted by the visit of his rich obnoxious uncle from Lima, who wants especially to meet a French girl. In the end, after the young woman's evasiveness, he decides to confront her. Entering unannounced, he discovers her in bed with his uncle. Only then does he learn what everyone else knew: the reason she avoided a relationship was that she is a call girl.

In the other stories as well, the characters' dreams tarnish quickly. "No hay milagros" (There are no miracles) tells of a Chilean and a Paraguayan who scratch out a living by a common occupation of the time, *ramassage*, going door to door to gather old newspapers and magazines to sell by weight as used paper. When they are offered 2,000 bottles to haul away, they think they've hit the jackpot, only to find that the bottles are flawed and it costs them all they have to keep out of trouble for their mistake. In "El sacón militar" (The military coat), a Honduran, now with a cushy government job at home, looks back on his sufferings in Paris: as he was doing *ramassage*, a lady offered him a winter coat left over from the American army. Though he needed a coat, he knew its Yankee origin would not be viewed well in the leftist political group he aspired to lead; all winter long he changes out of his coat before reaching the meetings, until the day a communist from the group spots him on his way home and he loses all credibility. In the last story of the book, though he remains offstage and unaware of the deed, the lovelorn narrator from the title story is even swindled by a compatriot. "Un chaleco color de rosa" (A rose-colored vest) relates the desire of a Peruvian poet to own a vest that he cannot afford. Passing by his embassy in a premature search for funds from home, he meets the remorseful uncle who, in parting, entrusts him with a gift of money for his disillusioned nephew; the poet takes it as a sign and spends the money on himself.

But *Pobre gente de París* offers more than so many tales of disappointment. Salazar Bondy shows the enduring seduction of Paris for such characters, how on the merest foundations—a slant of light, a change of season, a few remaining coins—hope springs anew. One has to indeed fall quite low, as Horacio Oliveira does at the end of the first part of Julio Cortázar's *Hopscotch* (1963), to be disabused of the dream of Paris. "In Paris everything gets resolved," Bryce Echenique has noted. Though time passes, the position of "marginality lets a person prolong their adolescence until death surprises them."[4]

By the 1960s, new factors, whose effect persisted for some two decades, elevated the status of Latin Americans in France. Politically, since the triumph of the Cuban Revolution, in an era when many of France's leading intellectuals were of the left, Latin America was viewed with greater interest, as a terrain of praxis, where the future was actively being created. French *tiers mondismo*, the affinity for Third World cultures, sought to embrace non-European causes the world over—although no one went quite as far as Régis Debray when he flew off to Bolivia to join Che Guevara's revolution and ended up in jail. Given the general atmosphere of bad governments and tyranny that only grew worse, the Latin Americans who came to live in Paris were often regarded with an added measure of respect, or sympathy, in the assumption that their exile was ultimately political. Moreover, Latin Americans and French shared a common struggle, to an extent, in their resistance to dominance by the United States. Against this background, Bryce Echenique set his comic novel of Latin Americans in Paris circa 1968, *La vida exagerada de Martín Romaña* (1981): the protagonist, a Peruvian student and would-be writer, collides with these very assumptions in his obsession with Hemingway's version of Paris and his inherent lack of a political purpose; when the events of May 1968 erupt, it is only to impress his wife and her friends that he attempts, clumsily, that he too came to make the revolution.

At the same time, Paris was becoming a crucial locus in the commer nomenon that was the Boom in Latin American literature of the mid–1960s. Several writers associated with the Boom were then living there—Cortázar since 1951, Mario Vargas Llosa since 1959, Severo Sarduy since 1960—and the rest (notably Carlos Fuentes, Gabriel García Márquez, and José Donoso) were frequent visitors. One of the most important Latin American literary journals of the time, *Mundo Nuevo*, edited by Emir Rodríguez Monegal, was published in Paris during its active two-year run and featured the Boom writers along with many others. A few years later, the ambitious if short-lived journal *Libre*, edited by Plinio Apuleyo Mendoza and also published in Paris, attempted similarly to present the broad sweep of current Latin American writing while transcending political differences. Through the 1960s and 1970s, French publishers were paying more attention to the literature, and French universities were hiring more Latin American writers. So that, for a while, the old dream seemed at last to be coming true: Latin American writers in Paris, or some of them anyhow, were taking their seat at the table of world literature.

And yet, almost in the same instant, the dream began to dissipate in the light of new possibilities. As writers became more established on an international scale, and as the political lines grew more complex and less polarized, other opportunities opened up: Franco died in Spain, other Western European countries developed greater interest, and publishers and universities in the United States were also catching on. Paris, seen as the focal point of the old attitudes toward Europe, as a place of initiation, was soon being dismissed by many as a relic of the past. Above all, with the decline of the dictatorships in the 1980s and renewed efforts at democracy in their countries, more writers were staying home or else returning from abroad. Ricardo Piglia, for instance, whose novel *Artificial Respiration* (1981) treats the period of repression, had chosen to stay in Argentina, while his compatriot Osvaldo Soriano, who wrote *A Funny Dirty Little War* (1983), also set in that time, returned from his exile in Paris after the military was defeated; in Chile, novelist Diamela Eltit and poet Raúl Zurita were among those who stayed under Augusto Pinochet's regime.

It is curious that most of the novels about Latin Americans in Paris end with the main characters either leaving or faced with the question of moving on. Plinio Mendoza contemplates that moment in his novel *Años de fuga* (Years of Flight, 1979), when the somewhat blessed interval of prolonged youth seems to have run its course. Here, Paris is where the Latin American characters go to escape the norms of family and career, as well as to live as intellectuals. But as the years pass, and certainties become riddled with doubt

—in this case, the political faith in revolutionary Cuba—the protagonist grows skeptical of politics and loses his sense of direction. At forty he thinks of returning to Colombia, which frightens him; he looks back on friends from student days in Paris, fervent leftists in their time who left behind all that to become lawyers and businessmen, or who were simply killed for their politics. None of these paths are for him, he recognizes, though the book leaves him on the threshold of making a change in his life. But even as he begins to imagine his departure, he knows there can never be another place like that: "Paris would always be Paris, you had to be a foreigner to know what this city was, to carry it always like a thorn inside, to love it."[5] More than the sentimental setting for a continent's coming of age, and even deposed from its pedestal of myth, Paris has remained important on the Latin American map, not just for a shared history but for the continued presence of many writers there today.

5

Interstitial Spaces

(Julio Cortázar)

Like many Argentines born in the first decades of the twentieth century, the period of greatest immigration from Europe and beyond, **Julio Cortázar** (1914–1984) was negotiating between the New World and the Old from the start—more than most, for he was born in Brussels where his father was on a diplomatic mission. By the time the family was able to return to Argentina at the end of the war, he was speaking mostly French. He grew up in a suburb of Bueno Aires, raised by his mother, who was of French and German-Jewish origin. He was an avid reader of Alexandre Dumas, Victor Hugo, Jules Verne, as well as Daniel Defoe. It was a time that coincided with the rise of the tango, with lyrics that often spoke of a longing for Paris, and the importation of French prostitutes who initiated many a young *porteño* (resident of the port city of Buenos Aires). Such was the prevalence of French culture in his education that Cortázar, like many others of his generation, did not really discover the literature of his own country until he was well into adulthood.

By his own admission, the revelation of the modern world came by way of another French book, Jean Cocteau's *Opium*, which he chanced upon in the 1930s in a Buenos Aires bookstore. There he first learned of the European avant-garde and names like Pablo Picasso, Raymond Roussel, and Rainer Maria

Rilke.[1] But it was through his readings of the writers and artists associated with surrealism—particularly the more extreme figures, Lautréamont as antecedent, later René Crevel and Antonin Artaud—that he began to develop his own aesthetics. More than just another vanguard movement, for him, surrealism was "an attitude, a world vision," that "connected traditional forms, melted them down, and fused them." What mattered was "the reencounter with innocence," its capacity to open a door onto a hidden reality, and its "collective effort to seek a restitution of all human activity to poetic dimensions."[2] Cortázar's entire literary production, as Evelyn Picon Garfield notes, reflected an affinity with surrealism in such terms: through his irreverent playfulness and humor, his "desire to transform reality instead of kneeling to it," his instinct for "irrational provocation," and his "preoccupation with the Absolute, here and now," as in the restless searching of his characters and his uses of the erotic, both narratively and linguistically.[3] The ultimate example of this attitude was Artaud, whose death led Cortázar to remark that "living is more important than writing, unless the act of writing is—as it is so rarely—an act of life."[4]

These lines, written in 1948, were like a declaration of principle, a way of recognizing his need to strike out for new territory. It was only in those years that he first gained confidence in the stories he was writing, with their disturbing strangeness often derived from dreams, in the spirit of Gérard de Nerval and Edgar Allan Poe.[5] After a decade mostly teaching high school and college in the provinces, he had returned to Buenos Aires where he took up work as a translator—like dreams, this profession proved to be an enduring mode of passage for his creative imagination. But the reigning atmosphere of the Perón era made it difficult to enjoy his aesthetic pleasures undisturbed and, moreover, he was eager to see Europe. Early in 1950 he made his first visit to Paris. On the boat going over he met the young woman who became the inspiration for La Maga, the muse of his best-known novel, *Hopscotch* (1963); in Paris they kept running into each other during the subsequent month, and two years later when he had settled there she found him a job as a packager in the Printemps department store and shared in some of his initial discoveries of the city.[6] In the interim, back in Buenos Aires, determined to make the break, he managed to secure a French government grant and published his first book of stories, *Bestiario*, shortly before leaving at the end of 1951.

That first decade in Paris worked a gradual transformation in Cortázar to deepen his previous affirmations. There, where he could absorb European culture to the fullest, it was rather his newfound fellowship with humankind that became the lesson. "From my country," he later wrote, "a writer went off for whom reality, as Mallarmé imagined it, should culminate in a book; in Paris a man was born for whom books must culminate in reality."[7] Paris was his "road to Damascus, the great existential jolt," after the more solitary life he had led in Argentina.[8] One outcome of this change in perspective by the 1960s was his growing political commitment on behalf of social struggles in Latin America, to the consternation of many critics. But taken as a whole, his writing showed a remarkable consistency to his original faith in the surrealist attitude. Paris remained at heart what it always had been for him: a propitious doorway, a place of passages. As the protagonist Oliveira saw it in *Hopscotch*, Paris was "a mandala through which one must pass without dialectics, a labyrinth where pragmatic formulas are of no use except to get lost in."[9]

For Cortázar, the apprehension of a hidden truth that he sought in his writing arose from a sense of displacement, an "interstitial zone," a state of being *in between*.[10] So much the better for a foreigner armed with the uncertainties of his Argentine identity, which itself came more into focus only through a self-imposed distance and the direct encounter with Europe. In 1953, Cortázar began working as a freelance translator and interpreter for UNESCO, frequently traveling all over Europe and beyond for international conferences. Besides the inherent advantages for travel, such a career nourished the fruitful ambiguity of place in which he found himself from month to month and conditioned his relation to time, as well, where he had to write in-between the irregular schedule of jobs. Translation served him as a conduit to writing on many occasions—in the mid-1950s, among other literary works, he translated Poe's stories—and that relationship with his native language also reinforced the "umbilical cord" to Argentina.[11]

What Cortázar came to call the fantastic with regard to his own stories, a realm he had known since childhood, was different from the Gothic or other fabrications; rather, it was contiguous with quotidian reality and accessible by way of a certain permeability, a kind of alert distraction. It defied any fixed definition in his view, but he did distinguish his notion of the fantastic from more intellectual formulations like that in Tzvetan Todorov's *Introduction à la littérature fantastique*, who saw it as the mode by which the writer, faced with the limits of taboos or censorship, transgressed the accepted laws of reality. This might be useful as a tool for reading some of Cortázar's stories, in the same way as Sigmund Freud's distinction of the uncanny, those encounters with the strangely familiar that awaken old fears—Cortázar had read all of Freud while still a provincial teacher in the early 1940s. But these explanations were too scientific, they did not respond to his experience. For him the fantastic was above all a feeling, the intuition of a parallel or alternate world that may at any moment interfere with or erupt into our own rational order of things.[12] He considered himself somewhat of a lightning rod for such events, and when a person is receptive on that level the occasions for what is normally called chance or coincidence proliferate.[13] In his view, certain situations encourage the interruptions of the fantastic, notably places constituting an in-between or passage, like the métro, buses, bridges, and also the arcades from nineteenth-century Paris that so fascinated Walter Benjamin (and of whom Cortázar makes no mention). In the tradition of the *flâneur*, he would take long walks through Paris, seeking out these fortuitous moments; often he liked to pick a place at random on the map, then take the métro to that neighborhood and go explore it.[14]

In his first three books of stories, all published in the 1950s, the interstitial truth revealed by the turn of the fantastic generally operated by way of narrative mechanisms that he largely abandoned later on. These books—*Bestiario*, followed by *End of the Game* (1956), and *Secret Weapons* (1959)—established his reputation, and it is mostly this period that critics yearn for when lamenting his subsequent literary experimentations and injection of political issues.[15] "Axolotl," from the early 1950s, is classic Cortázar: the narrator, by dint of going to watch for hours on end those prehistoric amphibians in the aquarium at the Jardin des Plantes, has himself become an axolotl. Yet his transformation is not the climax; rather it is revealed after a few lines, at the end of the first paragraph. The narrator continues to be a young man describing his research: "what obsessed me was the feet, of the slenderest nicety, ending in tiny fingers with minutely human nails." Soon, the narration switches briefly to the immobile axolotl's point of view, all while remaining in first-person. The gaze itself is the pivot, the point of entry, into a completely other sense of time; this switching recurs until the narrator contemplates what used to be his face now peering through the glass. "Only one thing was strange: to go on thinking as usual, to know."[16] But the axolotl-narrator concludes that no understanding is possible between them and imagines the young man, who no longer visits, will probably write a story about his former obsession.

Other stories from the same period offer comparable trap doors in ordinary circumstances. "A Yellow Flower" recounts a man's discovery of immortality while riding a Paris bus: there he sees a boy who resembles himself at that age, compelling him to befriend the boy and his family, the better to observe them. The more he learns of analogous events in the boy's life, the more he despairs at the prospect of "an infinity of poor devils repeating the pattern without knowing it."[17] Until, contrary to expectations, the boy dies from the flu and the man is able to enjoy a brief happiness knowing that he is the first mortal, that his own miserable life will end with him. In "The Night Face Up," neither the protagonist nor the reader can distinguish which is the dream: the pleasant motorcycle ride one morning and the accident that led him to the hospital bed, or his capture by the Aztecs one night in pre-Columbian Mexico and his preparation for sacrifice. Only as the executioner-priest approaches him with the knife does he realize "that the marvelous dream had been the other, absurd as all dreams are."[18] The fantastic, however, was not always the necessary result of Cortázar's interstitial perspective. In "Blow-Up," it is rather the precariousness of perceived reality that is emphasized, centered again on the transgressive nature of the gaze. The narrator, who is French-Chilean and a translator—and thus should be used to navigating the divide—is also an amateur photographer, and in this capacity he chances upon a couple at the tip of the Ile Saint-Louis. There, watching the woman about to seduce the frightened boy, he takes the shot, thereby intruding in their transaction; as a result, the boy runs off. Only later, idly contemplating an enlargement of the photo, does the narrator realize that a man he'd noticed in a parked car nearby was in fact part of the game, that the boy was being sought for him.

In the late 1950s, Cortázar made a breakthrough in his fiction that anticipated his later political engagement. Beginning with the long story "The Pursuer," inspired by the life of jazz innovator Charlie Parker, and consolidated by his novel *Hopscotch*, his writing became more centered on humanistic concerns, especially on a sort of metaphysical search for the new man: it was now the characters that determined the narrative situations instead of the reverse.[19] "The Pursuer" contrasts two quite different characters—the troubled saxophonist Johnny Carter, a supposedly ordinary fellow who seeks to "open the door" with his music, to reach the other side of reality, and his friend the narrator, who seems above all concerned with the success of his biography of Johnny. The musician is haunted by, and in pursuit of, another sense of time: he stops in the middle of playing to say, "I already played this tomorrow"; on the métro, in the space of just two stations, he relives in his thoughts a long sequence of moments.[20] Johnny's very nature is to view life at the interstices, a condition the narrator can barely guess at in his rational way, and that intensity of possible existences, where he is riddled with doubt as to the usual certainties about things, eventually wears Johnny out.

As his attention to Latin America grew in the 1960s, Cortázar tended to reflect more on the distances between Buenos Aires and Paris. A story from mid-decade, "The Other Heaven," sets up a parallel between the two places in two distinct times—Buenos Aires in the 1930s prior to Perón's rise to power, and Paris in the 1860s prior to the Prussian invasion—linked by the narrator, a young stockbroker (another middleman) who exists simultaneously in both locales, the narrative often shifting in mid-sentence. The transition is effected through its focus on arcades: the Güemes Arcade where he lost his virginity and still likes to wander, "an ambiguous territory . . . the treasure cave in which a glimpse of sin and mint drops deliciously mixed," and the Galerie Vivienne, where he befriends the prostitute Josiane.[21] The story is haunted by doubles, a favorite theme of the author, as by alternate worlds framed in the galleries' false sky. The narrator in Buenos Aires is engaged to be married, to embark on a conventional life, in the end reluctantly leaving behind that other heaven; but until then he likes to revisit his "secret homeland," in Alejandra Pizarnik's phrase, a place of exile that celebrates the imaginary.[22] There, in nineteenth-century Paris, the district is menaced by a serial killer of prostitutes known as Laurent, who is later caught, while the locals are also drawn to the mysterious presence of a tall man referred to as the South American, a clear echo of Lautréamont in his details and like the author a transplant. As Emir Rodríguez Monegal emphasizes, the story is finally about freedom through transgression—for the narrator, from his predictable routine, but also for Laurent with his crimes and for the South American whose vocation is writing.[23]

Another angle by which Cortázar found access to an interstitial vision was through alternate systems of reality. In the novels one form this took was in the ordering of different parts, using a collage technique to highlight the discontinuities and juxtapositions; there the system itself is permeable, most notably in *Hopscotch*, where he directly encourages readers to make their own order of the chapters. But in the stories each change in the old order follows its own marvelous logic. "The Southern Thruway," one of his masterpieces, offers a new glimpse of community that is evanescent yet within reach. On the six-lane freeway leading back to Paris from the south, traffic grinds to a halt one Sunday afternoon barely an hour from the city. Time and space become utterly transformed as the motorists only manage to move a few yards at a stretch until the next long interval of stasis. No one knows the reason for the blockage, but as the hours and days pass the people emerge from their cars, strike up friendships and even establish a general solidarity in their immediate groups: they organize the distribution of food, designate one car the warehouse and another the ambulance, trade provisions with others and send off members on expeditions to nearby farms. "At night, the groups entered another life, secret and private," as new relationships form in the pursuit of "some kind of happiness."[24] The story focuses on the unit around "the engineer in the Peugeot 404" who gradually gets involved with "the girl in the Dauphine" until they are planning a life together, when unexpectedly the traffic jam begins to give way, people dash back to their cars, which pick up speed, each at its own pace, and slowly the new community vanishes before his eyes.

Often the systematic reordering of things is self-willed, in the manner of an implacable private game. In "Manuscript Found in a Pocket" the narrator has developed a set of rules for chance encounters while riding the métro, starting with the crossing of deflected gazes through their image in the window. If the woman's response seems at all favorable, then he gets off where she does hoping that his predetermined connection to another line will coincide with hers, and only then may he speak to her. The day comes when he decides "to deny, one time, the law, the code," and approaches a woman who takes a different turn than he does.[25] Their relationship develops and he confesses about the game, whose rule he broke, as sadly they agree that a "legitimate meeting" is still possible. For two weeks they again tempt chance, but without success, and in despair he throws himself onto the tracks.

It was not until the 1970s that Cortázar's political concerns substantially entered his fiction, with the result that his exile at last became a political one in 1974. Yet, despite the feeling among some admirers that his activism had caused him to lose his way as an artist, his stories—even those with a clear political dimension—remained as always alert to the interstitial spaces where the fantastic intruded and reality showed its true aspect. In "Apocalypse at Solentiname," one of the stories that provoked the Argentine military junta to ban his books, the narrator, who is the author himself, returns from a visit to the poet-priest Ernesto Cardenal's Christian community in Nicaragua and back home in Paris proceeds to look at the slides he took. At first the pictures recall moments from his trip, but suddenly they begin to detail the massacre of that community as well as other tortures and horrors elsewhere in Latin America. When his girlfriend walks in to look at them, he has to leave the room, but she, of course, sees only the photos that he took. "Graffiti," from the end of the decade, is more subtly ominous in its silent game of forbidden communication on the neutral space of city walls. Under a reign of fear and censorship against such public displays, an artist goes about making colored sketches—sometimes abstract, and only once with a few words—knowing the authorities will quickly come and erase them. Then another sketch appears next to his, by a woman, and "a different time began . . . more beautiful and more threatening."[26] As their dialogue continues, he tries surreptitiously to see what she looks like, and when he does catch a glimpse, it is only as she is being hauled off in the police wagon. One of Cortázar's last stories, "The School at Night," merges the fantastic into a terrifying premonition of Argentine politics. Set in the teacher's college that the author himself attended in the 1930s, it begins as a schoolboy prank where the narrator and his friend break in after dark; however, a sinister underside is soon revealed as they discover some of their teachers and schoolmates engaged in a perverse and secret society that is bent on training the fascists of tomorrow.

The Argentine poet and critic Saúl Yurkievich, another longtime Paris resident, has noted that Cortázar's stories, being essentially self-contained, are not the work by which we really know him; rather, it is in the open-ended playfulness of the other writing, especially the novels.[27] Nonetheless, Cortázar himself insisted that both novels and stories came from the same central attitude, "to multiply their interstitial possibilities."[28] With *Hopscotch* it could not have been otherwise, for the book dwells upon an inherent division—between "the other side" (Paris) and "this side" (Buenos Aires), between the diverse wealth of his cultural heritage and the need to put all that into question—which it does not seek to reconcile so much as to elucidate the gaps, to create a polyphonic space. Cortázar saw it as a very Argentine book, precisely for its lack of certainties.[29] Based partly on his first decade in Paris, it could only have been written by an outsider. And living at a distance from his own country, as Karine Berriot remarks, he was able to play with the totality of his heritage.[30] Thus, he was in a favorable position to be innovative.

Hopscotch follows the metaphysical searches of an Argentine in 1950s Paris among a group of mostly foreigners, "people who only wanted to escape the ordinary routine of buses and history," who often gather to talk late into the night about jazz, modern art, Western and Eastern philosophy, and more.[31] Horacio Oliveira is too intellectual for his own good—he cannot act or make real contact with the world, and fails in his lyrical romance with the more intuitive La Maga—and his fall from grace is a hard one. As a result, he is picked up by the police and sent back to Argentina. The second part of the novel finds him in Buenos Aires, ever at a loss and reconnecting with his old buddy Traveler (who has never traveled), through whom he soon finds work in a circus and then in a mental asylum. There, still seeking a bridge beyond, a metaphysical breakthrough that remains out of reach, he suffers a sort of delusion of his own and the story ends with him perched on a window ledge, his friends below—the reader is given no clear indication if he will jump. But there is also a third part to the novel, "From Diverse Sides," comprising a hundred "expendable chapters" situated in the margins of the conventional order, according to a detailed page of instructions at the start of the book: some occur in a time and space in between the earlier chapters, others stand as further extensions of a scene or offer more elaborate ramifications of various reflections, while others are simply citations from diverse readings that draw the reader outside of the story even as they cast another light upon it.

Among other reasons for choosing Paris as his home, the city opened Cortázar to new rhythms of existence, including the pictorial rhythms of modern art that could only be experienced on site. Combined with his longstanding passion for jazz, which was far more available in Paris than in Buenos Aires, this led him to explore new approaches in his writing, to attain a kind of *swing* as in jazz carried by the shifting tensions in the rhythm. Jazz also showed the way to a certain freedom, as in horn players like Lester Young and Charlie Parker whose improvisations transformed old standards into new patterns of associations, providing another example to Cortázar of the permeability he favored, how with the porousness of a sponge he might take in ideas from all directions.[32] *Hopscotch* is the first full flowering of such porousness and of his efforts to accomodate a multitude of rhythms in the prose. One of the more evident aspects of the novel is the abundance of cultural and intellectual references made by the characters, which, in contrast to the intuitive figure of La Maga, soon appears as excess and serves in the critique of that very tradition; at the same time, especially when added to the heteroclite materials found in the expendable chapters—song lyrics, curiosities from newspapers, brief extracts from modern literature, and scientific treatises—it suggests just how wide the web of knowledge can be. Like no one before in Spanish, Yurkievich points out, Cortázar opened "literary textuality to the profuse proliferation of outside discourses."[33] But that attitude of porousness carried a danger in that it could get out of hand. "The saturation got to such a point," Cortázar later wrote, "that the only honorable thing was to accept without discussion that rain of meteorites that entered through windows, books, dialogues, ordinary coincidences, and convert them into passages, fragments, expendable or unexpendable chapters," in that way offering a glimpse of what lay beyond, concurrent with the book.[34] Indeed, embarking on his next novel, one of his purposes was to suppress the intrusion of such meteorites.

62: A Model Kit (1968) arose from two main impulses. The first was an intellectual proposition stated in chapter 62 of *Hopscotch*, wherein the reclusive writer Morelli—whose ideas the group loves to discuss—postulates a novel that would present "an *impersonal* drama," a constellation of human interactions beyond individual causality and psychology; in the characters something "subliminal would laboriously open up a road . . . everything would be a kind of disquiet, a continuous uprooting."[35] The other source, providing much of the specific flavor, was Cortázar's own experience as a translator, the resonant displacements in which one European capital with its ministries and hotels became superimposed over another, blurring together, suggesting a city beyond where all converge.[36] As in the previous novel there is an interchangeable aspect to the different parts, "especially on the level of meaning, where the opening for combinatory art is more insistent and imperative," he notes on the introductory page. "The reader's option, his personal montage of the elements in the tale, will in each case be the book he has chosen to read."[37] By creating the open structures of his novels, he sought to engage the active reader—another terrain, ultimately, for the exercise of his social conscience.

His most experimental novel, *62: A Model Kit* defies any straightforward synopsis; suffice it to say that the book constructs a more disturbing realm of the marvelous than the usual tourist of magical realism will encounter. In the ensemble cast—again made up mostly of foreigners, with a few French—Juan the protagonist is an interpreter whose profession marks him as the best disposed to navigate the burgeoning contingency of events. The story opens with a phrase overheard by Juan in a restaurant, "I'd like a bloody castle," itself a distortion of the customer's intent, who wanted his steak rare (*saignant*). The displacement of meaning "would suddenly cause the coagulation of other things already past or present."[38] These include: the image of Hélène before he entered the restaurant; the book by Michel Butor he was reading that refers to the writer François René de Chateaubriand as he hears the phrase with the word shortened from a *châteaubriand* steak to *château*; the associative leap to the bloody castle evokes the bloody Hungarian countess, Erzébet Báthory, who was likened to a vampire centuries earlier for her plunder and murder of young women; that echoes Frau Marta whom Juan spies on in her seduction of an English girl at the King of Hungary Hotel in Vienna, where he is working through much of the novel; this in turn echoes ahead in the story where Hélène unexpectedly and disastrously seduces her young friend Celia who has left home, even as Hélène—an anesthetist who that same day had seen a young man who resembled Juan die in the hospital—remains tragically destined to be with Juan despite a series of missed connections. Such communicative sparks tie in with still other events throughout the novel, which, as ever in Cortázar's long fiction, is given breathing space by a healthy dose of the comic and absurd. But it is Juan's in-between state, as with other characters, that allows him to perceive the multiple direction of forces and to sketch some sort of movement among them. In this respect, he shares a certain male condition with the protagonists of *Hopscotch* and *A Manual for Manuel* (1973), for they each occupy a space between two women: each must struggle to learn which, if either, is their true place.

In fact, *place* is the underlying problem for the characters in 62. It seems no one is really where they should be, or they are already on the way to somewhere else. Paris may be the affective center of the novel, with Vienna and London as the other settings, but there is another dimension where they mysteriously converge, the City—a dreamlike poetic space laid out like a vague amalgam of Paris, Buenos Aires, other capitals, which the different figures may chance to enter at any time, seeking one another or headed for an unknown rendezvous. Juan often goes by way of the hotels endemic to his work, "neutral territories from where . . . access to the city always seemed easier."[39] The City stands like a sort of exile beyond, a landscape of passage with its hotels and sidewalks, its canals and streetcars, equidistant from all other places yet embedded within each character that goes there. More than a novelistic convention, it arose directly out of Cortázar's own experience, which he visited in dreams throughout his life, to the point where he drew up a map of the place.[40]

Considering his increasing activity in support of Cuba and other social causes by then, it may seem surprising that he chose to write such an ahistorical, nonpolitical novel. But he always insisted that his artistic freedom was not to be compromised or obliged to serve any purpose other than its own. Even while working on the book he said as much in his letter to Roberto Fernández Retamar, reiterating his commitment. "Does it not seem paradoxical to you really that an Argentine almost entirely bent on Europe in his youth, to the point of burning his boats and coming to France without a precise idea of his destiny, should have discovered here, after a decade, his true condition as a Latin American?" Europe continued to be the optimal vantage point, for it allowed him to follow the Cuban Revolution from a "denationalized" perspective and to understand the roots of Latin American issues within a global context, due to the "mental ubiquity" that Europe afforded.[41] Nonetheless, Cortázar continued to be criticized by some on the Latin American left who felt he should relinquish his romance with Europe and come home.

In a 1969 polemic with Oscar Collazos, who argued for an art that was true to the Latin American social realities, Cortázar defended the literary experimentation of a novel like 62, which "was written as a probe, a first exploration of territory of difficult access." He lauded the appearance of "good novels immersed in the 'socio-cultural and political context,'" but what was needed above all were "the revolutionaries of literature more than the literati of the revolution."[42] Several years later David Viñas charged that Cortázar incarnated "the old Argentine myth of sanctification in Paris" just when leading French intellectuals were announcing that Paris was finished as a center. Cortázar's spiritual journey to France, according to Viñas, was like the inverse of Régis Debray's journey to Latin America to materialize the revolutionary spirit developed in Europe.[43] In response, Cortázar insisted that he did not come to Paris to sanctify anything, rather because he was suffocating under the Perón regime, which did not allow him to live as he pleased. What had to be understood, he said, was to what point Paris was and had been a "detonator" for many aspects touching on Latin American consciousness and that Europe was in a way the "coauthor" of his books, especially *Hopscotch*.[44]

By this time his last novel, *A Manual for Manuel*, was about to be published. Partly a return to issues and techniques explored in *Hopscotch*, it was his only novel to make politics one of its central concerns. Here too the protagonist Andrés is caught in "the not very friendly confrontation between the old man and the new," as he struggles to understand what sort of bridge may be built, a problem demonstrated to him by the music of Karlheinz Stockhausen.[45] Above all, the novel offers an alternate writing of history, on several levels. The main action of the story—which does not develop until almost halfway through the book, in favor of more humanistic questions—involves the kidnapping of a Latin American diplomat in Paris whose ransom is the liberation of leftist guerrillas imprisoned in Latin America. That the group perpetrating it should hardly seem the terrorist type, or that their plot somewhat succeeds, is a measure of what lies behind the official version of such news items. Throughout the book, the ongoing project among the group of friends—as in the previous novels, a seriocomic band of mostly Latin Americans and other foreigners, plus a few French—is to assemble another book, the manual for the baby Manuel's future, a sort of history via press clippings of what really went on in Latin America and Europe. This construction of the future book remains open to debate among the group as to its full nature, with the clippings themselves inserted directly into the narrative.

Again producing a collage novel, Cortázar surely reveled in the provocation of his hybrid form. Yet, in another note to the reader on the first page, he states that after a long convergence, such mixture of historical reality and the purely imaginary seems rather natural to him.[46] It was consistent with the surrealist attitude to transform reality, to break down old habits and restore a poetic dimension to life. In the novel this also characterizes the group's activities prior to the kidnapping. These "responses" aim to disrupt the working order of society, to let the irrational intrude, as a ubiquitous form of guerrilla theater: one person suddenly starts to scream during Brigitte Bardot's sex scene in a movie theater, another goes to a nice restaurant and insists on eating his dinner standing, others alter packs of Gauloises by replacing the cigarettes with half-smoked butts and slipping the packs back into circulation on the market.

In a paper delivered at Cérisy in 1978, Cortázar called for writers to turn away from the negative value of exile, to profit instead from "an opportunity for self-examination." He urged the exile, in a "deliberate act of distancing," to use humor as a resource and to reinvent himself by opposing the conventional.[47] It was around then that he first planned a trip with his wife that became one of his last books a few years later. *Los autonautas de la cosmopista* (*autopista*=highway) (1984) is another collage book or almanac, in the form of a travel diary, with its echoes of Marco Polo and other intrepid explorers, that followed a mad plan: taking the southern thruway they made an "atemporal voyage" in their camping van from Paris to Marseilles, but in a way that turned inside out the usual pattern and became a journey utterly of interstices. According to their rules, they had to stop at every rest area along the way, at the rate of two per day, staying overnight at the second. The trip lasted thirty-three days, a medieval velocity that allowed them to see the *other* thruway and to experience the rest stops as the archipelago of their vacation.[48] Like the truckers they met whose phantom city each night changed anew, there they continually discovered another, transient human community.

6

Transgressive Gestures

(Severo Sarduy, Copi)

If Cortázar flourished in the space *between* cultures and places, **Severo Sarduy** (1937–1993) and **Copi** (1939–1987) could well be said to have thrived in a space *beyond*. Both drew strength from their positions as outsiders, in relation to their adopted home and also their native culture. Their writing proved boisterously defiant of social norms, populated by outrageous characters whose gender, sexuality, and very identity remain often ambiguous, never stable. Each subverted the public's easy certainties, but their most fundamental transgressions were effected through the use of language and formal expectations. Sarduy cast his lot with that lineage of writers who were above all preoccupied with problems of meaning and representation in language, drawing constant attention to the surface of the text. Copi, writing in French, kept shattering theatrical and narrative conventions, while effectively refusing any assigned place as an artist.

In a sense, as exiles, both writers lived outside the law—the law of their native lands—since their first transgression, like many Spanish-American writers and preceding all else, was to have left. Sarduy, the son of a railroad stationmaster in Camagüey, a provincial city in the east of Cuba, arrived in Paris in 1960 on a scholarship to study art criticism; he never returned to Cuba except once toward the end of his life, when he went to visit his dying mother.[1]

Copi, born to a prominent family in Buenos Aires, spent much of his childhood in Uruguay and then Paris, during the Perón years; in 1955, the family returned to Argentina where he wrote his first plays, but in 1962, he left again to settle in Paris. From the start of their new lives, both writers maintained a sort of distant intimacy with their native cultures, profiting from that remove to redraw their own national borders.

Despite the freedom it bought him as a writer, Sarduy recognized, in a late text, the responsibilities that came with exile, particularly within the Latin American tradition of Paris: "To arrive . . . at this exile, voluntary or not, is at the same time to embrace an order, to integrate oneself: to accept as well, which is the hardest, like the delegation of a continuity, that you cannot be unworthy of those who came before, you have to write as they did, or better, you have to give this distance—from your native land—consistency, texture, you have to create a *meaning* with this *lack*." Defining oneself within that experience ends up inevitably an individual response. "Among artists, the categories of exile are as specific as their own styles. None of them are alike. . . . As for me, I simply consider myself someone who *stayed*, or else—I come from an island—an ex-islander (*un a-islado*)." But more than the physical distance from the familiar colors and flavors and sounds, "the true leap is linguistic: leaving the language—sometimes it leaves us—and adopting French." Citing some of the Spanish-language writers who made such a leap—Jorge Semprún, Hector Bianciotti, Fernando Arrabal, Eduardo Manet—he sees that move as "the very example of will and courage." Finally, Sarduy questions whether geographical exile isn't a mirage after all, if true exile isn't "something that has always been inside us, like a part of our being that remains obscure . . . which is that land we have to leave within ourselves."[2]

Sarduy had been active as a young writer contributing poetry, fiction, and critical pieces to Havana journals in the late 1950s, before and especially after the Cuban Revolution. Among his collaborations in 1959, the first year of the new government, he became art critic for the weekly *Lunes de Revolución*, edited by Guillermo Cabrera Infante; though Sarduy left Cuba by the end of that year, he continued sending articles. His decision to stay on in Paris after the fellowship, as Roberto González Echevarría points out, was not yet, in 1960–61, considered an act of desertion, as it would be later in the case of many others.[3] Indeed, when Cabrera Infante opted for exile in 1965, like Nivaria Tejera that same year and Manet in 1968—these last two had each spent much of the 1950s in Paris and returned to Cuba to take part in the revolutionary process—they were all erased from the official histories of Cuban literature. This became Sarduy's fate as well, ultimately, despite the fact that he remained outside of politics and never publicly criticized the Cuban government.[4] Still, the choice to remain reflected his situation in both places: immersed in his studies at the Ecole du Louvre, he was making new friendships that included the philosopher François Wahl, his lifelong companion who introduced him to Roland Barthes and the journal *Tel Quel*; away from Cuba, he viewed with caution the rapid changes taking place there, where *Lunes* had disbanded and the literary figures who helped him previously no longer held the same influence.[5]

In regarding Sarduy's novels, from *Gestos* (Gestures, 1963) to *Pájaros de la playa* (Beach Birds, 1993), the most salient feature may be the disruptive nature of his prose. The narrative line incessantly folds back on itself or spins off in new departures, undermining every level of illusion, shifting scenes without transition, mixing the most disparate references from high art to popular culture, crossing discourses in a fluidity of time and space that defies the traditional order. This practice, where the play of language—of writing—is foremost, reflects the plasticity of thought he achieved through his attention to other disciplines, notably painting, as well as the freedom gained by claiming both a geographical and literary space of his own. In his work he remained independent, of the *Tel Quel* writers as of his Latin American contemporaries, even as he posited, in a 1967 essay on Maurice Roche, "a new literature in which language will be present as . . . a surface of unlimited transformations." The characteristics of such writing, as he developed it in his own novels starting with *From Cuba with a Song* (1967), would include "transvestism, the continual metamorphosis of characters, references to other cultures, the mixture of languages, the division of the book in registers (or voices)," all exalting the body through their dance and gestures.[6] Implicated within all this was the very body of the writer, who "is a *material, situated* subject and not an 'inspired' floating author," as he told Jean-Michel Fossey in 1973, citing his own example: "I write naked, and sometimes I dance around looking for the words, looking for them until my body turns into a language and the language on the page turns into a body."[7]

But his sense of rupture, a writing whose constant changes disrupt narrative continuity, was more than an aesthetic tactic or even a result of exile: it connected directly with some very Cuban qualities in his "interpretation of reality as the product of explosions." González Echevarría traces this view to Sarduy's first text on art in 1957, where he champions the abstract aspects of a Camagüeyan painter whose landscapes are like so many bursts of light and color. He later develops the concept in his book-length essay, *Barroco* (1974), drawing a parallel between the big bang theory of the origin of the universe and the ornamental effusions in baroque art as generated from an empty center.[8] More immediately, such eruptions may also be found in the rhythms of Cuban humor, fundamental to Sarduy in both life and art: the mocking verbal jests known as *choteo*, the penchant for nicknaming as "to smash every attempt at solemnity and grandiloquence."[9]

His preoccupation with the surface of writing derived partly from his interest in abstract art, but was also nourished by the French writers he frequented. In the early to mid-1960s he studied structuralist methodology with Barthes at the Sorbonne, where he took courses as well with Roger Bastide on the African component in Latin America, reinforcing his own investigations into Cuban identity.[10] He began collaborating with *Tel Quel* in 1965, and the following year with the Paris-based journal that favored the Latin American writers of the Boom, *Mundo Nuevo*. The pieces published in these journals made up his first book of essays, *Written on a Body* (1967), where he articulated important aspects of his poetics. In regard to writing's surface, he understood what was at stake. "One of our culture's persistent prejudices demands that the *support* be obliterated from all artistic production"—the canvas and pigments in painting, the armature in sculpture, the page and "graphicness" in literature. These are "concealed in order to achieve an illusion of space, an original *logos*," so as to "organize" the object. "The reason for such censorship is that civilization—and above all Christian thought—has destined the body for oblivion, for *sacrifice*. Consequently, everything that refers to the body . . . is ultimately considered a transgression."[11]

While the association with *Tel Quel* granted Sarduy new intellectual tools to further his own concerns, he remained an outsider and never ceased to think of himself as typically Cuban, in the rich tradition of the Spanish baroque, especially Luis de Góngora. González Echevarría makes the important point that "the non-European modern world—the postcolonial world, the Third World—is absent from *Tel Quel*, with the exception of Mao's China, reified and distant."[12] For Sarduy the inescapable difference was language. Though he identified with the theoretical research of the group—how the text involves a symbiotic relationship between reader and writer, how the production of meaning is open-ended and multidirectional, how the doubtful authority of a unifying subject may affect language—his view of the results was distinct: "I found luxury, proliferation, humor, uproarious laughter."[13] In other words, it sent him back with renewed enthusiasm to harness the energy of the baroque.

At the same time, despite his Latin American friendships, he himself was rather an "anti-Boom" writer in that his more radical practice turned away from a mimetic approach to fiction.[14] He did not hesitate, therefore, to tease his readers, along with his friends, as in this footnote from *Cobra* (1972)— "Moronic reader: if even with these clues, thick as posts, you have not understood . . . abandon this novel and devote yourself to screwing or to reading the novels of the Boom, which are much easier."[15] Still, he was instrumental in presenting their work to the French public, due to his position as editor at Le Seuil (home of the *Tel Quel* writers), where he codirected the Latin American collection for more than twenty years. There he helped publish many important writers: García Márquez's *One Hundred Years of Solitude*, José Lezama Lima's *Paradiso*, José Donoso's *The Obscene Bird of Night*, the Brazilian writer João Guimarães Rosa, fellow Cubans like Heberto Padilla and Reinaldo Arenas, as well as his own work. In his last years, he tried to relaunch Roger Caillois's old series at Gallimard, with La Nouvelle Croix du Sud. But Sarduy's literary methods served as a provocation to Latin Americans, for he saw writing as the ultimate battleground. At a time when many leftists were losing faith in Cuba, he suggested to Fossey, "Every regime rests on writing. A revolution that doesn't invent its own writing has failed. . . . What's the point of all those acts of 'confrontation' except for writing, because writing is the force that demythologizes, corrupts, mines, cracks the foundation of any regime?"[16]

Regardless of his opinions about the Cuban Revolution, and its opinions of him, it galvanized his inquiries into the nature of Cubanness and how that might be reflected in writing. In a long essay about Lezama Lima, whose *Paradiso* with its "multiple sediments" makes the collage tradition an essentially Cuban trait, Sarduy defines Cuban reality as "not a synthesis, a syncretic culture, but a superposition. A Cuban novel must make explicit all the strata in that superposition, must show all its 'archeological' planes."[17] This was in effect a statement of purpose for his own second novel, *From Cuba with a Song*, which he was then writing; but along with other abiding concerns such a view was already present somewhat in his first novel.[18] Set just before the Cuban Revolution, *Gestos* wavers at the edge of abstraction to focus on collective gestures. The fervor that gave rise to momentous events is palpable in the very texture of Havana life: the restless movements of people through the city, the brisk rhythm and interchange of voices, the itinerant singers, the weariness and waiting, all offset by a vivid juxtaposition of colors and architectural details in rooms, façades, streets. The characters remain unnamed—including the protagonist, a cabaret singer by night and washerwoman by day—as if to de-emphasize individual destinies. Thus, in the last chapter like the first, after the bomb she set at the behest of those who recruited her blows up the electrical plant, the woman seems much the same (since her own destiny is not really the novel's concern): fed up and with a headache, unsure if she'll sing that night. As the Barbadian novelist George Lamming says in another context, about the particularities of the Caribbean novel, which would include Sarduy's book, "Community, and not person, is the central character."[19]

In writing *Gestos*, Sarduy wanted to produce "a book of action writing." His obsession at the time was the action painting of the abstract expressionists, especially Franz Kline; a decade later, with his interest in Buddhism, it would be Mark Rothko's canvases.[20] Some critics have also seen the *nouveau roman* writers reflected there: the minute attention to objective details as in Alain Robbe-Grillet, the hidden subconscious movements of Nathalie Sarraute's tropisms.[21] But these abstract techniques help convey a specific figurative reality, the cultural layers brought into focus as the woman moves through the streets and as repercussions from a series of bombs are felt among neighbors ever skeptical of official reports. Almost at the center of the novel, before the sequence of the woman going to plant her bomb and with the city already in disarray, a carnival procession at once parodies the old order and shifts the balance irrevocably toward greater disturbances. As the woman is told in the following chapter, on hesitating at her assignment, "This is your great opportunity to do theater."[22] Indeed, by the end of the story the city has become a patchwork of fires, like so many crumbling stage sets, transformed by a sort of comic chaos.

Within the scope of his first novel, Sarduy employed several elements that would become constants in his fiction irrespective of their theoretical value. These derive from a theatrical dynamic that is multiplied and refracted, emphasizing the performative aspect of narrative, writing as spectacle or as specular experience. Here again, Sarduy shares in a Caribbean aesthetic, one that is polyphonic, contrapuntal, and based in ritual, which pertains to the mixed roots of the cultures and the importance of traditional practices.[23] Each of his protagonists is engaged in a performance, usually on a stage, albeit sometimes against their will: young Cocuyo, whose first fear is of people looking at him, ends up repeatedly spying on others unperceived. Through the identifying gaze there is a doubling—the washerwoman who is a cabaret singer, and who is also a terrorist—the same and yet different, a mask and concealment, the better to reveal that measure of difference. Sarduy's texts parody and exaggerate, they make a show of signifying. Underlying all this is the musicality of his writing, the way he breaks up or combines the prose rhythms and shapes the movements of his narratives, as well as the frequent interpolation of Cuban song lyrics that place the texts in the context of popular culture, never far from Sarduy's mind. Which leads, then, to his sense of voice, and by extension, to hearing.

Voice in his work is less a feature for constructing characters than it is a thread or musical figure that generates text through the weave and response of other voices. In "The Beach," one of several radio plays he wrote in the 1960s and 1970s, the fragmented story develops through the repetition and overlapping of roles, the parties to events shifting gender, the events themselves recurring in different places. The beach effect renders the flux of what is heard, or overheard, "the open sea bringing back the voices."[24] Rather than characters, the actors are more like "bearers of text," Sarduy says in his notes, and with the "superposition of voices" the sequences proceed through a "melodic organization."[25] In fact, *overhearing* might be thought of as a crucial gesture in his work, with all it implies: hearing what one is not supposed to or hadn't intended, like a secret spectator; hearing through or beyond, across boundaries, like the diagonal thinking of Caillois that he admired, or like the layering of cultural strata that he experienced both in Cuba and as a foreigner in Paris; hearing in excess, as to playfully distort or reflected in the baroque's superabundance of signifying. As he wrote in a sequence of poems inspired by Franz Kline (in translation these were his first contribution to *Tel Quel*): "The ear stuck to the wall./Listen./Something is going to break. Something/grows."[26]

Though it pretends to treat the archaeological components, *From Cuba with a Song* is a relentless parody that puts into question the mythologizing forces of a culture. In three fables reflecting the Chinese, African, and Spanish strands of Cuban reality—the elements of Sarduy's own personal mythology—the desired object proves elusive, like the fiction itself. So the General lusts after Lotus Flower, a singer at the Chinese opera, who is really a transvestite, a made-up image of exotic charms, fleeing from his advances; so the mulatta courtesan Dolores Rondón hungers after power through the rise and fall of the senator, Mortal Pérez; so the chorus girls Help and Mercy search across Spain for an absent lover that becomes a quest for salvation and a pilgrimage through Cuba with a dilapidated wooden Christ. Marked on all levels by its theatrical methods, the text turns representation inside out, lifts the curtain, permits every invasion of other texts, from ancient Hispano-Arabic poets to Columbus's diary to a modern soap commercial, and animates his own ideas developed elsewhere: Help "composing the Lord's texts on her naked body," replete with recorded soundtrack, to win over the masses.[27] The Dolores Rondón section with its two bickering narrators takes the form of a wild dramatized commentary (first written as a radio play) on a *décima*, a traditional ten-line verse stanza, written for herself as a preposthumous epitaph. Not only the unity of the text is exploded but so are received images, like the Orientalist send-up early in the novel and the Spanish phantasmagoria later; it is "an exaltation of the surface" that he practices, as it will be in *Cobra*, with "costume jewelry India."[28] Even décor itself is suspect, precisely for what it leaves out, the movement hidden by its seeming stasis: the backdrop at the Chinese opera that Lotus Flower uses for camouflage, in the same way that Colibrí in a later novel will vanquish his opponent by feigning stillness to blend in with the mural; or like the figures in the Spanish carpet whose gestures remain incomplete, obstructed by unraveling and repairs. What emerges, in González Echevarría's phrase, is "the residue of history," a playful mosaic circling around a lost origin.[29]

In contrast to the anonymity of characters in *Gestos*, their perpetual metamorphoses are a keynote in the next book. Help and Mercy—appearing in all three fables and referred to by various nicknames (the Divine Ones, the Fates, the Flamenco Girls)—are shameless in their transformations, leaping to it at a moment's notice; in subsequent novels they reappear transfigured, like the twins with healing powers in *Maitreya* who become fat sopranos after puberty, and again with their own names in Sarduy's last novel. This talent for metamorphosis among characters develops into the fetish-names of later protagonists—Cobra, Colibrí (Hummingbird), Cocuyo (Firefly)—where each incorporates the illusion of stillness in movement, free from entrapment, escaping any easy identification: like Sarduy the exile.

In its French translation, Roland Barthes praised *From Cuba with a Song* as "a hedonist and therefore revolutionary text," through which the "Cuban language has subverted our horizon" and revealed "the baroque face of the French language."[30] All the greater was his enthusiasm when *Cobra* came out in 1972, translated by Philippe Sollers with Sarduy, which developed his methods on a wider plane, well beyond Cuba. Barthes described *Cobra* as "a marbled, iridescent text," even "a paradisiac text, utopian (without site), a heterology by plenitude." The novel was perceived by the French as a *tour de force* and awarded the Prix Médicis for best foreign novel. (Cortázar won the honor two years later with *A Manual for Manuel*.) "Language reconstructs itself *elsewhere*," wrote Barthes, "under the teeming flux of every kind of linguistic pleasure.... *Cobra* is the pledge of continuous jubilation, the moment when by its very excess verbal pleasure chokes and reels into bliss."[31]

The novel was set in motion—burst out of the air—by a phrase Sarduy heard on the beach at Cannes, about a famous transvestite: "Cobra was killed in a jet over Fujiyama."[32] At the start of her slippery journey of incarnations, Cobra the protagonist is the queen of the Lyrical Theater of Dolls, the greatest artifice wrought by her manager, the Madam: this launches a series of relationships through Sarduy's four subsequent novels involving some version of performers and tyrannical managers, each a reflection of the work trying to break free of its creator. Cobra wants to be perfect, or rather divine, and suffers extreme measures to transform her ugly feet; she and the Madam's efforts result in miniature duplicates of themselves, but the monstrous disobedient copies cast doubt on the supposed originals. Ultimately she wants to become her simulation, a real woman, so she, her dwarf Pup, and the Madam go off to Tangier for a strange operation—even then, she is dissatisfied, a sad echo of her former glory. The second part of the novel continues her journey as through a looking glass, where Cobra reappears as a man, unchanged it would seem, in a Paris leather bar initiated as the fifth member of a motorcycle gang with fetish names; after they go riding to a Buddhist monastery, Cobra's corpse is laid out in ritual fashion, his body dispersed. One last time he reemerges among five fugitive distillers, refugee lamas from Nepal after the Chinese invasion, only to disappear again in the final "Indian Journal"—a correction in part of Columbus's error with the discovery of the 'real' Indies.

With its proliferation of references, its appropriations and tributes to other artists, *Cobra* is the most baroque of Sarduy's fictions. It was no accident, he reminds us elsewhere, that the baroque style first developed with the rise of the Jesuits: all ornament and artifice was intended to convince.[33] Today, however, "being baroque means to threaten, judge and parody bourgeois economy ... at its very center and foundation: the space of signs, the language, symbolic pillar of society ... To waste, dissipate, squander language solely in function of pleasure ... is an offense against the good sense ... upon which the whole ideology of consumption and accumulation is based."[34] The neobaroque, then, "reflects structurally the discordance, the rupture of homogeneity, of the logos as absolute," and thus "a desire that cannot reach its object."[35] In the novel's many levels of textual play, Rodríguez Monegal counts at least eleven transfigurations of Cobra. But "just as Cobra is always a man, essentially a man, in spite of tons of body paint ... the text is always the same despite the metamorphoses of its episodes, places, and personages," remaining "immobilized on its ever-changing surface."[36] Some years later, in *La simulación* (1982), Sarduy articulated this notion in terms of travesty. "The transvestite does not copy; he simulates, since there is no norm . . . to determine his metaphor." His pursuit is "of an infinite unreality . . . to be more and more of a woman, until the line is crossed and woman is surpassed." The goal, finally, is "a kind of disappearance" into the model's image, and so "his fascination with fixity."[37]

It is curious to note a chance symmetry that occurs over the full three decades of Sarduy's novelistic production: *Maitreya* (1978), at the exact middle of this span, marks the beginning of a return from his furthest reaches. So much was he identified with the audacious *Cobra* that he wanted to shake off its image, and so he set out to write a parody and inversion of his own novel, systematically tracing the opposite route.[38] *Maitreya* begins in a Tibetan monastery at the death of the Master during the time of the Chinese invasion, and proceeds toward the cacophonous West in search of the future Buddha. The first surprise in the opening pages, with the description of the monks and their ritual, is the almost naturalistic prose—an increasing element in Sarduy's arsenal, though never innocent. A bit more linear than the previous books, the narrative finds the young incarnation of Buddha with the old Leng sisters, who take him south away from the eager refugee monks and enshrine him in an island ashram. At length, the boy tires of the game, refusing to play the guru, and declares it to be his last cycle: that night he will enter nirvana. The Divinity does not correspond to expectations, and so the mystery remains intact. But if the first part of the novel is about a repetition in time, the second part, as Sarduy has noted, is a repetition in space.[39] In Cuba, the chubby Chinese mulatta twins at first mock their gifts for healing as the boy had done at the ashram; later, as prodigious sopranos—guided by the dwarf who is their manager—they perform mock socialist tributes at the local Chinese opera house. Dubbed Ladies Divine and Tremendous, they continue north to Miami and New York, launching a sex sect based on fistfucking. Lady Tremendous flourishes as a Wagnerian diva in a gay bar and after reducing her sister to a mere prop, she and the dwarf go off to the desert where they set up a house of fistfucking for wealthy petrodollar magnates. In a final ritual, orchestrated by the dwarf, her big Iranian chauffeur performs the act on her, whereby she gets pregnant and soon gives anal birth to a child, an odd freak who betokens the strange decline of them all.

In the search for the future Buddha, the "signifying absence that is Maitreya," Suzanne Jill Levine points out that "desire is always mediated, its object always deferred." The series of displacements that is unleashed, therefore, becomes the sinuous plot of the novel.[40] Exile—of Tibetans as of Cubans

—is figured into the space of a journey where identity is perpetually negotiated as a mirrored play of perspectives. Hence Sarduy's longstanding interest in Diego Velázquez's painting, "Las Meninas." The doublings are inevitably distortions—in *Maitreya* and *Cobra*— which take their revenge by rendering the model suspect: like "the power of an *ex-centric* discourse, a runaway, the opposite of instituted law," that he describes in an essay on Juan Goytisolo. "To look on from expulsion . . . is already to call into question the oppressor's territory." History is "seen from the shifting periphery," and in the resultant stereophony, the nomadic voice becomes "freed, decolonized" through "the deterritorializing act of writing."[41] What Sarduy wanted to achieve in *Maitreya*, he has said, is "an enormous laugh"—linking at once the Buddhist sense with that elaborated by Mikhail Bakhtin, as carnival, circus, or in the spirit of Witold Gombrowicz where the normal order is likewise inverted.[42]

All the same, exile is also a process of nostalgia and melancholy, and in *Colibrí* (Hummingbird, 1983), he holds before him the image of Cuba as a Caribbean space. Set on a river delta in the jungle, the novel is dominated by the natural world. Yet realistic as the descriptions of landscape seem, they are a composite of place and artifice: the surrounding locales Sarduy visited in those years (Mexico, Puerto Rico, Venezuela), the prehistoric nature found in the tradition of books portraying a return to the sources (especially Alejo Carpentier's *The Lost Steps*), as well as Wifredo Lam's painting, "The Jungle." Among other themes, the novel is also an allegory of power. The labyrinthine site of Colibrí's repeated escapes, the jungle stands in contrast to the Big House where the Regent and her sidekick the Big Dwarf entertain their wealthy clients: on a stage with an exotic backdrop ferocious wrestling matches are held, and there the protagonist arrives, slight of build, who defeats the fat Japanese. Now the favorite, Colibrí rejects his new status and opts for flight—his talent for simulating fixity in movement serves him at each turn. The Regent sends her hunters after him, but Colibrí keeps getting away. The narrator, meanwhile, can't help intruding, but the story is "robbed" from him too in one chapter, where the chase is diverted through an Alpine summer landscape. When at last the hunters catch up with him again, it is to help him take power: he in turn proves more ruthless and intolerant than the Regent.

In Sarduy, the return to his geographical roots by way of a more conventional literary form must also be seen historically, as González Echevarría observes: the early 1980s saw *Tel Quel* disband, the move away from theory and experiment toward a more autobiographical writing, and the deaths of

Barthes, Jacques Lacan, and Michel Foucault.[43] Absence dogged him, as in his "Tibetan Book of the Dead"—an address book bought in Tibet—where he dared not erase the names of deceased friends who were becoming so numerous, he says, that the book was approaching fiction. He worried about his "lack of close ties: the phantom that haunts every exile."[44] Diagnosed with AIDS in the mid-1980s, he perceived the disease as "a stalking . . . as if someone, at any moment, under any pretext at all, could knock on the door and carry you off forever . . . For how long will you escape? Everything gathers the weight of a threat. The Jews, it seems, know this feeling well."[45]

Cocuyo (Firefly, 1990), the tale of a boy coming into adolescence and also into awareness of the perfidy of the world, is a novel shot through with anxiety—clearly rendered by the French title, taken from its first chapter, "So that no one will know I'm afraid." Yet even while the threat of asphyxiation recurs often, the writing here and in his final novel tends to breathe more, as if by necessity, and is more at ease in the realism of its descriptions. Family is the first source of anxiety: their gaze immobilizes the boy, and after he is reduced to mute mechanical gestures by the shock of what he sees during a hurricane—a man in the street beheaded by a flying sheet of zinc roofing—family members ridicule him mercilessly. So he tries to kill them by lacing their tea with rat poison—even his sister, the only one who took pity, who returns periodically in his thoughts as the merest ghost of a guardian angel. Only he fails, and they all end up in the hospital. Escaping there, his family left behind, Cocuyo begins to understand that exile will be his lot, without a resting place. The course of his journey, with disturbing dreamlike turns, is set in fragments of Havana from the Batista era where, nonetheless, ships arrive with slaves who are sold at public auction. A motherly old black woman brings him to a sort of orphanage for girls, where a white woman, Lady Kindness (*la Bondadosa*), lets him sleep in one of the offices. He develops an attachment for one girl, Ada (or *Hada*, fairy), and discovers the fragility of the body, which includes the changes wrought by puberty. But each time his desire would bring him closer, he finds her dressed in white and in the charge of authority figures who violate her, first by piercing her ears, later at an underground auction, and in the end across the bay at the Pavilion of the Pure Orchid, a house of voyeurism for viewing naked virgins. Each time he must convince himself that it's not real, in order to survive, feeling manipulated and ever more certain of the human need for cheating, for meanness. Only when he escapes from the Pavilion does he realize that he has been injured, determined to leave his wounds as "marks of the lie, the signatures of indignity in my body."[46] Swearing to return and exterminate everyone, he is left lying on his back, face up toward the burning stars.

Despairing as the novel may be, it does still close with its gaze to the light, and this appears to be Sarduy's own victory. Citing the "writers of subversion" —Antonin Artaud, Georges Bataille, William Burroughs—François Wahl says that Sarduy "read them with passion, but he couldn't bear to slip toward that metaphysical tragedy that transgression held for them. His dimension—not always euphoric—was life, and in life the search—not exactly the attainment —for serenity."[47] *Pájaros de la playa* (Beach Birds, 1993), published a month after his death, is a luminous novel about dying, set in an island sanatorium where the terrain recalls the Canary Islands. Beneath the glass cupola the young patients gather, prematurely withered by "the disease" (*el mal*), to soak up the curative light. Careful attention is given over to the trials of the body: the shell that's left of one person, the spirit gone, is a "pure simulation"; others retain only the vulture-like sharpness of their gaze; for some, merely to stand up from bed requires enormous effort.[48] The book is a curious weave of past motifs and methods. As in his first novel, the collective experience stands as the foundation, most patients glimpsed anonymously; some characters reappear, like the ambulance drivers Help and Mercy, or the blonde patient who recalls Ada, while others are figuratively evoked; the fetish name for the new doctor, the Horse, who becomes the lover of the protagonist Siempreviva (everlasting). An old lady with her perpetual performance of reminiscences and fashion shows, Siempreviva wishes to keep the young patients company, until her affair makes her seek rejuvenation at all costs, which of course ends badly. Intermittently, between various narrative departures and comic turns, the "cosmologist's diary" offers the author's own reflections on death and the body: how illness offers a sense of connectedness to all around; how decay advances on the body surreptitiously; how disillusionment will be all that is left, since he had thought that in humankind there was a part of God; how the slogan for his remaining days has become, "Train yourself not to be."[49]

Such was Sarduy's own project at the end: beyond remorse, to depart empty-handed. Yet he kept writing, just to write—reflections, aphorisms, poems. In his final months, he wrote a series of epitaphs for himself in the form of *décimas*. Above all, he retained that humor worthy of a mambo mystic:

> A gulp of cheap rum,
> a good leftover, a mass
> and a dry unhurried toast

to appease the absent
but ferocious gods:
to the one who died of laughter![50]

• •

Throughout his career, **Copi** too laughed at death, and at every taboo, leading his characters each time to the brink—and then pushing them further or bringing them back for more. He left scant record of theoretical reflections separate from his own practice, nor did he frequent the sort of French intellectual circles that spent so much time brooding over the creative process. Overall more accessible than Sarduy, his writing nonetheless marks a path of constant provocations, sparing not even his most natural allies: neither his compatriots nor the gay community, not his publisher nor the most noble leftists escape his caustic wit. Yet Copi was well liked, for he often placed himself, or versions of himself, at the heart of his most outlandish adventures—whether as actor in his plays or as narrator bearing his name in several novels.[51] Brilliantly inventive, he thrived on setting his own rules, or breaking any that got in his way. And as a cartoonist, by which he first gained renown in Paris and kept a loyal following for two and a half decades, his economy of style matched subtle timing with a deep capacity for empathy and outrage to produce a unique brand of humor.

His colorful and peripatetic upbringing no doubt predisposed Copi to the risks he courted as an artist. Born Raúl Damonte, he was the son of a politician and journalist who was forced into exile in 1945, when the family settled in Montevideo. His mother's father had founded the liberal newspaper *Crítica*, which enjoyed the biggest circulation in its day but suffered first from the family feuding for control and then at the hands of the Peronists. His maternal grandmother was a noted feminist, anarchist, and playwright in Buenos Aires —of "light sinister comedies, lesbians cheating their husbands in the 1920s and 1930s"—who loved the plays Copi wrote as a teenager and found in him a certain mischievousness that she recognized as her own.[52] It was his grandmother who gave him the nickname Copi as a child, though accounts vary as to its significance: according to the French press, his name meant 'little chicken,' not surprising given his wiry physique (and a little chicken was a frequent secondary character in his best-known comic strip); his brother Jorge says it referred to the tuft of hair (*copo*, also snowflake) that stuck up on top of his head, and it may have indicated, as well, the paleness of his complexion.[53] In 1952, his family moved to Montparnasse, after Copi's father received the honorary title of Uruguayan consul in Reims, a post that consisted of traveling a few hours once a year to order champagne for the Uruguayan government.[54] In Paris, besides going to school, he went constantly to museums with his parents, and to the theater. His father tried to make a career as a painter there, until deciding at last to bring the family back to Argentina and fight against Perón. At fifteen, Copi was helping his father run guns across the Uruguay River. Settled back in the capital after Perón's fall, his parents separated and his younger brothers were sent off to study with the Jesuits, so Copi, with his Parisian ways and in full adolescence, was well disposed to enjoy the big city.[55] In the latter half of the 1950s he began to publish his drawings and write his first plays. And he went often to the theater, at a time when small independent companies were at their height in Buenos Aires—a formative experience he had in common with Jorge Lavelli, who became his most frequent director through the subsequent decades in Paris.[56]

Copi returned to Paris on vacation in 1962 to see theater and ended up staying; he went back just twice to visit Buenos Aires, in 1968 and 1987, the year he died. Back home, his father was no longer able to send him money, having sought asylum in the Uruguayan embassy, so to make ends meet Copi sold drawings on the Pont des Arts and at cafés in Saint-Germain-des-Prés and Montparnasse. Soon he was publishing his drawings in magazines, and in 1964, *Le Nouvel Observateur* asked him to contribute a weekly comic strip, where for the next ten years his trademark, *la Femme assise* (the seated woman), appeared. In 1966, his first theatrical sketches in Paris were produced, directed by Lavelli and Jérôme Savary: in one piece the only prop was a bathtub, which was supposed to contain the playwright Arrabal working as an actor, until Copi had to replace him. These plays were more or less regarded as *happenings*, but Copi did not like the association and later explained his attitude saying that "in the *happening* nothing happens."[57] Whatever the form or style, he recognized the need for story—and all his work, especially the fiction, is remarkable for the density, the abundance, of his imagination.

The comic strips, collected in nine books over twenty years, were like his narrative workshop—but stripped down, wasting not a word or visual flourish in the unraveling of an emotion, a philosophical paradox, a social issue. Later, they appeared regularly in *Hara-Kiri*, a journal of risqué humor, the newspaper *Libération*, the magazines *Charlie Hebdo* and *Gai Pied*, and even *Paris Match*. His comics work as a sort of minimalist theater or *arte povera*, usually carried by a simple dialogue, even a monologue: with *la Femme assise* her interlocutors vary, often a chicken or duck or snail, though sometimes her daughter or others. *La Femme assise*, possibly inspired by Copi's favorite aunt, who was confined to a wheelchair for forty years, touches on a universal figure in Latin or Mediterranean countries and beyond—the woman of indeterminate age who sits in her chair and watches the world go by.[58] Copi dispenses with extraneous decor, only the woman at right seated in profile, hands folded on her lap. The most prominent feature is her big nose, with a dot or small line for her eye, five limp strands of hair and a pouting mouth; there is no top to her head above the eye, just as the chair is rendered only by two lines, the back and the back leg, with her seated body framing the rest. She is a figure outside of time, to whom things inevitably happen: as with most of Copi's protagonists, no sooner does she present herself than the world sweeps her up in its mystery.

Even as he was experimenting in the mid-1960s with his theatrical sketches, Copi was perfecting the art of the response, the pregnant silence, the poignancy of the slightest gesture, in his comics. He delighted in piercing the bubble of human illusions, but not without some tenderness. In one episode, the woman is snoozing in her chair when a little angel flutters down, settles at her feet and takes a nap. She watches, and pats the angel on the head, who begins to snore. That makes her laugh fondly, until a voice from above is heard, "Loulou, come back up here!" Before her eyes the angel flies away, and she is left more alone than before. In another, the woman gives a speech and the snail expertly plays its role as her public. "Time, for example," she begins; the snail waits. "It's always one day after the next. And who profits from it?" She pointedly holds up her finger. "The bourgeois!" she answers herself indignantly, and the snail marks a pause before cheering three times, "Bravo!" That in turn pleases her, and she leans toward the snail, "Here's your twenty centimes." Copi plays self-referential in another strip, where the woman is reading the *Observateur* and calls out, "Copi, come here right now!" The little chicken walks in from the left, "What's going on?" She is irate: "Why did you give me such a big nose?" The chicken laughs. "I'm not laughing!" she says and stares him down. "It better be the last time!" "Oui, Madame," he replies and walks away. In the last picture, her nose is three times larger.[59]

The first play where Copi began to integrate his interests in avant-garde theater into his own aesthetics was *La journée d'une rêveuse* (The Day of a Dreamer, 1968). Built from an unexpected sequence of scenes, it underlines a near-constant in his plays: no matter what rules they break, and how surreal or absurd their atmosphere, they still partake in the old unities of time and place. But these unities are scarcely a matter of the historic realm or of daily life; rather, they spring from an insular created space, like that made by the exile.

Moreover, that space is a function of distance, wherein the characters seek to reconnect with the world on their own bloody terms: the antechamber before death and history in *Eva Perón*, a frozen Siberian outpost in *The Homosexual*, an Alaskan cabin in *The Four Twins*, a spaceship in *Loretta Strong*; later, a high-rise suburban apartment in *A Tower Near Paris*, an empty theater after midnight in *La Nuit de Madame Lucienne*, and the hospital clinic in his last play, *Grand Finale*.[60]

In *La journée d'une rêveuse*, Jeanne—developed from the seated woman in the comics—inhabits a small, sparsely furnished house surrounded by a park. "To each their own morality," she says. "Mine consists in never leaving the park."[61] By way of strange disturbances, her day takes her from morning until night, with its prospect of death—the only time she fails to find the right dress for yet another costume change. The play begins in slapstick: not one but five alarm clocks awaken her. However, the repetitions turn ominous, as if to threaten a loss of identity. She goes to write in her journal: the pages are already filled, describing how she got rid of the clocks. A man lands in the tree beside her house, then four more men; all claim to be the true postman, the rest being false. Likewise, the woman herself is hardly the true Jeanne, since her mother and sisters also bore the name. Throughout the day, faced with such intrusions, she laments that she cannot even get her laundry done. At length her infant son appears, whom she soon sends out into the world with a suitcase of melon slices and her motherly advice. Other characters come and go, referring to their travels in the world. Reminded of her son, she says he "grew up so quickly I can't even remember his face. But that's natural. How can one have the same face in different places?"[62] She barely has time to bid her son a last farewell before the day slips away from her.

Eva Perón (1970) was the work that gave Copi notoriety as a playwright. A great success, it scandalized French critics and caused masses to be held in Buenos Aires; one night, a far-right commando stormed the Left Bank theater and burned down the set.[63] When the Théâtre National de Chaillot revived it as a classic in 1993, it was so elegant that it nearly lost its edge.[64] Not least of the offenses in the original production is the fact that Evita was played in drag. Though nowhere indicated in the text (Copi provided minimal stage directions for his plays), César Aira makes the convincing argument that it was systematically implicit: if she isn't "the Saint of the Humble, the Champion of the Workers . . . neither does she need to be a woman." Nor does she have to die, as the myth requires.[65] She survives as image, ruthlessly constructed and maintained by the character to the point of faking her own cancer and killing her nurse at the end of the play, her aide adorning the corpse with a wig in her stead as she escapes. From the start, as though continuing from the close of the previous play, the piece is about dressing: already cursing in the first line, she searches frantically for her presidential robe. Outside, the people wait as she plans the spectacle of her demise, berating her entourage, especially her mother whom she accuses of wanting only the numbers to her Swiss bank account. As for Perón, he is little more than a wooden puppet in a world of his own, without much to say until the journalists rush in around her corpse and he rises to the occasion with his demagogic speech.

Because of the play Copi was banned from Argentina for fifteen years, and even then it was not until after his death that his work, mostly the later pieces, drew some attention there. Still, in a 1981 interview he insisted that he had no quarrel with Argentina; not only were his roots in the trenchant irony of Argentine theater, he worked largely with other Argentines in Paris. "I'm an Argentine citizen," he said, "I have an Argentine passport." Though he did make use of it in his work, especially in the fiction, nationality was not a prime concern for him. "Argentine artists are nomads; they're born there by chance and continue their journey anywhere in the world, like all artists do." What interested him most in theater was to try something different each time, to explore what was possible and hadn't been done.[66] He fit most comfortably, if anywhere, in the international avant-garde typified by Samuel Beckett and Eugène Ionesco, but also to a closer lineage in that ultimate reaction against intellectual dogmas, the Panic movement, founded by Arrabal, Roland Topor, and Alejandro Jodorowsky in Paris in the early 1960s.[67]

His next plays had nothing to do with his native land, though all the characters are exiles of one sort or another. Moreover, the plays take up again the theme of dressing and twist it ever further. *The Homosexual or the Difficulty of Sexpressing Oneself* (1971) mixes farce and melodrama on the Russian steppes where everyone fights back the hungry wolves and the three main characters have each had sex change operations in Morocco. Irina and Madre were deported to Siberia, while Madame Garbo, in a tale recalling some movie with that other Garbo, landed there for love of an officer, giving up her career as an artist. Again, the play begins on the tracks of the previous one: *Eva Perón* closes with the mother playing her role, crying "Mon Dieu!" before the corpse and the crowd, and *The Homosexual* opens with Madre also filling her role, concerned that Irina keeps skipping her piano lessons with Madame Garbo. It soon develops that Irina is pregnant, but by whom? Madre turns out to be not her mother but her lover, as is Garbo, who claims the baby is hers. Each inhabits an ambiguous zone of confused gender: it is not quite clear who still has what between their legs. Though Irina aborts, Garbo wants to run off with her to China, which Madre reluctantly accepts—only Irina vacillates, obstructing any move through acts of self-abasement and mutilation, as a test of the others, to the point of cutting off her tongue. Once more the mother, stern and protective, has the last line as she indicates Irina opening her mouth despite her inability to speak.

The Four Twins (1973), with its two sets of twin sister outlaws, opens with one of them fighting off the barking dogs as she enters. The first pair are bandits, their gold and jewelry stashed everywhere, while the second pair are failed gold diggers, which is how they end up in the wilds of Alaska: all are heroin addicts, constantly shooting up. Throughout, in an endless round between sisters and pairs, they try to cheat each other out of the loot and escape to sunnier locales, killing each other off along the way. Here, within the comedy of extremes that so amused him, Copi took the pattern of repetitions and multiple variations that he often used and placed it at the core of the piece: thumbing his nose at fictional illusion, he resurrects the murdered characters so many times the viewer loses count. Such resurrections occur in many of his works, but never at the fever pitch of *The Four Twins*—where, of course, the characters each walk out the door in the end.

Increasingly, as Copi moved more into fiction in the 1970s, his writing came to resemble a sort of controlled delirium. *Loretta Strong* (1974) was the first of three dramatic monologues he performed over the next decade, marked by a fluidity of voices and events; he brought the piece to the United States, Spain, and Italy.[68] Loretta Strong is an astronaut on her way to Betelgeuse to plant gold, who sends out a hallucinatory stream of messages. Recounting it all to Linda in another satellite, she battles the Monkey Men from the Polar Star and ravenous Venutians, engages in cannibalism and strange sex, and fights invading rats, though one climbs up inside to fecundate her, whereupon she gives birth to monsters and explodes over and over until it is as if she herself were being born. César Aira links the velocity of events in the play to a mechanism central to Copi's work, common to the imaginative games of children and the reality of comics: it is enough to imagine a possible development for it to already be happening.[69]

Fantastic voyages abound all the more in Copi's fiction. His first short novel, *L'Uruguayen* (1973), an epistolary tale, is addressed to the narrator's old mentor back in France whom he takes every occasion to abuse, celebrating the distance between them. He relates an utterly surreal Uruguay, and is quite unable to recall why he went there.[70] Thus, another important theme in Copi's work is introduced: the problem of memory. The narrator has almost no memory left, so he asks his reader, in a like process, to cross out the lines as he reads them. In the grand tradition of the traveler's tale, especially the accounts of New World explorers—which echo throughout Copi's fiction, to both confirm and mock European presumptions of difference—the narrator details the strange habits of the Montevideans: their language (a child's Spanish constantly reinvented), their lack of smell, their childlike way of appropriating territory. After his dog digs a bottomless pit in the beach, getting lost there, he finds Montevideo buried in sand, an empty desert. To orient himself he draws streets, houses, even pedestrians, in the sand, greeting them when he passes. Food being a problem, on the beach he discovers his dog's crater now teeming with chickens —no sooner have they run off toward the city than they're cooked. The sea advances and recedes, carrying away the sand, leaving a city of corpses that a municipal crew crudely replaces with so many stuffed bodies. The sole survivor, he takes up residence in the fanciest hotels, keeps a fixed schedule and reads old newspapers. Eventually, the people come back to life stranger than ever, and he is declared a saint by the president. The pope of Argentina arrives, a white slave trader known as Mister Puppy, and steals away the president, leaving the narrator—the traveler, the outsider—to run the country.

In this and subsequent books, a striking feature of the writing is that the entire text is laid out as a single block of prose. Though supposedly letters, they leave no gap between them: "Until tomorrow, old imbecile. Good morning, idiot."[71] Events follow upon one another in a rush of continuity, because at all costs, according to Aira, the story must go on, thereby triggering the absurd: "within a situation there can be no blanks, hence the instability, and even the horror." This drive, more acute in the novels, he describes as a baroque tendency in Copi.[72] Distinct from Sarduy's neobaroque, as a pleasureful squandering of language, a structural discordance, with Copi it is rather a function of narrative, of content, and the multiple possibilities that rise up from the telling.

Le bal des folles (The Queers' Ball, 1977) is at once about the task of writing a novel and the tragicomic love story it relates, the two deliriously feeding (or bleeding) into each other. To meet the demands of his publisher, Copi, the narrator, holes up in a backwater Paris hotel for two weeks. The narrative entails a premise of false starts: it's his third time trying to write the novel, but he keeps losing his notebooks and cannot remember what he wrote; he wanted to write about transvestites, but that just leads him to the story of Pierre, his

Italian lover, who estranged him from his friends. He circles around the story —their meeting in Rome, Pierre's desire to become a woman—and introduces his rival, a woman whose only success as an actress is playing Marilyn Monroe in gay bars; she marries Pierre and turns Copi's flat into drag queen central. At last reconciled, the two men make love and Copi explores Pierre's erotic navel, plunging his whole hand there to achieve orgasm in his arm. The narrative shifts to the present, with the (false) news that Marilyn was found hanged in a Roman prison cell; he recalls their visit to her at the Chelsea Hotel in New York, where she wins back Pierre and fights with Copi, who gets bitten by her pet boa and has to have his leg amputated. In Ibiza to convalesce, they meet a hippie sculptor from Baltimore, Michael Buonarro ti, and Pierre becomes a drugged-out guru; Marilyn arrives to be his priestess and humiliates Copi by blackmailing him into marriage.

Back in the present Copi the narrator loses track of the days, given the intensity of his work and his substance abuse, but discovers that Marilyn's mother happens to be the baker's wife across the street. He goes and brutally murders her, and kills twice more, including his publisher whom he runs into at the steam baths; there in "queer hell, two floors below the Place de l'Opéra," he decides to stick around and finish his novel, but is disturbed that he cannot account for the past few days.[73] He kills again and again, and outside calls his friend Marielle, his interlocutor through the novel, relieved to discover that his rampage was only a dream: despite his amnesia, his manuscript is found by the hotel's concierge who passes it on to his delighted publisher. But there are more endings, to both the love story and the writing of the novel. In Rome, Pierre recovers to the point that he wants a sex change to become a Carmelite nun, and in a final night of love Copi sinks his entire arm into Pierre's navel reaching all the way until he holds his heart; the next morning Pierre is dead. Michael and Marilyn, who marry and have a daughter Pierina, run into Copi at an old hotel where he goes to sleep off his artistic ordeal. He finds them annoying, goes out to a gay nightclub and brings back a Sicilian dwarf; they've left Pierina in his care, so he has the dwarf sodomize her and disposes of her body, then delivers a final chapter to his publisher, a job well done.

Rather as in Sarduy's fiction, there is a catastrophe at the heart of each of Copi's novels, a disaster not of the characters' own making. That catastrophe may be seen ultimately as a figuration of exile, for it signals a radical break, even a series of breaks, from all that went before. And yet, as Aira observes, in contrast to the dreamlike or absurd narratives of Kafka and later writers, Copi's characters show a sort of "magic adaptability" to deal with whatever comes their way. Instead of a realistic character lost in a dream, here it is rather "the dream man (like the dream of being a woman or an artist) dominating all the capricious flux of reality."[74] Or as Colette Godard puts it, "Copi doesn't exorcise nightmares, he becomes familiar with them."[75]

La Cité des Rats (1979) is another novel told in the form of letters, this time by a rat—Copi's totem figure, often appearing in his work, a sort of icon of the margins. Copi here is the recipient and editor-translator, entering the story from all sides (preface, notes, afterword), since rats supposedly see backwards from humans and their writing must be deciphered. Gouri the narrator has lost the cozy comforts of his friend Copi, who would carry him up five floors in his grocery cart and read him English novels: Copi is stranded upstairs with broken ribs and the concierge's cat won't let Gouri pass. From the Rue de Buci he and his buddy Rakä, a worldly rat, go sunbathe on the Ile de la Cité and meet two sisters who live with their mother, the Queen of Rats, among the roots of a willow. The text constantly plays on the idea of cuteness in the little creatures, with their surprising perspective on human objects and clever adaptions of human refuse to fit their humanlike needs, even borrowing from popular culture: as formal attire to dine with the sisters they swipe two Mickey Mouse suits from a toy shop window.[76] Yet it is hardly a story for children. The sort of innocence granted the rats makes the many accounts of human cruelty all the more terrible: the child that taunts them, the murderous wino who saves them from the river, the crowd that thirsts for the wino's beheading, not to mention child abuse and other tortures. Even the death of the humans' God fails to impress them, but then the fearsome Devil of the Rats appears (later revealed as Gouri's father): they are the chosen to found the City of Rats. The Devil makes the Ile de la Cité break free of Paris, sailing down the Seine like a ship toward the ocean, full of rats and a throng of human outcasts (jailed prisoners, mental patients). On the open sea their Paris island in exile is the only landmass left, and the American and Russian navies that threaten are destroyed by the Devil. When the water recedes, they discover the New World; the humans set off in search of El Dorado and the rats head toward a waterfall to found the City of Rats, only to find the ancient ruins of a labyrinthine city, which Gouri and Rakä explore. Climbing to the top, at the end, they chance upon a miraculous passage back to their sewer on the Rue de Buci, followed by one of their adventurous new offspring.

Certainly Copi flourished in Paris, but what was his relation to his native culture during all those years? Despite the hostility provoked by *Eva Perón*, he was no less caustic in later works. A short play in 1978, *La Coupe du Monde*, a satire of machismo and nationalism set during the World Cup soccer championship in Buenos Aires, led one Argentine daily to remark, "Once again Copi denigrates his homeland."[77] The fact that he wrote in French, obviously no barrier to his Argentine critics, reflected the inherent decision to stay where opportunity presented itself and he could live as he pleased; in contrast to his mother tongue, he referred to French as his "mistress tongue" (*langue maîtresse*), thereby suggesting the greater freedom and fantasy it offered him.[78] Being a foreigner as well as gay only reinforced his interest in marginal characters and situations. The disaster of Argentine politics, especially the infamous decade under military rule, further marginalized him: most of his friends and family eventually left. And yet it was during that period, in the late 1970s, that he wrote his only works in Spanish. In 1978, he wrote the gaucho-style verse play *L'Ombre de Wenceslao*, performed at the La Rochelle festival for a public of Spanish cleaning ladies and their children, and in 1980, he wrote his "barbarous tragedy" *Cachafaz* in the same style. Set in a Montevidean slum, it tells of an outlaw and his transvestite lover who feed the starving neighborhood by killing the police and turning them into sausages.[79]

La vida es un tango (Life is a tango, 1979), the one novel he wrote in Spanish (and translated into French), takes place mostly in Argentina on three decisive and carnivalesque days over a span of seventy years. By far his most historically-grounded story, it nonetheless flaunts its irreconcilable chronologies. In the first half of the book, provincial schoolteacher Silvano Urrutia is nineteen when he wins the young poet's prize at the Buenos Aires daily *Crítica* (the paper founded by Copi's grandfather), which publishes his epic and pays his long journey south for what becomes a day and night full of sex and intrigue; Hitler has just invaded Holland, and by chapter's end Silvano is amazed at how precariously both the paper and the country are run as the police crack down on the daily and wrongly accuse him of murder. In the second chapter, his Paris exile, set during the height of the student revolt in May 1968, he hardly seems a decade older; his relationships with two women there and his young son cause him to vacillate about returning to Argentina, but the sobering end of the festivities decides for him. The last chapter finds him living on inherited land back in his native Paraná on the day of his hundredth birthday, in the year 2009; escaping the local celebration of him and the visit of two women from his past, he finds a childhood grotto, has a youthful vision there, and dies.

What has been said of his final novel, *L'Internationale argentine* (1988), could also be said of *La vida es un tango*: that Argentina and its representation, instead of being a problem as it was for many before Copi, is rather a joke.[80]

His antirealist, exaggerated narratives, no matter how much they draw on the "real" world, demand to be read ironically. Moreover, these two books especially, as to an extent all his novels, play off of an element in the myth of exile that goes back at least as far as the story of Ulysses: the return of the exile as conquering hero. During the Paris chapter of Silvano's story, he receives a letter from the newspaper publisher who once welcomed him to Buenos Aires, urging him to come back and run for president.[81] This recurs as the main theme of *L'Internationale argentine*, set entirely among Argentines in Paris who each seem sillier than the next (with a tweak at Borges in the guise of the stern Raoula Borges, his supposed daughter by the cleaning lady at the National Library, who can recite the Koran and the Chinese alphabet): an apolitical and minor poet, Darío Copi, whose arrival twenty-five years earlier resembles the author's, is approached by an unimaginably rich black man, Nicanor Sigampa (the Argentine branch of an internationally powerful family), who insists on bankrolling his candidacy if only he'll accept. Just as Copi becomes most convinced of his capacity for the job, his mother reveals to him his Jewish ancestry, and Sigampa's family—now recognizing the impossibility of success in Argentina—drops him like a stone; the narrator, in an attempt on the mediocre bureaucrat promoted to replace him, is shot to death on the final page.

Implicit in Copi's attitude as an exile, part of what gives his humor its edge, is his absolute refusal to belong—much like Groucho Marx, who disdained any club that would have him as a member. *La guerre des pédés* (The War of the Fags, 1982), even more than *Le bal des folles*, is centered on gay life in Paris (and beyond) in that it largely entails a community response to events.[82] A certain political consciousness takes precedence in the efforts of gay militants to confront the disruptive and dangerous Brazilian transvestites who have invaded Montmartre. Yet Copi remains wary of this crusade, and the protagonist, René Copi, a French cartoonist, suffers from divided loyalties. In an interview at the time that he wrote the novel, Copi rejected the view of homosexuality as constituting its own world or as a "condition" that might change one's vision of things.[83] The novel complicates matters because Copi the protagonist is smitten with passion for the jewel of the Brazilians, Conceição do Mundo, not least for her enormous sexual organ; the sadistic extremes she and her group practice on their clients make her the enemy to Copi's friends.[84] But when he consummates his love for her, a surprise awaits him: she turns out to be a real hermaphrodite, and he discovers heterosexual intercourse as well.

The real enemy is her father, Vinicio da Luna, a macumba sorcerer who bought her from an Amazon circus when she was a child. Vinicio poisons Copi's friends in his apartment, and later, when prominent leftists and gays hold a meeting there, he machine-guns them all (Foucault, Duras, Daniel Cohn-Bendit) and springs Copi from their surveillance.[85] They drive to his mother's house in the country, where Copi had sent Conceição for her protection. His mother is utterly charmed by Vinicio, who intends to marry her, and even when Copi and Conceição are caught screwing in the garden she remains unfazed, only worried about her roses. Vinicio's plan for control is global, interstellar: his Amazons blow up not just key Paris sites (Saint-Laurent headquarters, the Comédie-Française), but also Brasilia and the Statue of Liberty. When Copi tries to escape with his love, they end up in a massive freeway accident and are soon brought aboard a spaceship where his mother and Vinicio await them—their destination, the moon. In the fantastic voyage that follows, Copi feels nostalgia for the dying earth as he learns that life is now on the moon, where the Amazon jungle has been transported since it is the lungs of the world. Just as the Amazons begin to eat his mother, he and a pregnant Conceição are rescued by a crew of herculean moustache men from the Homosexual Interspatial, which includes some old Paris acquaintances; they built the spaceship stolen by Vinicio. But contrary to expectations, Copi does not choose to join his saviors. Despite Vinicio's escape with Conceição into the jungle, she triumphs and chops off his head. In the end, Copi is left with her at peace in the jungle as the Homosexual Brigades take off for other planets.

Though most of Copi's fiction was published in Spanish translation by the Barcelona publisher Anagrama between the late 1970s and the late 1980s, his work has remained poorly known in Spanish-speaking countries. With respect to his native land, as Gustavo Tambascio notes, the provocative nature of his work exceeded the limits of the tolerable: without looking to send a message, he placed "before the eyes of those who 'had seen nothing' the mirror of the atrocious . . . speaking in his insouciant way of how easy it is to kill."[86] It was only with his play La Nuit de Madame Lucienne (1985) that Argentina began to reclaim him, after its Spanish-language premiere there in 1991.[87] Slightly more restrained in its use of the grotesque, the piece is a masterful layering of theatrical illusion in which the promise of real life keeps receding. A play within a play (within a play), it is set in a theater at three in the morning where the Author, the Technician, and the Actress rehearse an unfinished play that must open in a week. The rehearsal keeps getting sidetracked until the threatening entrance of Vicky Fantomas (Maria Casares in the original production), a disfigured actress and striptease artist, who reveals that Madame Lucienne, the cleaning lady, presumed to be working in the building, is dead.[88] Vicky further reveals that she and the Actress were the twin daughters of Madame Lucienne; the Actress denies it, then admits all. Soon everyone confesses their guilt, whereupon the Actress kills the Author, the Technician kills the Actress, Vicky kills the Technician—and then they are alive again, commenting on the play. They bid goodnight to the Author, and then the cleaning lady enters: she complains to him of the theater's falseness and how all her personal details are copied by the play. "You're going to regret the theater life!" she warns, waving a gun, and after shooting him, she declares the end, not just of the play, but of theater itself.[89]

In a curious way, Copi denounced theatricality as well when it came to dying. Stricken with AIDS, he wrote his last play, *Grand Finale* (its French title: *Une visite inopportune*), as a sort of defense against all the histrionics and staging that surround the approach to death. Besieged by a wisecracking nurse, a naive journalist, the unexpected visit of hysterical opera diva Regina Morti, a deluded doctor, and the patient's own faithful lover, Cyril the playwright wants only to die in peace—but not without offering a last flourish or two of his own. Premiered early in 1988, a month after Copi's death, it was the most successful of his plays internationally.

Outside Looking In: Paris, City of Exiles

Over the past century the number of foreigners in Paris has roughly doubled. Today the city holds the greatest number of Chinese in all of Europe, it is one of the capitals of the Armenian diaspora, and it also contains a major North African population.[1] While former colonies in Africa, the Caribbean, and Southeast Asia provided one type of source for the waves of immigrants and exiles, many who first came as students, it was also official French policy since the end of World War II to encourage immigration according to a general hierarchy of preferences. Predictably, northern Europeans were at the top, then northern Mediterraneans (Piedmont, Lombardy, Galicia), followed by Slavic peoples and everyone else after. Between the wars Italians made up the largest immigrant community, often intermarrying with the French and becoming naturalized citizens. After Franciso Franco took power, many Spanish republicans arrived, and in the 1960s, many more Spaniards came, mostly for economic reasons. By the 1970s, it was the Portuguese who were coming in large numbers.

With regard to writers specifically, in the postwar decades, Paris has been home to a wide diversity of figures from abroad. It was the destination or way station for many fleeing the Soviet-bloc countries of Eastern Europe. In the 1950s, Czeslaw Milosz lived in Paris, where an important Polish community received him.[2] Later, in the 1970s, Milan Kundera left Czechoslovakia to settle there, and the Yugoslavian writer Danilo Kiš arrived, as well. Some of the most important Middle-Eastern writers have also resided in Paris. The Iranian novelist and short-story writer Sadeq Hedayat, an intermittent resident, took his own life there in 1951 and is buried in Père Lachaise. In more recent decades, the Syrian poet Adonis has been living in Paris, and so has the Palestinian poet Mahmoud Darwish.

Of the identifiable communities of foreign writers in Paris, probably none has received more press over the years than that coming from the United States. Indeed, the American occupation of Paris has grown steadily in almost every conceivable form of enterprise through the half-century since the war. But what constitutes a community when it comes to writers, beyond sharing the same national origin or language—the Americans have long engaged in a certain commerce with British, Irish, and other English-language writers there, while remaining inevitably distinct—is not easily defined. Usually it is the critics or journalists who contrive some further definition by which to view a group of writers who, though perhaps friends, may share fewer similarities than differences. In the mid-1980s, for instance, at a moment when five literary journals were being edited by Americans, several articles in the United States were proclaiming a new American expatriate literary renaissance in Paris.[3] The truth was, little in style or substance unified the writers beyond their passports.

Between the world wars, if some of the Americans in Paris could be grouped loosely as modernists or of the Lost Generation, still the differences between writers like Gertrude Stein, Ernest Hemingway, Djuna Barnes, and Henry Miller, were significant. Exile, then as now, was rather "an enabling exercise, an ironic means of inserting the self into the world," as J. Gerald Kennedy suggests.[4] Often it involves a kind of disaffection, and maybe a later reckoning, with one's native culture. Even in those for whom it was less a matter of choice than of survival or circumstances (as for Witold Gombrowicz in Argentina), exile has always entailed a process of individual responses and individual agency, so that the writer as foreigner accepts no affiliation entirely, including nationality. As in the earlier period, attempts to typify the American residents of Paris in the first postwar decades were possible only insofar as they identified various clusters that might also partake in groupings of French or other foreign literary people. In the 1950s and 1960s, the principal criteria related either to publishing—Maurice Girodias's Olympia Press, literary journals like *The Paris Review*—or to experimental affinities, as for John Ashbery and Harry

Matthews with their interest in French modernist Raymond Roussel, or like the writers living at the Beat Hotel (William Burroughs, Brion Gysin, Allen Ginsberg, Gregory Corso, and Harold Norse).[5] Approaching the subject from another angle, Michel Fabre's study of black American writers in France, during the last century and a half, offers criteria hinged on race—reactions to racism, the effects of a mixed heritage, the perceived obligations of the black writer—but aside from those linked to the Harlem Renaissance, subsequent figures each decided their own terms. The differences between Richard Wright, James Baldwin, and Chester Himes, for instance, were legendary, and later the poet Ted Joans forged alliances with surrealists and the Beats, along with jazz musicians and mentors like André Breton, Aimé Césaire, and Langston Hughes.[6]

But whether or not a group identity holds sway, what is the responsibility of the exiled writer, if any? Albrecht Betz, studying the German intellectuals who fled the Nazis and lived in France during the 1930s, cites the case of Gottfried Benn, who took issue with the émigré writers, claiming that events in Germany could not be discussed by those who left, only by those like himself who stayed and lived through them. Nowhere outside of Germany except in France, at any rate, could the exiled writers publish as much as they did, including some 300 books in that decade. For the politically engaged writers, the development of the Spanish Civil War brought the dilemma into focus: was only content important, rather than literary quality? As in comparable situations, the problem remained—how to manifest one's commitment? what sort of actions? should they be personal or collective? And concerning the novelist, should one seek a radical form or a more conventionally accessible form?[7]

Since World War II, in terms of exile due to political reasons, the largest wave of Latin Americans departing for Europe occurred after the military coup in Chile in 1973. This migration included many people fleeing dictatorships in Argentina and Uruguay as well, some having sought refuge first in Chile under Salvador Allende. The social experiment that was the Popular Unity government found sympathy with the French left—just when the Cuban Revolution was becoming increasingly problematic—so that for a while these exiles, despite their hardships, were seen overall as the heroic fighters for a shared ideal. During that period numerous concerts and public events rallied people to the cause, as leading figures in the new song movement from the Southern Cone settled in Paris: the group Quilapayún, and Angel and Isabel Parra, from Chile; the Cuarteto Cedrón from Argentina; Daniel Viglietti from Uruguay. By the 1980s, however, the glow began to fade, and the exiles' continued presence—like those from Eastern Europe—became rather a reminder of the failed aspirations toward a new society.[8] Ana Vásquez and Ana María Araujo, working in the Paris region with exiles from the Southern Cone in the 1970s and 1980s, distinguished three stages in their experience: the arrival, marked psychologically by traumatism, mourning, and a strong feeling of guilt; ensuing processes of transculturation; and, as the situation became prolonged, one's own identity as well as the initial collective project were put into question.[9] From the start, beyond any European roots in their own families, the exiles learned to define themselves by their American difference. Forced by circumstances to postpone or abandon the dream of returning home to pick up where they left off, gradually they built new lives.[10] But for many, even the myth of return faded in favor of a different view of exile: as "the freedom to live another way, to build an identity out of wandering where one dies and is reborn several times."[11]

Given the political orientation of intellectual life in Paris, especially in the 1960s and 1970s, when most figures identified with the left, it was sometimes difficult for Latin American writers to disentangle themselves from politics, all the more so when they departed from the script of expectations. Such was inevitably the lot of the few Cuban writers who came to Paris, at a time when many French as well as Latin American intellectuals still considered Cuba the beacon of the future for the continent. Nivaria Tejera (b. 1933) in particular suffered the difficulties of this situation, having experienced a series of exiles by the time she settled in Paris in 1965. Though she was born in Cuba, her journalist father soon moved the family to his native Canary Islands where he was imprisoned after the Spanish Civil War broke out; on his release in 1944 they returned to Cuba, where she eventually began as a writer. In 1954, fleeing the Batista regime, she went to Paris: there she frequented the surrealists, had a show of her drawings, published in journals like *Les Temps Modernes*, and finished her first novel, *El barranco* (The Ravine), based on her childhood when her father was in prison. Maurice Nadeau, who proved instrumental in the careers of other Latin Americans in Paris (Hector Bianciotti, Silvia Baron Supervielle), published her novel in French translation in 1958 with Les Lettres Nouvelles. After the triumph of the Cuban Revolution, she took the first plane back. Joining the new diplomatic corps, she returned to Paris as a cultural attaché in 1960 and stayed for two years, later going to Rome in a similar post. It was there that she decided to break with Fidel Castro's government, feeling suffocated by the growing atmosphere of repression, and opted for Paris.

But in Paris, hers was an unpopular position, and despite her contacts she has maintained an uneasy relationship with literary circles there and abroad. Her rejection of the Cuban Revolution no doubt played a part in the controversy around her winning the prestigious Biblioteca Breve prize in Barcelona in 1971 for her second novel, *Sonámbulo del sol* (Sleepwalker in the Sun).[12] In a poetic, densely textured prose that characterizes all her work—she acknowledges affinities with Nathalie Sarraute and Samuel Beckett—the novel follows the jobless narrator on his rounds through the overheated streets of pre-revolution Havana. Publication of her later work became ever more difficult, despite enthusiastic readers, and reacting to the political and social posturing around her she grew withdrawn. *Fuir la spirale* (Escaping the Spiral, 1987), a fragmentary narrative directly concerned with exile, never found a Spanish publisher and only came out in French after some seven years of wandering. Her next book, *J'attends la nuit pour te rêver, Révolution* (I Wait for the Night to Dream of You, Revolution, 1997)—a novelistic essay denouncing the Castro regime, drawn abundantly from her own experience—also remains unpublished in the original and took nearly a decade to appear in French.[13]

Other writers were more fortunate, and less abused, in navigating the political assumptions about Latin Americans in Paris (perpetuated, it must be said, both by French and other Latin Americans). Eduardo Manet (b. 1930) had, like Tejera, lived in Paris in the 1950s and returned to Cuba to work for the revolution, but when he defected in 1968 it coincided with the production of his first play in Paris. Though he actively campaigned against Castro over the next decade, he did so in coalition with anti-Soviet intellectuals of the left. Above all, as a playwright and novelist he built his career writing in French, and his books never treated Castro's Cuba directly, except in a late novel, *Rhapsodie cubaine* (1996), and even there, the story deals more specifically with Cuban exiles in Miami. With respect to Chile, for example, the poet Luis Mizón (b. 1942) arrived in Paris in 1974, having lost his university teaching job after the coup. Having no desire to profit from his special status as an exile nor to become politically engaged, he found, on the contrary, that by not playing the role it often caused consternation among those around him. In his new life he also de-emphasized his work as a poet, until word got out and Roger Caillois chose to translate him, the last such work done by Caillois; since then, nearly all his writing has appeared first in French translation, mostly by Claude Couffon (perhaps the most active translator of Latin American literature since World War II), or bilingually.[14] Later, in 1984, the Nicaraguan writer Milagros Palma (b. 1949) settled in Paris with a comparable perspective, refusing to abide by the standard political assumptions. Having lived in Paris as a student in the late 1960s and 1970s, she then did anthropological research in Colombia and Nicaragua, where she tried to establish herself in the early 1980s, only to find that little was possible without first joining the Sandinista party. Not wanting to be distracted by politics from her chosen work, she returned to France and founded her own publishing enterprise with two imprints, Côté–femmes (women writers in history and women's issues in traditional societies) and Indigo (foreign literature); the hundred titles to date include several of her ethnographic studies and also her five novels, which do not shy away from political contexts on their own terms.[15]

Among some Latin American writers in Paris, especially within the scope of a declared political commitment during the 1960s and 1970s, a recurring issue had to do with a form of guilty conscience, the need within or without to justify one's years abroad, all the more so if the exile was not forced. One famous polemic in the late 1960s arose when the Peruvian novelist José María Arguedas criticized Julio Cortázar and other writers associated with the Boom for their European exile, as if that made them less authentic or they were shirking their duty at home. Cortázar insisted it was really a matter of taste and personal needs, that writers must be judged by their works, not where they chose to live, and that "we 'exiles' are neither martyrs, fugitives, nor traitors."[16] Another Peruvian of fervent political convictions, Manuel Scorza, who wrote part of his cycle of novels on indigenous struggles in the Andes while living in Paris, dramatizes such personal choices in his last novel, *La danza inmóvil* (The Immovable Dance, 1983), which follows the opposite paths of two friends, an ex-revolutionary who stays in Paris for love and a *guerrillero* fighting in the Peruvian jungle.

Beyond the political questions, though, many writers feel uneasy about absenting themselves from their native culture in favor of the microcosm that is Paris. In Roland Forgues' *Bajo el Puente Mirabeau corre el Rímac* (Beneath the Pont Mirabeau Flows the Rímac, 1987), the eight Peruvian poets he interviews, residing in Paris for over a decade, all sound this theme in some way. Yet weighing the alternatives, they would rather contend with the tribulations of life as foreigners. José Carlos Rodríguez points out that not only is publishing difficult in Peru, but there is no work, and a university job, when available, pays poorly.[17] For José Rosas Ribeyro, he already felt estranged while still in Peru, due to the social and cultural differences.[18] And if the old myth of Paris no longer holds, Armando Rojas recognizes that he was able to meet people from all over Latin America there and the city provided him with the necessary isolation and distance to consider his own culture. Like others before him, he took advantage of these opportunities to engage the larger cultural dynamic of Paris by also founding the elegant bilingual literary journal *Altaforte* with other Latin Americans, publishing eleven issues during the early 1980s.[19]

Julio Cortázar, Saint-Germain-des-Prés, 1961.
Photographer: Jerry Bauer.

Alejandra Pizarnik.
Photographer: Daniela Haman.
Courtesy of Yucef Merhi.

Octavio Paz, early 1960s.
Courtesy of New Directions Publishing Corp.

Mario Vargas Llosa, 1960s.
Photographer: Baldomero Pestana.

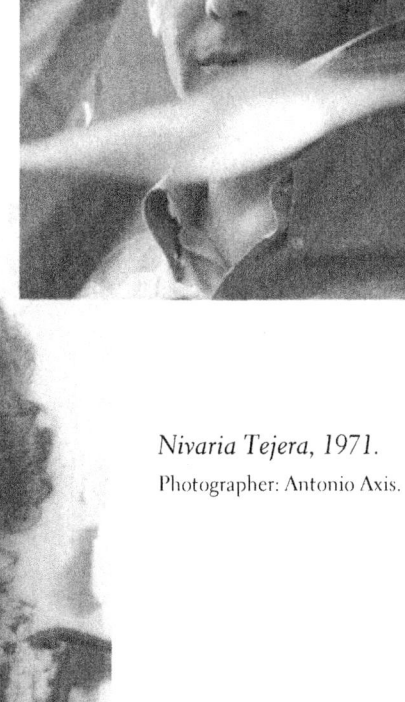

Nivaria Tejera, 1971.
Photographer: Antonio Axis.

Miguel Angel Asturias.
Photographer: Antonio Gálvez.

Pablo Neruda, Chilean Embassy library, Paris, 1972.
Photographer: Jerry Bauer.

Severo Sarduy, 1972.
Photographer: Denis Roche.

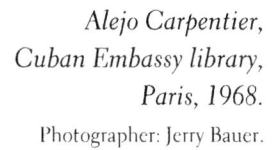

*Alejo Carpentier,
Cuban Embassy library,
Paris, 1968.*
Photographer: Jerry Bauer.

Gabriel García Márquez, 1970s.
Photographer: Ignacio Gómez-Pulido.

Julio Ramón Ribeyro (foreground), Alfredo Bryce Echenique, 1974.
Photographer: Baldomero Pestana.

Copi, 1980s.
Photographer: Jorge Damonte.

Juan José Saer.
Photographer:
John Foley Opale.

Luisa Futoransky.
Photographer: Tamara Pinco.

Rubén Bareiro Saguier.
Photographer: Angela Mejias.

Edgardo Cozarinsky, 1991.
Photographer: Pepe Fernández.

Hector Bianciotti, 1990s.
Photographer: John Foley Opale.

Eduardo Manet.
Photographer: Angela Mejias

Silvia Baron Supervielle.
Photographer: J. F. Bonhomme.

7

The Privileged Eye: Writing from Distance

(Julio Ramón Ribeyro, Juan José Saer)

Early in 1967, after more than a decade in Paris, **Julio Ramón Ribeyro** (1929–1994) wrote in his diary: "What am I doing far from my country, in a city where I have only two or three friends, forcing my wife into a life of seclusion, in two rooms with leaks and cockroaches . . . ? Who has exiled me and why? What am I looking for?"[1] By then he had written four books of short stories, his three novels, and five plays, all set in Peru—well over half of his collected output. While his school friends back home were thriving—he had studied law to please his father, yet never practiced—he was hardly known outside his own country where all his work was published. His mostly realistic style, about luckless protagonists edged out by a changing society, placed him at a disadvantage internationally in a market that craved the grand, exuberant narratives of the Boom writers. Still, his situation in Europe had improved slightly: though always broke, he did have a steady job (often the night shift) in the Spanish-language bureau at the Agence France Presse, employer to many Latin American writers through the years.[2]

Ribeyro seemed naturally to find himself in circumstances where he did not quite belong. In the 1930s and 1940s when he grew up, Lima was already becoming transformed from an old colonial city into the sprawling metropolis of today, with the massive migration of people from the Andes. He himself came from a sector of the old middle-class on the decline, displaced by the new entrepreneurial class that was modernizing the capital. His paternal ancestors had attained high positions in government and the university, but what inheritance remained by the time of his father—who never finished law school—was all spent in bohemian pleasures, which included learning three languages and extensive reading, well before his mother entered the picture. In going off to Paris, Ribeyro was not only evading the expectations of his class in order to devote himself to writing, he was also fulfilling a wish that his father was unable to realize; father and son had both been avid readers of French literature. There was, of course, a long tradition of Peruvian writers who went to Paris—the French-Peruvian social activist Flora Tristan (grandmother of Paul Gauguin), the García Calderón brothers in the era of *modernismo*, César Vallejo and surrealist poet César Moro between the wars—but from the start Ribeyro questioned what he was doing there. Weeks after he arrived in the summer of 1953, life in the Latin Quarter struck him as "a bad comedy," his peers "drunk with independence" and without much of interest to say.[3] Yet six months later, he wrote to his brother: "The great error of human nature is in adapting. True happiness would consist of a perpetual state of initiation, successive discovery, constant enthusiasm. And that sensation is only produced by new things that offer us resistance or that we still have not assimilated." The ideal was to be "the eternal foreigner, the eternal apprentice."[4]

In the five and a half years that he remained in Europe during the 1950s, Ribeyro survived largely on fellowships, living in Madrid, Munich, Antwerp, and Berlin, besides three stays in Paris. Whenever he was away from Paris, it was not long before he plotted his return. He was supposed to write a thesis on Flaubert when he first went there, only to abandon it as too big a project. Eventually, he took a variety of odd jobs in Paris—as the concierge in his hotel, doing *ramassage*, unloading freight at a train station—and his finances grew so dire that he even sold the books he had been carting around in his suitcase, partly to buy cigarettes, which for him were essential to writing. He had already envisioned his purpose as a writer in the letter to his brother, when he was not yet twenty-five, stating that the task was difficult due to his "distance from Peruvian reality. I need to see things from close at hand ... I'm convinced now that we must write about what is happening in our country." This was in contrast to his early stories that were not localized, the characters rootless. But he had to find "the right measure between the regional and the universal, the anecdotal and the transcendent."[5] The problem of distance, however, did have its benefits, as he reflected ironically later that year, on receiving press clippings from home that described him as the best young short-story writer in Peru: "Undoubtedly it's a great advantage to stay away and publish little."[6] And he soon understood why he worked better in Paris. On another visit to Madrid he found himself unable to concentrate, becoming more extroverted, quickly identifying with the spirit of the city. Paris, by contrast, was "a great school of solitude. The resistance of the surroundings obliges a person to define himself, to measure his strength, to fortify his convictions."[7]

Though the grants were really pretexts for him to keep on writing and gather new experiences, Ribeyro did briefly study journalism, photography, and printing. All the same, returning to Peru in 1958, he seemed in his own eyes a man without a future—no diplomas, no profession—yet could not bring himself to complete the academic credential he might need. After a year, ambivalent about his past in Lima, seeking a foothold in the present, frustrated by his prospects in a society where literature hardly counted, he began to think of going back to Paris, but it took him another year to make the journey. In the end, he remained nearly all his adult life in Paris. Still, he never considered himself an exile: it was simply "a series of circumstances" that permitted him to stay so long.[8]

Following the decade at France Presse, in 1970, he joined his country's delegation to UNESCO where he worked for twenty years, ultimately as the Peruvian ambassador there. Even in this new career he felt out of place, certain that the old gentlemen of the organization's executive council must be wondering how he ended up in their midst. His early story "The Insignia," from before he first went to Europe, had turned out prophetic: the narrator, having stumbled into membership in a secret society, rises through the ranks to become its leader without ever learning what the group stands for. "The truth is," Ribeyro wrote in his diary in 1972, "I know very little about this organization whose most hermetic circle I've penetrated. I don't know why I am there, nor how, nor thanks to what merits." Declaring it all a farce, he longs to be elsewhere: a small hotel room, a beach, a remote village in Peru to work as a schoolteacher.[9] But it was easier to dream of Peru from afar, and if he had any doubts, a trip to Lima in 1973—on the occasion of the publication of his collected stories—confirmed it. He had been seriously ill that year, and was eager to visit old haunts, to see friends and relatives. The attention, however, tired him out, and fame left a bad taste in his mouth, as if he had become just another product to be sold. He was happier back in the obscurity and isolation of Paris than "applauded, regaled, prostituted in Lima."[10] His position of choice, after all, was at the margins, and in Paris he could preserve "that attitude of being a man from the border," from a culture at the periphery.[11]

In Ribeyro's fiction, as Susana Reisz has noted, there is a constant "tendency to register the other face of things, the voices—or silences—of others, the diversity of forms of experience and systems of values."[12] Considered the preeminent writer of short stories in Peru, his nine collections are dominated by an urban social realism that alternates sometimes and even dovetails with a mode of the fantastic. In effect, they are as two sides of the same ironic perspective, where the absurd conditions of life are often so extreme that there may be little difference. "The Insignia," in treating the narrator's rise through the secret society, reveals to us, in the words of Washington Delgado, "a banal and meaningless world, the same world basically as in his realistic stories."[13] By contrast, a sort of fable from the late 1950s, "The Banquet," approaches this convergence from the precarious and overblown reaches of Peruvian high society. A *nouveau riche* businessman hosts a lavish banquet for the president, to whom he is vaguely related, after pouring his entire fortune into renovating the house, hiring cooks and waiters and orchestras, all for the prospect of an ambassadorship in Europe and other benefits. The event a success, at midnight he makes his requests, and the president assures him it will be taken care of tomorrow. Elated, the businessman and his wife stay up until dawn planning their future, only to wake up ruined on reading the newspaper headlines: "Just before daybreak, a government official, taking advantage of the reception, had led a coup d'état, forcing the president to resign."[14]

Yet the distinction between realism and the fantastic, as Alfredo Bryce Echenique cautions, is hardly adequate to describe the wide range of registers employed by Ribeyro throughout his career.[15] In a clear, economical style that shunned the fashions and vanguards of his day, he sought above all to give his characters a chance to be heard, choosing as the general title to the volumes of his collected stories "La palabra del mudo" (The Speech of the Mute). He explained to his publisher: "most of my stories are the expression of those who in life are deprived of speech, the marginalized, the forgotten, those condemned to a harsh existence."[16] Then as now, Peru was a deeply divided society where, according to Julio Ortega, "there hasn't been, in fact, a nation. That 'imaginary community' has been an absence, a deferred consensus, a mutually exclusive fragmentation of classes, ethnic groups, visions, and regions."[17] Ribeyro's first book, *Los gallinazos sin plumas* (The Featherless Buzzards, 1955), written during his initial stay in Paris, focused directly on characters from the poor and working class struggling for the merest shred of hope to escape their miseries.

In the title story, about human scavengers in the slums of Lima, two boys sift through the garbage cans on elegant streets for scraps to feed the pig that their cruel grandfather wants to fatten enough to sell. As the pig grows insatiable, the boys must search further in the garbage dump by the sea. Each in turn gets sick, so the grandfather feeds their stray dog to the pig. They end up trading blows, and when the crippled old man trips backward into the pen of the voracious pig, the weakened boys desperately take flight. Brutal as the story is, Ribeyro endows it with a poetic grace, especially in the recurring note of that enchanted hour of dawn when they set out to work, an interval of possibilities. Writing in a café, he would surprise himself in the mirror making sympathetic expressions, and he noticed, too, a curious correspondence with his current status, which he thought might lend a touch more truth: as the concierge in his Latin Quarter hotel, one of his tasks was to make sure the building's trash bins got picked up.[18] Another story in the collection also struck a resonance with his life, in that it had to do with debt, and his own fear of bills coming due, the rent in particular.[19] "Junta de acreedores" (Meeting of creditors) portrays the owner of a local grocery shop at the final reckoning with his creditors, who prefer to squeeze him dry. His business has declined due to competition from the Italian immigrant nearby, and only the Japanese-Peruvian creditor is humane enough to consider a compromise, though voted down and mocked by the others. The grocer tries throughout to at least preserve his dignity, convincing neither his family nor himself, and at last, feeling broken like an object, he heads off toward the sea and possible suicide.

Living the dream of Paris and facing its own harsh realities, both in the 1950s and later, Ribeyro knew there was no real escape from such a society as he had left behind, even for more fortunate individuals like himself. Rather, Paris provided the necessary remove from the subjects of his interest, the better to imagine them. "I was freer, more independent, in the sense that in Lima I had lots of friends and relations, a lot of commitments, and the possibility of isolating myself was more difficult. While in Paris I could stop seeing everyone for weeks on end. . . . Also, the fact of being far away allowed me to see things with a bit more clarity. Because I wasn't confused by a lot of small details."[20] If his innate social conscience was perhaps sharpened by the contrast of Europe, all the more so in witnessing the fate of Algerians in Paris, he remained well aware of a basic paradox. Even as he signed manifestoes in support of Cuba during the Bay of Pigs invasion and later in favor of armed resistance in Peru, he was ever skeptical of the effects of such acts and of writers' attempts to dabble in politics. "What sense, what decency can there be in preparing this declaration in Paris, listening to [Louis] Armstrong and drinking a glass of Saint Emilion?"[21] But this also reflected his reticence to take firm positions, whether in regard to his own life or in his judgments of other people. As he wrote in the mid–1960s, "I have always fled every test, every confrontation, every responsibility. Except that of writing."[22]

Ribeyro's sentiment of not fitting in found its natural justification in Paris, though admittedly he never tried much to adapt to the culture and his closest friends there were usually Peruvian. As a writer, however, this feeling no doubt reinforced his empathy for those set apart or seen as foreigners within Peruvian society. His stories treating race relations in Lima show particular insight into the nuances and different levels of rejection. "Of Modest Color," from 1961, tells of a twenty-five year-old painter, Alfredo, who feels out of place at a typical party in the middle-class Miraflores district, where he accompanies his younger sister. As the party warms up, his very position out on the terrace shows him at odds between two poles: the dancers inside cutting loose to the fashionable Afro-Cuban music that he does not like, in that it suppresses "the censorship of the timid, hypocritical inhabitants of Lima"; below on the sidewalk, the "ordinary people excluded from the festivities of life" peering up through the railing, with their "greedy eyes, drawn heads."[23] Taking refuge in drink, he is reminded with each encounter that he does not share the values of the guests, neither in social etiquette nor aspirations. All the same, he decides that he must dance, and finding none who will accept, he enters the kitchen and presses a maid—"the black girl"—to join him. Happy at last, he leads her to a more secluded area, only to be discovered by the shocked revelers who kick them both out. Proud of his gallantry, he convinces the girl to go for a stroll by the dark sea wall, where they get picked up by the police. His rebellion against his own class proves hollow in the end, for the police challenge him to take his supposed girlfriend to a well-lit local park: there his courage vanishes before all the confident young people milling about, and faking an errand, he sneaks out on the black girl who leaves in turn, never having really expected otherwise.

Alfredo's cowardice, as James Higgins indicates, betrays his class prejudices in that he draws on his social advantage to use the girl for his own ends, with no concern as to her feelings or the loss of her job.[24] In a similar way, the protagonist of "La piel de un indio no cuesta caro" (An Indian's skin is cheap), written the same year, also bends to the will of his milieu. A young architect, at his country house in a cooperative club headed by his wife's uncle, employs a teenage Indian whom he wants to bring to Lima and send to night school. When the boy dies—electrocuted by a poorly installed power cable on the club's grounds—the architect seeks justice, ready to refuse the promise of new contracts from the club. But after the uncle quickly arranges matters—the death certificate revised, the power cable repaired, even a check to the family for the burial—the architect is left with no objective ground to stand on and so resolves to go join the party at the club. Of course, beyond the class and racial inequalities, these stories mainly concern liberal protagonists in weak-kneed resignation at their defeat; but in another story where the disadvantaged character tries to affect his own prospects, the outcome is bleaker still.

"Alienation," from 1975, lays out its tragedy at the start: a mulatto named Roberto López longs "to resemble less and less a defensive back on the Alianza Lima Soccer Team" and more and more "a blond from Philadelphia." In order to prosper he decides it is not enough to just be white, he must also become a gringo. He ends up a "fragmented being," his "rosy dream [turned] into a hellish nightmare."[25] His ordeal begins as a teenager when he desires Queca, whose beauty transcends class and who rejects him because of his looks. First, he imitates the way gringos dress, dyes and straightens his hair, powders his face, losing friends and his job for his pretentions. Then he learns English from American westerns and detective films, finds work waiting on Americans, becoming known as Bobby, and enrolls at a language school where he befriends someone like himself. Renting a room together, their gringo haven, they dream of escaping to the United States and save every penny. But severe difficulties and disappointment greet them in New York, until they opt for the only solution: to avoid deportation, they enlist as soldiers and go off to Korea. Months later, the friend returns to Lima without an arm, but Bob López dies in action, blown up in an ambush.

The hardships Roberto suffers in the States, notes Higgins, is a variation on a central theme in Peruvian narrative of the 1950s: the dashed hopes of provincial immigrants who came to Lima for a better life.[26] Yet the sacrifice of his identity sets the story also within the larger theme of displacements that marks the book in which it appears, *Silvio en El Rosedal* (Silvio in the Rose Garden, 1977). Ribeyro explores this dynamic in many directions: the departure from mundane habits, where a classics professor is forever changed by stepping out into the modern city ("Terra Incognita"); the dispossessed marquis in the lost grandeur of Miraflores, obsessed with bringing down the newer family that supplants him ("El marqués y los gavilanes"); the army captain posted up north by the desert, confirming his authority in the struggle against solitude ("Cosa de machos"). In two cases, displacement becomes his method within the very expectations of the narrative. "El carrusel" (The carrousel), like an endless chain that turns circular, moves among several cities and fifteen narrators, where everyone, in effect, is a traveler, as each paragraph introduces a new character who proceeds to tell another story. In the elegant tale "Sobre las olas" (On the waves), Ribeyro seems even to invert his own image as a pessimist in a world where the strong alone survive: on a visit to his dying grandmother by the sea near Lima, the narrator strolls along the beach and spots the first swimmer of the season bravely going out beyond the breakers to calmly swim about. But the wind rises, the sea grows rough and the swimmer starts to tire. No one is in a position to help him, there is no lifeguard, and by the time a launch arrives, the swimmer has drowned. The narrator returns to the house imagining the worst, only to find his grandmother, who had been feverish and delirious that morning, sitting up and smiling, arms stretched out to him, "as though she had emerged triumphant on the crest of a wave."[27]

The title story of the collection takes a more existential view of displacement, in another version of Ribeyro's constant question to himself: what am I searching for? All that Silvio had ever wanted was to play the violin and be an elegant *Limeño* (resident of Lima), but his Italian immigrant father made him work in their hardware store until he inherited The Rose Garden, the most coveted hacienda in the Tarma valley. Out of his element, slowly Silvio learns to administer the property, and to appreciate the country life with its solitary pleasures. From a little tower on the grounds he discerns a pattern in the rose garden behind the house and tries to decipher its coded message, as if it offered the key to his life. His quest inconclusive, it does provoke him to resume playing the violin. But after initial enthusiasm he grows dispirited, feeling emptiness all around. Then his cousin writes from Italy; she arrives with her daughter and makes the hacienda prosperous again; he is convinced that they are the true meaning of the message. To celebrate a local fair and his beautiful niece's sixteenth birthday he throws a grand fiesta that all the big ranchers attend, their sons dancing eagerly with her. Withdrawing from the party, Silvio takes his violin and climbs the little tower again, but there he no longer sees a secret message in the rose garden, nor in his life, which he finds liberating: "Picking up his violin he fit it against his jaw and began to play for no one, in the midst of the uproar. For no one. And he felt certain that never had he done it better."[28]

Ribeyro himself later reflected: "I have never been able to understand the world and I will leave it carrying a confused image. Others could or believed they had solved the puzzle of reality and managed to discern the hidden figure, but I lived among scattered pieces, not knowing where to place them. . . . Because of that, what I've written has been an attempt to give life some order and explain it to myself, a vain attempt that culminated in the elaboration of an inventory of enigmas."[29] But if one *Limeño*'s unwanted displacement proves fortuitous in the title story, another's lifelong dream of a voyage turns fatal in "Juventud en la otra ribera" (Youth on the other bank). An education bureaucrat from Lima, going to a conference in Geneva, stops over in Paris for his first visit—at an age (past fifty) he considers already too late. At a café, however, he meets a young painter, a woman who ends up showing him around Paris, fulfilling his old bohemian dreams for a few days, and even sleeping with him. But she is not to be trusted, as she helps her friends in trying to swindle him of his money, which he manages to avoid, until on his last day there they catch up with him in the forest of Fontainebleau, where she has brought him for a picnic, and finally they take his life, as well.

Here, at least, the protagonist finds a brief happiness in his belated adventure, even if he is deluded and it leads him to his death. But in the dozen stories of an earlier book, *Los cautivos* (The Captives, 1973), based largely on Ribeyro's experience in the 1950s and written in the 1960s, the encounter with Europe offers little more than false illusions and rancor.[30] At best, there are glimpses of solidarity in the shared miseries of foreigners: the old Algerian laborer who takes pity and carries the wounded protagonist to safety, the young man clearly not cut out for the heavy work at the train station ("La estación del diablo amarillo"); the Spanish woman, obsessed with swiping travel posters from the Paris streets because she is too poor to go anywhere, and her frustrated suitor, the narrator, who ends up also stealing a poster, an image of her home town, to complete her collection ("Papeles pintados"). The title story becomes like a lesson in reading for the narrator who discovers, at a boarding house in Frankfurt, an enormous garden teeming with birdcages. What starts as an entry of song and color takes on a somber resonance when he chances upon a photograph of the owner—whose sole interest is his captive birds—as an officer in uniform standing guard before a much larger cage at Auschwitz. Even more than the stories set in Lima, these stories are about limited and shrinking horizons, which become evident in contrast, through the experience of the foreign. Thus, the Lithuanian salesman (whose upstairs neighbor, Señor Ribeyro, can be heard on his typewriter) is reduced to hardly venturing from his two rooms, alone and abandoned by his wife in France, the possibilities of his life playing out only in his tragicomic fantasy as he lies dying on the floor, a suicide ("Nada que hacer, monsieur Baruch"). Or the exiled woman, for decades an anonymous translator at the Agence France Presse, who still dreams of returning to her youth and Spain as "it could have been," but she never will ("Las cosas andan mal, Carmelo Rosa").[31]

These were practically the only stories that Ribeyro set in Europe. By the late 1960s and especially later, his writing grew more subjective and autobiographical, so that some of the European stories fit into this trend, in that they looked back upon an earlier time in his experience. Once more, it was the necessary distance through which he imagined his narratives, since he was attracted far more by the past than the present. The material had to settle enough in his memory, "for it to decant a little and the essential appear."[32] Many of his stories are drawn from his childhood and adolescence, and in general, the Lima he writes of is mostly the city he knew up through the 1950s, when his neighborhood in the Miraflores district was still marked off by the streetcar tracks from the working-class neighborhoods around.[33] Two stories in particular that followed this new tendency held a special charm for him, though he saw them as perhaps too personal, less stories than autobiographical tales, "fragments of the memoirs that I will never write."[34] In their treatment of family history, they illustrate again Ribeyro's ability to bring realistic subjects to the edge of the fantastic.

The wardrobe at the center of "El ropero, los viejos y la muerte" (The wardrobe, the old folks and death), from 1972, must have indeed borne the weight of the past for he refers to it back in his diary of 1958, after returning to Peru, aimlessly wandering through the family house and wanting already to leave again.[35] The story recounts how the massive three-chambered piece of furniture, inherited from his father's grandparents, had followed the family with each move, until it took up nearly half of the bedroom in Miraflores. "A veritable baroque palace," with its many parts and its secret passage, the narrator and his siblings liked to play inside it. Covering its door that faced the bed was a mirror where his father would gaze, more than at himself, at those who had seen themselves. "His ancestors were captives there, in the depths of the mirror. He saw them and saw his own image superimposed on theirs, in that unreal space, as though . . . by some miracle they inhabited the same time." One day his father invites an old friend over to enjoy the garden, and the kids must entertain the friend's boring son. The new boy finds a soccer ball, so they go out to the street to play, but then the boy gives a prodigious kick and the ball clears the garden wall, disappearing into the house. Incredibly, the ball flies through the open bedroom window and breaks the mirror, the wardrobe losing the radiant life it once contained. Their father nevermore dwells on his past, facing only the future now and his own death.[36]

"El polvo del saber" (The dust of knowledge), from 1974, also reaches back to the narrator's great-grandfather, whose personal library of some 10,000 volumes becomes a family myth of lost patrimony. At the patriarch's death, the library ended up with the narrator's great-uncle, a professor who had no children and was married to a rich and difficult woman whom he often cheated on. The narrator's father, who had ruined his health moving those books and spent the happiest years of his life reading from them, would have inherited the library except that his uncle died suddenly, intestate; the widow, out of spite, never let the family have a thing. Like his father, the narrator in turn used to pass by the house, to gaze through the fence and dream of recovering that legacy. Years later, as a university student, he goes to study with a friend who lives, it turns out, in that same house, which the aunt's heirs had converted into student lodging. Recognizing the old furniture from family photos, he inquires about the library but no one knows anything about it, until he asks the caretaker. She recalls the roomfuls of old books and the trouble it took moving them out to the former servants' quarters; she hands him the key and says to help himself. What he finds is masses of moldy paper that crumble at his touch. "The coveted library . . . once a source of light and pleasure was now excrement, decrepitude. With great effort I managed to disinter a French book, miraculously intact, which I kept, like the bone of a magnificent prehistoric animal."[37]

In Ribeyro's final two books of stories, the turn toward the personal grew more direct, often dispensing with the pretense of a narrator different from the author. Grouped as the fourth volume of his collected stories, it was clear that at last the general title, *La palabra del mudo*, applied to him: he was the mute or silent one attaining speech. *Relatos santacrucinos* (Tales of Santa Cruz) treats the neighborhood where he grew up in the Miraflores district. The most unified of his books in tone and setting, its ten stories arise from the same retrospective gesture, reviving a lost world, a more close-knit sense of community. These constitute the precarious sense of place and belonging that was always denied his other protagonists by the subsequent forces of change. "Mayo 1940" sets the turning point at a dramatic moment, depicting his own family in their daily routine of school and work the day an historic earthquake shook the city. Though the family and their house all escape unharmed, nothing would ever be the same. "It was like a signal that marked a fracture in time: our childhood had ended, Lima would soon lose its charm of a tranquil colonial city."[38]

Other stories in the book try to revisit that enchantment long after, only to accentuate his loss. "La música, el maestro Berenson y un servidor" tells of the author's early appreciation for classical music, initiated by his father and developed by way of a school friend, and especially the arrival in Lima of Berenson, a refugee from Vienna who transformed the symphony orchestra into a top-rate ensemble. For years Ribeyro attends the orchestra's performances with his friend, until their devotion is shaken by a disillusioning encounter with the maestro. Some two decades later, on a trip back to Peru, he discovers Berenson reduced to a mere hack, conducting Beethoven in a large private home but waving his baton to music coming from a stereo. The book's closing story, "Los otros," emphasizes his perspective from the present by glimpsing in local friends the ruins of their youthful splendor. But what about the others? he asks. He proceeds to tell the separate stories of four who died young, arriving at the end of his narrative by the empty seawall, recognizing the same colors of the sunset, hearing the same roar of the sea rise up, as in his childhood. "For a moment I wonder what time I'm living in . . . present and past seem to merge in me . . . The others no longer exist. The others are gone forever from here . . . except perhaps from my memory and from the pages of this story."[39]

Despite working at UNESCO, which never interested him much except as a nice livelihood, Ribeyro began to feel more keenly the distance from Peru and to think of returning. He had long been doubtful about the European capacity to see Latin America in other than the broadest terms, as in the 1960s, when it became the setting for many intellectuals' dreams of revolution. By the 1980s, he would note in a fragment, on chancing across a llama kept by some acrobats performing on a Paris street, a role previously reserved for bears, goats, monkeys—"Prefiguration of what awaits us: our culture, our symbols, or rather the symbols of our culture, converted into circus objects, trinkets for the public square. The little white llama, with the bluest eyes, was wearing a collar of awful plastic flowers and watching the traffic scared, wondering what in hell it was doing there, so far from its Andean plains. Poor Peruvian animal! Life isn't easy in your pampas either, you carry heavy loads, climb steep slopes. But you are not a foreigner."[40] Bound up with these sentiments was the physical fact that from the early 1970s until the end of his life he remained in fragile health, above all due to his tenacity as a smoker. The title story of *Sólo para fumadores* (Only for smokers) is thus a marvelous accounting of the habit that caused him such trouble, to which he always remained faithful despite doctors' warnings. By way of a smoker's pleasures he offers the unique itinerary of a life, tracing the different brands of cigarettes he took up, the places and periods where they fit in, the implications of their image or provenance, and how it was all indispensable, even elemental for him, as for many other writers.[41]

Part of what had attracted him to Paris, the intense cultural life, was another reason why he thought of leaving. He had grown tired of "being a consumer of culture, having to be up to date with everything."[42] One of his last stories, "La casa en la playa" (The house on the beach), from 1992, describes the utopian search that resulted in these later years. One summer in Lima he and a sculptor friend, saturated with the cosmopolitan life in Europe, decide to pursue their old idea of finding a deserted beach to build themselves a house, a peaceful refuge. But their impossible, near-mythic quest turns out ever elusive, and each summer they must venture further. Their first choice, once an isolated spot, is now a middle-class outpost. The next year, starting 200 miles south of Lima, they come upon an enclave of fishermen who hardly welcome their approach. The time after that, they discover another group of fishermen, so they move further off and get stuck in the sand when the chassis of their Land Rover strikes a hidden rock, no one bothering to help them. The following year, with two women friends, they head even further south, only to have their expedition entirely derailed by a jug of exquisite homemade Pisco brandy given by a friend. The next year, they agree to look for an island—not exactly the accessible spot desired—and catching a ride on a tugboat, they land at a magnificent place that was once active in the guano trade. Just when they seem most certain, the sea lions on a neighboring island launch into their daily deafening uproar. A few years later, they resolve to try once more, heading north this time. And what if we don't find that deserted beach? asks the narrator. "What's it matter," says his friend. "Our house will just exist in our imagination. And for that very reason, it will be indestructible."[43] Ribeyro himself, after retiring from diplomatic work in 1990, bought an apartment in a seaside section of Lima where he spent about half of each year. He died there at the end of 1994, six months after a new edition of his collected stories was published in Spain.

• •

By the time he left Argentina for Paris in 1968, **Juan José Saer** (b. 1937) had already written six books of stories and novels set in a fictional version of his native Santa Fe. Some thirty years later, still in Paris, he continues to anchor his writing in that "zone," as he calls it, the region northwest of Buenos Aires along the Paraná river coast that includes the city of Santa Fe. By way of this locus, through an ongoing series of interlocking texts with recurring characters and situations, he has elaborated not so much the representation of a province or the intricacies of a national identity as he has a nuanced reflection of the wider world, in his experiments with narrative techniques and the shifting play of perspectives.

The son of Syrian immigrants, Saer grew up in a small town and later the city where he and his siblings were educated. Up through the 1960s, when he began teaching literature at the film institute there, Santa Fe was bustling with numerous cinemas, theater companies, and bookstores, such that he felt at no disadvantage with respect to the capital. If Santa Fe eventually took on mythical proportions in his writing, he saw the reason as simple enough: "When I was young, I had never left Santa Fe. I think I was nineteen when I first visited Buenos Aires, and then I didn't go back there until I was twenty-six. But at the same time I read a lot. So, all my representations of the world—from Athens in the classics through Chandler's Los Angeles and Faulkner's Yoknapatawpha—all those were my own experiences of Santa Fe. Certain houses in the novels reminded me of houses in Santa Fe. In that way, all those cities kept acquiring a sort of density."[44] Before moving to Paris he always lived in the same province, and that trajectory is indicative of his poetics, according to novelist Ricardo Piglia, who likens Saer's treatment of Santa Fe to James Joyce's Dublin, Cesare Pavese's Piamonte, or Thomas Bernhard's Salzburg. "From that local space the nation is seen as an extraneous territory, a land occupied by the official culture. The artist resists in his zone, establishes a direct tie between his region and world culture."[45]

That Saer has ultimately produced most of his work outside the place where it is grounded is less a matter of choice than of chance. Although he was thinking of leaving Argentina, and he had begun to read the *nouveau roman* writers —Nathalie Sarraute, Alain Robbe-Grillet, Michel Butor—whose methods were to mark some of his own fiction, he had not thought to go to Paris until a friend encouraged him to apply for a six-month grant, which he won. His wife at the time later joined him, and gradually the elements of a life fell into place there: he began to teach literature at the university in Rennes (where he has commuted from Paris ever since), his wife gave birth to a son, the political situation in Argentina deteriorated.[46] On the relation of his fiction to Santa Fe, he has said that by then "the lines were already drawn . . . I was prisoner of the things I was writing. In the sense that I always felt the obligation to take up again things that I had done, to do them differently, or to try to say them better."[47] His first book, *En la zona* (1960), introduced situations and characters —the dynamic figure of the writer Carlos Tomatis—that he still comes back to even in his most recent novels. While it was not his intention to write a chronicle of Santa Fe, a prime objective has always been to use a colloquial language, one that has the oral intonations of the locale, which he could then modify stylistically.[48] Except during the decade of military rule, he has returned to visit Santa Fe every two or three years and kept in regular contact with people there.

Nonetheless, the distance has yielded certain advantages, in his view. Being outside made it easier to shake off the nationalist rhetoric, and to imagine the American space, in its historical dimensions, without the strong element of pathos supplied by the official vision.[49] At the same time, the comparative experience of two different societies helped him to see Argentina better in its entirety, and to put certain values of European culture more into perspective.[50] The encounter with the foreign became a test of his own sense of reality, leading to a new "apprenticeship of the known made relative by the unknown."[51] But the distance served also to reinforce a dominant function in his imaginative process: the role of memory. Saer's fiction is notable throughout by the highly detailed descriptions of objective reality, be it the smoky ambience of a billiard table (*Cicatrices*), a man lighting a cigar (*La pesquisa*), or a long walk down the main thoroughfare of the gridlike city streets that provides the foreground for another story told second- and third-hand (*Glosa*). Even with the texts he wrote while still living there, he did not physically go back to the places where the stories occur. It has more to do with "the mechanisms of memory," he says, with "the settings of memory. . . . In my imagination I can locate a scene in a specific place, and most likely I haven't visited that place for years."[52]

In "Recuerdos" (Memories), a brief text from the first book Saer wrote entirely in Paris, *La mayor* (The Premise, 1976), his narrator dwells on the different kinds of memories and how they exist beyond the human capacity to remember them. In effect, of all that is external to us, memories could not be more remote. "An ontological scandal separates us from them," as they resist our efforts to construct our lives like a narrative. Given the need to put some order to them, chronology proves inadequate. He proposes a "new narration," without beginning or end, that would instead be circular in its approach. "The position of the narrator would be like that of the child on a merry-go-round who tries to grab the ring at each turn. He needs luck, dexterity, continual changes of position, and still most of the time he may well come up with his hands empty."[53] Saer himself has employed a circular form of narrative in most of his novels—especially *Cicatrices* (Scars, 1969), *El limonero real* (The Real—or, Royal—Lemon Tree, 1974), *Nobody Nothing Never* (1980)—but here, more than the pursuit of memories, it is rather additional details, different angles of vision, a further fold in the narrative complexity, that are apprehended with each pass in the telling. Throughout, he tends to de-emphasize the importance of anecdotes and events in favor of a greater focus on the act of writing, of articulating perception, and a constant reflection on the nature of representation.[54] As Piglia notes, in Saer "to narrate is really *to illuminate* a story that already exists."[55]

The repetition of narrative material, Mirta Stern has shown, both within and among Saer's works of fiction, generates each time new possibilities and prevents the text from ever becoming formalized in a definitive way. Each text partially erases those that came before, just as it is in turn transformed by subsequent texts. *Cicatrices*, for example, is comprised of four first-person narratives that intersect only occasionally until each converges, directly or obliquely, in the same event: Fiore, who shot his wife to death in a drunken fight the day before, jumps to his own death from the judge's office during the inquest. This incident turns out to be of passing significance to the others as all but the final story, which is Fiore's own account, end somewhere beyond the tale of his demise, while his version closes when he goes home after killing his wife. Stern remarks that each of the narrators is obsessed with the desire to erase some aspect of their past or their immediate reality that has left a scar in them.[56] Indeed, in the final moment, Fiore shuts his eyes, only to open them and find the external world unchanged, so that he must yet erase himself.[57]

Saer's art of retelling, while enabling a story to elude fixity, at the same time grants it the resonance of a myth: like a story passed on, with its variants, still fresh in the air. *El limonero real* takes his method of circular narrative to its most absolute, telling the same essential story eight times. He himself has described the formal subject of the book as being "precisely that impossibility of exhausting the signifier and narrative as well."[58] Set among the inhabited islands in the Paraná river, from one dawn to the next, it tells of Wenceslao, who goes to visit his brother-in-law's family on a neighboring island where all the relatives gather to celebrate the last day of the year. On Wenceslao, whose own wife refuses for the sixth year in a row to join her sisters because she is still in mourning over the death of their grown son, falls the task of slaughtering the lamb for the annual feast, in an echo of the biblical sacrifice that betokens the renewal of life. The novel is suffused with motifs signaling the theme of the eternal cycle, starting with the tree of the title, which contains all its phases simultaneously: green fruit and ripe, budding flowers and a carpet of fallen petals underneath.[59] Each repetition advances the story a little further until his return home, shifting narrative styles and modes of consciousness as it continually branches off into other related stories past and present, layered with recurring images like that of the dead son as a child running off down the path to dive into the water.

Implicit in the form of this novel, as well as several of its characters' circumstances (sons or daughters who go off to the city; Wenceslao, who leaves his wife back home), is the theme of departure, which figures prominently in subsequent books.[60] As Saer and many others recall, his is a generation dispersed into exile, often well before the dictatorship that took hold in the 1970s. When it has to do with a geographical departure, the reference in his fiction is usually Paris, thus Europe poses the inevitable counterpoint to Santa Fe. In the story "A medio borrar" (Half erased), from *La mayor*, Pichón Garay—whose cousin the judge was one of the narrators in *Cicatrices*, and whose family descends from the city's founder—makes the last rounds with his friends in the days before leaving for Paris. In all the later fiction with a contemporary setting, he remains the one who went off to Paris, never entirely absent for the others in Santa Fe. At lunch with his friend Héctor, he imagines his native city existing without him and decides that "a city is an abstraction that we agree on to give a proper name to a series of fragmentary, disconnected, opaque, and largely imaginary places," while Héctor calls up memories of his own three years in an almost mythical Paris.[61] After, Pichón is struck by the thought of the rooms in his house that "go on being in their place, empty of me. . . . In this world, I am the least real. I have only to move a little to become erased."[62] When the bus takes off in the end, he sees the wintry city closing behind him "like a sphincter, a circle, bidding me farewell, leaving me outside."[63]

Throughout its many texts, *La mayor* proposes a constant questioning as to what trace, or scar, is left behind when the perceiving consciousness moves on: what is the nature of memory, and how does its reality compare with that of the ever-moving present? In the title story, the unnamed narrator, who is the writer Tomatis, tries and rejects the Proustian mechanism of the biscuit dipped in tea, saying for him nothing emerges, no flow of memories. By a meticulous observation of external details as he moves through the house, he seeks to capture some trace of the ineffable, a glimpse beyond the present moment. Only when he undresses for bed and lies down in the dark does something like a dream or a memory rise up: a familiar city street amid the noonday bustle, a boy in a bus aiming his camera toward the narrator. It is all so vivid that he wonders, is it a memory, and from what world? The shorter texts take up similar questions. In "Discusión sobre el término zona" (Discussion about the term zone), set a few months before Pichón's departure, he states that a man should remain faithful to a region, to which his friend replies by exposing the problematic of such a concept. It's impossible to delimit a region, says the friend: where does the coast end and the pampa begin, or the city and its outskirts? After five years in Paris, in "Me llamo Pichón Garay" (My name is Pichón Garay), he recalls a visit from Tomatis, whose own subsequent departure left him riddled with memories and an uncertain sense of self. By contrast, Tomatis's admiring young friend Angel Leto, almost an innocent when a narrator in *Cicatrices*, is seen in "Amigos" some fifteen years older, at a point when his destiny has taken a decisive turn. Active in the radical underground, hiding out in wait for the moment when he must kill a man who betrayed the cause, Leto reflects on how death, time, can never entirely erase the human presence—be it his intended victim, or a childhood friend, or even himself—which can only be eliminated from the immediate field of action.

The ensemble of Saer's fiction, as a single project, has developed in multiple directions to elaborate an ongoing "topography of the zone, with its privileged and recognizable places," as María Teresa Gramuglio describes it.[64] He "displaces the traditional totalizing forms of representation" with "a detailed and reiterative registering of perception" that allows him to treat the more elusive aspects of reality—time, space, being, things.[65] But the way the individual works fit together evolves organically and is hardly schematic, as Saer explains: "Each novel is like a fragment that I set about installing in the fissures left by the previous narratives. The work, then, is a kind of mobile wherein each piece that is added modifies the rest, and each piece functions like a digression. But the fragments never manage to close the whole thing, rather they introduce more uncertainties. In my texts, the sense of time is compressed or stretched out, so that I can always add new fragments (novels) that compress the time stretched out in other fragments (novels), or vice versa."[66]

In "A medio borrar," for instance, the one person Pichón does not get to see before leaving is his twin brother Gato, who has been living in the family bungalow outside the city in Rincón, a town along the river; each makes the effort to go find the other, but at the same time, thus their failed reunion. *Nobody Nothing Never* takes place entirely in and around the bungalow in Rincón, with Gato and his lover Elisa as the main characters; she is Héctor's wife, and has been seeing Gato at least since the time of the previous story. Another character, Wenceslao's limping nephew, was seen earlier among the nearby islands of *El limonero real*. In the novel, Pichón has been in Paris long enough to have sent his brother a novel by the Marquis de Sade, which enters the narrative as a stark contrast to the parched and barren terrain of the story's own time. Later, in a flash forward midway through another novel, *Glosa*, it is revealed that Gato and Elisa, who by then had left her husband, were disappeared (by the military dictatorship) from that house in the late 1970s. In one of Saer's most recent novels, *La pesquisa*, set in 1987, Pichón has been living in Paris for twenty years and returns for a visit to sell the house in the city, now that his mother has died, as well as the empty bungalow.

On the other hand, a character's reappearance may occasionally provide a new version in part, as with Angel Leto. In *Cicatrices*, he is eighteen and from the city, but in a novel written nearly two decades after, *Glosa*—set in 1961, as the continuation of an early novel, *La vuelta completa* (The Full Turn, 1966), which took place six months earlier—he is twenty-one and has moved there only in the past year; in both he has a problematic relationship, though each time different, with his recently widowed mother. During another flash forward in *Glosa*, it is learned that since his descent into clandestine activity as a militant—first portrayed more vaguely in "Amigos"—he has always carried a capsule of cyanide, in case of capture. A few months before he finally takes the poison, he goes to visit his old friend Tomatis, who is in the midst of a depression and living at his mother's house, described earlier in "La mayor." Saer's next novel, *Lo imborrable*, takes place some months after that visit, focusing for once directly on Tomatis, who is now tenuously on the mend. But even in the two historical novels from the 1980s, Santa Fe—which is never named in any of his fiction—remains the site of crucial encounters. Set in the sixteenth century prior to the city's founding, *The Witness* tells of a Spanish expedition that was killed, and eaten, by an indigenous group of people. The only exception is a cabin boy kept for ten years as their guest of honor, and who narrates the story as an old man. *The Event* takes place in the mid-nineteenth century during the first wave of immigration, when a mysterious European comes to settle in the growing city; his best friend is of the Garay family.

In his essay "El concepto de ficción," Saer offers a general definition of fiction as a "speculative anthropology." A mix of the empirical and the imaginary, fiction asks not "to be believed as truth, but rather as fiction." It is a "specific treatment of the world, inseparable from what it treats," and by its very nature points up the complex notion of truth. Indeed, the verifiable remains outside of fiction's concern, and that is part of the reason why we admire writers like Miguel de Cervantes, Laurence Sterne, Gustave Flaubert, and Franz Kafka: because their work does not depend on what can be verified, nor does it resign itself to the function of mere artifice or entertainment.[67] Yet he makes the distinction elsewhere between the novel, which he considers a purely historical genre, and narrative, "a mode by which man relates with the world. Being a narrator demands an enormous capacity for availability, uncertainty, and abandon," irrespective of nationality. "All narrators live in the same country: the thick virgin forest of the real."[68] Saer's own practice often results in a heightening of reality, so that from one instant to the next the narrative gives way to a meticulous description of external details where time seems barely to move, probing them for meaning, thus building a kind of tension and suspense. By contrast, the most frequent textual material in his work is the running dialogue or debate among friends, be it on the occasion of a party, a meal, or a chance encounter. Between these two poles, as it were, the story weaves its path.

Though his fiction is rooted in local practices, local intonations, and the descriptions of landscape, of streets and roads, reflect the region and city of Santa Fe, it is rather by way of atmosphere, even weather, that Saer invokes a deeper resonance of Argentina in his time. Suggested previously by Leto's clandestine situation in "Amigos" and the area falling apart from winter floods on the eve of Pichón's departure in "A medio borrar," or even earlier in *Cicatrices* among the darkening autumn rains where several characters were disappointed ex-union members, in *Nobody Nothing Never* the tone becomes more ominous. Written in the late 1970s during the decade of military dictatorship when Saer visited just once, the novel is dominated by the midsummer heat that crushes the land and people alike. The intense sunlight renders characters sluggish, their thoughts and actions sketching a reduced orbit of details, as the narrative itself returns over and over to the same few days, advancing from different angles and by way of forays through the recent past, to amplify the disturbing circumstances: along that stretch of coast, in the last nine months, seemingly random horses have been brutally killed at night, as the present of the novel begins with news of a tenth horse found. Tilty, on behalf of his uncle (Wenceslao, or Layo), has brought a horse to be kept safe in the yard of the Garay family bungalow where Gato is living. Repeatedly, the horse in the yard and Gato lock gazes, as if to question whether he is really friend or foe.

It is not until halfway through the novel that the full story of the murdered horses is recounted, and even at the end the perpetrator remains unknown.

Various hypotheses are put forth, including the comic touch of Tomatis's investigative newspaper article which explains the relative value of horses by noting that in France of all places, the country of Descartes and Voltaire, "there were special butcher shops where the one thing sold was horse meat."[69] Nowhere does Saer make a direct connection between their deaths and the reality then prevalent beyond the fiction—the repression in Argentina, the people who were disappeared—but the ambience of fear, the sense of menace in the air, seem comparable. Among the slaughtered horses is that of the local police chief, whose name is Horse Leyva, known as a torture specialist who can make suspects confess. Despite his tighter security methods he is gunned down in a guerrilla-style attack in front of the police station. The army in turn arrives and closes off the area, yet the next morning—as Gato and Elisa leave for the city and a long overdue storm brings relief from the heat and tension with the first drops of rain—there is no visible sign of the killing. Such is the "illusion of continuity" in the obliterating heat of that "unreal month"—the phrases keep recurring—that external reality, like memory itself, almost ceases to cohere. The perception of an incremental series of details, within the scope of different characters' experience, leaves the prospect "that nobody, nothing, at no time has ever been in the vast, unstable empty space."[70]

The illusion of emptiness, by contrast, as a vast terrain full of possibility, marks the starting point of *The Witness* (1983). Posing as a historical novel in the tradition of European explorers' narratives, it seeks rather to subvert the convention by questioning lines of filiation. Saer himself has remarked that he purposely included many anachronisms, in matters of thought and language, to show precisely that his aim was not to create a historical reconstruction but rather a metaphor for our own time.[71] The original Spanish title, *El entenado*, means the stepson: a fifteen-year-old orphan when he signed on to a ship bound for the New World, the narrator comes to know such respect for the indigenous people who capture him that ever after he feels closer to them than to the European world he must later return to.[72] They become his lost origin, the home discovered in exile. As an old man writing of them, recalling his fear after they kill his companions and carry him off, he realizes "that the crying child lost in a strange world is unknowingly witnessing his own birth. We never know when we might be born."[73] The recent past before his capture—the captain and crew, the journey across the ocean—seems like "an ill-remembered dream," and that idea recurs often in his account (as it does wherever Saer treats the passage of distance and time), that "the memory of an event is not sufficient proof that it really happened."[74]

Thus, the narrator's curious detachment as he watches them prepare and grill the bodies of his former shipmates, and then gorge themselves on the meat. Digesting their feast, they sink into melancholy and a confused guilt, followed by a bout of alcoholic excess and a desperate, indiscriminate orgy. After, they lie about like "sick abandoned children," and only with their recovery do they become polite and hardworking again, so that the narrator remembers them overall as "the most chaste, sober, balanced beings I have ever encountered."[75] He learns, through his long captivity, that the whole process is an annual instinctive summer ritual, the struggle with their dark inner depths: their triumph is in having risen from eating each other, way in the past, to eating outsiders. Each year one outsider is spared, taken as an honored guest to witness their struggle, and eventually released, laden with gifts, back to his own people. The narrator is kept for ten years only because it is not until then that the Indians spot other Spaniards along the river, who soon hunt down the Indians and kill them all. At his departure, the narrator recognizes that the Indians want him to tell their story to the world beyond, so that they might live on. A foreigner everywhere, for the rest of his years he wanders about Europe remembering them, to whom he owes his own life.[76]

A different reflection of exile, merging with circumstances of immigration, *The Event* (1988) takes another European departing for brighter prospects to the New World. Bianco—whose name and exact origin remain uncertain, and who speaks several languages, all with an accent—has become famous demonstrating his powers of mind over matter in London and Prussia, until he is denounced as a fake at a meeting in Paris rigged by the positivists. Determined to refute them in writing, he has not advanced much by the end of the story; on the contrary, in the six years since moving to Argentina—which was, like other Latin American societies in the nineteenth century, substantially influenced by positivism—he is vanquished over and over by matter. Having received a land grant in exchange for recruiting Sicilian peasants to settle the pampas, he amasses a small fortune by cattle raising and other ventures, and builds a house in the newer part of the city. One evening, returning unannounced from the empty expanse of his land where he likes to go meditate, he surprises his young wife, Gina, in warm conversation with his best friend and business partner, Garay López. The thought of what he glimpsed—her "expression of intense pleasure," his "wicked smile," their cognac and cigars—will gnaw at Bianco until he is almost mad with jealousy.[77]

His problem is one of perception, of interpretation, and the signs are too ambiguous. Nor can he bring himself to confront them about what may have been an innocent moment. Yet it adds to his suspicion that she has long been undermining him, as in their failed telepathy experiments. When she later tells him she is pregnant, he believes his doubts have been confirmed (though he made love with her the morning after his return): the deception has been made manifest in blood and tissues. Indeed, he grows so obsessed by the possibility that he prefers it to be true, and resolves to trick his friend into a confession. Garay López—who works as a doctor in the capital, having escaped his cloistered family, one of the oldest and richest in the region—returns for another reason, however: he has fled an outbreak of yellow fever but ends up bringing it with him, infecting the entire city. That is his confession. Bianco tries one last time to know the truth, only to find his friend too far gone, whose ravages represent "that material conspiracy malevolently opposed to his desires."[78] Bianco in turn must flee for his life, this time taking Gina to his little cabin on the pampas. There he senses that it has all been a dream, that he is fast asleep beside his mistress in Paris. Gina's voice brings him back to the material reality: they are survivors, and about to start a family.

Saer, who has always gone his own way as a writer, produced his most linear narrative in *The Event*.[79] Even so, the circular method of previous texts remains operative in his recuperation of moments from the past decade in Bianco's life, his treatment of memory, and his development of philosophical issues. Some months later his next novel, *Glosa* (Gloss, 1988), signaled a return not only to the Santa Fe of his own time but to his dominant concern with language as a process of exchange and how the uncertainty inherent to one narrative may affect others. Here too, the circularity seems relegated to the background, yet it keeps intruding on the linear aspects. Of intricate structure and richly layered, *Glosa* is divided into three parts, each marking off a stretch of seven blocks that Leto walks along San Martín, the main street, having gotten off the bus before his usual stop one bright spring morning on his way to work. By the second block he runs into the Mathematician, fresh from a tour of Europe, who accompanies him the entire route and never manages more than a postcard-like account of his trip: "Prague, most of Kafka's work becomes clear when you get there; Bruges, they painted what they saw; Paris, an unexpected rain."[80] Throughout, their principal subject of discussion is the sixty-fifth birthday party for the writer and former union organizer Washington Noriega, a gathering that unites nearly the whole web of Saer's characters, which both of them missed—Leto because he wasn't invited, as the youngest and newest in the wide circle of friends, and the other because he was in Europe. Still, the Mathematician launches into an extended description of the event, because he heard about it from Botón, who was there, and this becomes so amplified by other versions—especially that of Tomatis, who was also there and who joins them in the middle stretch along San Martín, contesting the details—that long after, their memory of the party will endure more intensely than many of their own experiences.

Glosa stands as a sort of skeleton key to the full range of Saer's methods and materials: a polyrhythmic narrative where the ostensible line is more like the edge of a prism, constantly dispersed in the play of light and color. Like Leopold Bloom's trajectory through Dublin and other voyages on a local scale, the Avenida San Martín provides the illusion of continuity despite many interruptions and digressions. On the most immediate plane, there are numerous external details about buildings, pedestrians, traffic patterns, and the changing aspect of the street. Meanwhile, Leto probes his own family mysteries through a series of recollections, working back from his mother that morning to his father's suicide the year before, as he engages with his friend's descriptions of the party, reconstructing it in his mind to fill the gaps of places and characters he doesn't know firsthand. The Mathematician, with regular modifications and reinterpretations of Botón's account, and his later refutations of Tomatis's version, acknowledges the problematic nature of his source even as he continues weighing the variants. When at last they go their separate ways at the Plaza de Mayo, the seat of secular and religious power, the two friends recognize the privileged hour spent together although they will never be that close again.

Twice in *Glosa*, in the second and third parts, amid what is otherwise a luminous novel, the narrative jumps forward seventeen years to the late 1970s to reflect at length on how the repression in Argentina affected some of the characters: the Mathematician, exiled to Sweden, who on a visit to Pichón in Paris will recall key phrases from Washington's party; Leto, his transition into the unreality of life underground, who will leave little trace of himself. By setting *Lo imborrable* (The Indelible, 1993) in the winter of 1980, a period when he himself stayed away, Saer takes up the implications of this dark time more directly. Curiously, the new characters here seem strangely oblivious to the sinister forces regulating their lives, but Tomatis, in his precarious recovery from depression, is not fooled: for him, "in the times as they are, most people are still reptiles."[81] The people he meets seem only interested in their careers, in marketing successful enterprises, pretending that all is right with the world, while he remains well aware of the shame that marks the daily social fabric where others are disappeared, thrown alive from airplanes into the sea. He knows that if the streets are often empty it is due to more than the weather, and he sees other friends also falling apart. His third marriage failed the year before, partly from such questions of conscience, precipitating the depression while his eight-year-old daughter went off with her mother to a fashionable summer resort.

In this novel Tomatis struggles to reintegrate a sense of self, hence his doubts as narrator in using the first-person pronoun. As a cure he takes to writing sonnets, a favorite activity from adolescence: the effort at working language into verse and rhyme, autonomous form, puts "a brake to the dispersion, due to the heroic prestige of all measure, [which] now indelible" pacifies him.[82] But what helps above all is his encounters with external details. Strolling through the city, he is reassured by his interest in the irrational, which can reunite him with "the contradictory thickness of the real world."[83] On a drive out of town, in the silent marshy terrain he feels unexpectedly at one with the world and the present moment. And at the end, at a party hosted by the publishers of Bizancio Books—a series of leatherbound highlights of Western literature comprising mostly second-rate writers—who have been courting him all along for his involvement, in a place teeming with unreality amid local big shots, Tomatis returns to being a normal person by ordering the first alcoholic drink since his depression.

La pesquisa (The Investigation, 1994) signals a return as well, but of a broader sort: the return from exile, if only for a visit. Or rather, the return of a character to his roots, both transfigured by the intervening time, an encounter between presences and absences, and thus a search for continuities. The novel emphasizes a dual mind from its first word, "There," as Pichón recounts a series of brutal murders of old ladies that took place in Paris, in his neighborhood, ending in December at the start of winter, while he sits with Tomatis and Tomatis's friend Soldi at a bar and grill in Santa Fe, at the end of March, where it is not spring but autumn and still hot. The Paris story dominates the novel, and as in *Glosa*, story and narration are clearly relegated to separate spaces, with a frequent questioning as to the nature of the telling: what is my part in all this, Pichón asks, how do I know so much and present it so clearly, when at the time it is experienced in fragments?[84] Narrative implies a certain organizing principle after the events, and as an outsider, even after twenty years, he may better perceive the society in which the crimes occur (not so long before, in his native land comparable crimes were perpetrated as a matter of state policy). When Pichón reaches the dénouement, where the devoted inspector is revealed as the assassin—in schizophrenic lapses that respond to his mother's abandoning him as a child—Tomatis lights his cigar and offers an alternate solution, where the inspector's partner and best friend plausibly framed him.

Regardless of the truth of the story, for Pichón "only the present seems real."[85] On the pretext of selling off family properties, he has come back to revisit the near-mythical places that long ago formed him. To his surprise, in the first weeks he feels rather an absence of emotions, sapped of strength, with the fragmentary gaze of a foreigner; by contrast, the time passes quickly for his teenage son who is new there and eager for discoveries, adapting easily in the company of Tomatis's daughter the same age. That day, all of them had traveled upriver to Washington Noriega's old house, now occupied by his daughter, who lets them examine an unpublished novel that Washington may not have written, discovered by Soldi among his posthumous papers. To Pichón the whole terrain, even the trees in the patio, seem unrecognizable. Nor can he summon any emotion on glimpsing, from the river, the family bungalow in Rincón where his brother had vanished.[86] Only when they reach port in the city at dusk does he realize in a flash why his return has left him indifferent: because he is finally an adult, which means understanding (as in *The Witness*) that "one is born not in one's native land but in a larger, more neutral, unknown place," a home that is neither geographical nor verbal, but rather physical, chemical, cosmic.[87]

8

Tsuris of the Margins

(Luisa Futoransky)

Contrary to the usual trade routes of culture for an Argentine writer, **Luisa Futoransky** (b. 1939) had traveled the world over and lived abroad for more than a decade before moving to Paris in 1981. In the early 1960s, she ventured to Bolivia and Brazil and later to other reaches of Latin America, in between studying opera in Buenos Aires and working at the National Library under Jorge Luis Borges; by the end of the decade, she made her first visits to Europe and to Israel. In 1971, on a Fulbright fellowship, she went to the United States as a poet in residence at the University of Iowa. From there she was offered a study grant to write in Rome, where she stayed for two years and worked as an assistant director of opera. This in turn led to a position at the Opera of Tel Aviv for a year. Amid these comings and goings, she also managed to visit Madrid, Greece, and Indonesia. By then, with the military dictatorship in Argentina, she chose not to return and instead cast her sights further, to the Far East; at the end of 1975, meanwhile, her family, as well, decided to leave Argentina and emigrated to Israel. In 1976, she was hired to teach and stage Italian opera in Tokyo, and stayed four years. After, she went briefly to Paris, but accepted the chance to work in Peking for the Spanish bureau of Chinese radio's international service, remaining for a year and a half.

Paris, then, represented a second phase in her exile. To some degree, it completed the movement common to many like her, especially in Argentina: the return, to a different Europe, of children or grandchildren of immigrants —who were, in her case, fleeing pogroms in the Ukraine and Bessarabia. Yet, after two decades, Futoransky's situation there is hardly more secure than it ever was. Perhaps that is because she never expected to stay, but by the 1980s, most of the plum jobs for Latin American writers in Paris had long been filled. Never so fortunate as to land a spot in a publishing house, a university, a cultural or diplomatic organization, she has survived precariously, often working two jobs (at the Centre Pompidou and at Agence France Presse, during the past decade), interspersed by occasional residencies, awards, and small commissions. In the larger picture, moreover, as a foreigner and as a Jew, she came at a time when the old ghosts were again rattling their chains with the rise of Jean-Marie LePen and the National Front in France and the revival of a xenophobic nationalism throughout the continent. Add to this the fact that she arrived in Paris past forty, a woman alone and "not at all skinny," as she puts it, and the multiple dimensions of her marginality— physical, cultural, geographical, historical—begin to emerge.[1] Such conditions of not belonging, viewed with irony, humor, and compassion, entered directly into her writing as the means by which she might nonetheless make a place for herself. It was in Paris that she matured as a writer, where she became a novelist and wrote much of her strongest poetry, plus two nonfiction books that explore supposedly women's subjects—hair, honeymoons— in penetrating cultural analyses.

Before Paris, Futoransky had published four books of poetry that marked a process of opening out toward the world. The circumstances of her first book, *Trago fuerte* (Strong Drink, 1963), hinted at what awaited her as a writer, but echoed too the persistent obstacles to cultural exchange between the countries of Latin America: visiting Bolivia, she had given the manuscript to an editor, only to receive ten copies of her book some time later and never another word from the publisher.[2] Opening with a few lines from *The Song of Songs*, the book traces the quest that love implies and the difficulty in learning to love not only another person but also oneself. In *El corazón de los lugares* (The Heart of Places, 1964), the journey describes a wider realm, extending across the American continent and beyond; here the poet seeks to enter something deeper than the self, a mystery that can only be approached through traveling, in this way likening her experience as a Jew to that of the Gypsies. *Babel, Babel* (1968), by contrast, immerses itself in the specifics of history, achieving a tone of testimony mixed with prophecy. The poet wants to challenge God, who seems so far away in a world where love is lacking and disasters multiply.

With *Lo regado por lo seco* (The Watered for the Dry, 1972), her first book after leaving Argentina, she began to explore the condition of exile. She considers the figure of "stupid Ulysses, spouting literature" while his wife enjoys herself at home.[3] For Ulysses, however, the voyage came to an end, whereas Futoransky herself finds that it always starts over again. Perhaps Israel could be her new home, she seems to wonder, and here she devotes many poems to the subject. She recognizes that "each land has its favorite fruits and . . . there is no place like this for the vines of dementia."[4] Elsewhere, after a night spent with a man who was probably an Arab, she imagines the child she might have had, who no doubt would have been a rebel. The land is full of uprooted peoples, and she feels tenderness for them all, with the cruel history that has been their destiny. Yet, this is not enough in the end to make it her home: she wants more from the world than to be united with that history.

Partir, digo (To Leave, I Say, 1982), her first book from Paris, collects the poems from a decade of her most distant travels. Here she enters fully into the theme of exile. As in the textures of her prose, memory and imagination mix constantly, distinct moments and voices from along her route recalling one another. This weaving back and forth is also employed from book to book, by taking poems from earlier collections and presenting them, usually revised, in the new context. "Vitraux of exile" appeared in the previous book after a series of poems on Israel, yet in opening *Partir, digo*, it draws attention to the primacy of exile and to the currency of foreign terms: instead of the Spanish word *vitrales* (stained-glass windows) she uses the French *vitraux*, thereby casting her reader off-balance, who is made into a foreigner with the first word in the collection. Moreover, in its tone of reckoning after so much wandering, the poem holds added weight revisited ten years later:

> You learned at the cost of your youth
> and most of your innocence
> that to be alone in a forsaken suburb of the pampas
> or in splendid Samarkand
> holds the same dimension of oblivion or tragedy;
> ....
> because to say country is to whisper barely
>   seven letters
> and through them the density of secret combinations

> gravestones of strangers bearing our name
> and pale photos that preserve the echo of
> > your passage
> toward love or despair.[5]

Launched by the retrospective impulse, the book proceeds like a report from the front, reflecting on what she found and what she missed there, recognizing the persistent need to press on. But more than a dialogue with places and figures from the recent or distant past, Futoransky creates in her writing "endless lines of flight where the language establishes relations of intensities, of elements of force that show us the immaterial life pulsating between the words," as decribed by Elia Espinosa.[6] That pulse is a function of the traveler's desire, her search for an earthly and spiritual love that could offer a key to her existence, but which cannot be framed within any preexisting story. The long poem that closes the book, therefore, "End of the Poem," draws on motifs from myth, history, fairy tales, opera, and tales of chivalry, yet always the speaker refuses the part apparently assigned to her. Once again, the only role that will fit pertains to departures:

> at any rate the wandering jew sets off with her knapsack of baubles and trinkets along the narrow path of the moon; she's afraid of an autumn leaf, the name of the winds, her inability to read compasses, to keep walking; tell me why she doesn't stop and wait for the sun to come out, I know, the terror would be the same, but clearly to disappear on horseback, slowly through the narrow pass, in silence and shadows, is a fine end of the poem.[7]

When Futoransky left Peking and came to Paris, she already had the project of her first novel, *Son cuentos chinos* (Chinese Intrigues, 1983).[8] At that point in her life, and for her as a poet, writing a novel posed the new challenge in its requirements of endurance and application. Besides, as a longtime reader of Henri Michaux and as a Latin American woman who had worked in the Far East, she wanted to respond in a way to his books *Ecuador* and especially *Un barbare en Asie*, based on his own travels half a century earlier. Like her subsequent novels, it is drawn largely from autobiographical experiences and concerns the uncertain existence of foreigners in general and Latin Americans in particular as they try to build a life. Not of a temperament to puzzle out a sustained plot, Futoransky deals in short takes, constructing each narrative like a different mosaic to offer a multiple vision of places, times, and voices. *Son cuentos chinos* takes the form roughly of an intimate journal that allows her, on behalf of the protagonist, Laura Kaplansky, to bring up at will: memories of her Jewish childhood in Buenos Aires, her tangles with the Chinese bureaucracy in Peking, her amorous adventures with two African diplomats, and reflections on the years in Japan where she had to leave behind her dog, Tango. There are also past loves, friends who help her, the differing views of Chinese women colleagues, other foreigners with their own peculiar problems, and her parents faraway who do not understand her, each as though speaking another language and her in the middle translating it all. A sort of orchestrated scrapbook, it incorporates, as well, a host of other brief texts—Zen commentaries, Ecclesiastes, Borges, Ray Bradbury, Gerald Durrell, Felisberto Hernández, and Marguerite Yourcenar. These reinforce or play off of neighboring passages like musical figures, just as she does in reapplying motifs and one poem entirely from *Partir, digo*.

Pervading the novel is a sense of the forbidden, the family and social injunctions against what may be said or done, and the ensuing fear that one has nonetheless broken some rule. At the same time, in the protagonist, there is the will to escape, to define her own terms, cost what it may. But she cannot start over from zero, she realizes, as she once had hoped, for there is always a past that dwells like a secret voice inside. Beginning with her earliest childhood memories, she recalls her parents at home worrying about the war and the rumor that concentration camps are being set up in the north of Argentina. Worse for her, though, is the perfidy of her father, whose other woman she meets one day while strolling with him and about whom she must never speak at home. Later, she steps over the line altogether with her short-lived marriage to a *mestizo* and non-Jew, for which she is effectively disowned. Since childhood, everything for her has been precarious: even to the present day she attaches things to the wall with thumbtacks, not frames or nails, nothing permanent. In China, on the other hand, she is baffled by the otherworldly realities of working in the state radio offices; not only are photocopy machines unavailable, they have no use of carbons either, the better to employ ten times the amount of people needed. What, she keeps asking, is she doing there where she does not speak the language and must seek permission for every move? The appeal of exotic places, she is reminded, becomes complicated on contact. At first, the idealist, she wants to work in the same conditions as the Chinese, but as winter sets in and with no office heater, she soon abandons that notion. Moreover, as a foreign worker, she finds herself trapped in a familiar hierarchy, affecting the quality of her lodgings, the public hospital she can use, and other privileges: as a Latin American she is cast generally with the rest of the Third World, the status of Anglo-Europeans beyond her reach.

Throughout, ever curious about the world around her, the narrator finely observes the habits, manners, and hobbies of the Chinese, and how these compare with her own experience or with other places she has been, like Japan. Among the most startling is the matter of women's rights and restrictions on sexuality: premarital sex, early marriage, even making love more than twice a week are discouraged by the revolution; as for abortion, her Chinese colleague who confides in her cannot believe that in Laura's country it is forbidden whereas in China it is obligatory. Try as she might to comprehend the differences, Chinese ways often remain inscrutable to her, based on old codes that no longer seem to have a purpose except to control people—much like codes in her own culture. But what, she wonders, still ties her to Buenos Aires after so long away? Her passport, her language, a "packet of ghosts," and the "four or five friends" whom she sees now and then somewhere in the world; that's all, and the bones of her grandparents buried there.[9] Ultimately she is riddled with the absences of her past—the routes she took to school, the cafés that nourished her literary passions—as she tries to reassure herself that people do still remember her. She mourns as well the exile from her father's love long ago, a wound that pains her yet, and laments the passing of a special romance in Italy, fragile intimacies in Japan, until she pulls herself back into the present, proudly waiting for her lover in Peking.

With this novel Futoransky may be seen among other recent Argentine writers practicing an ironic sort of orientalism that allows them, as Francine Masiello notes, to "pick up on a fascination for otherness and use the distance between cultures to explore the construction of meaning, to explore their own conditions as 'other' in the society in which they live." Above all, the Orient, in such terms, "offers a site to emphasize voice over form, performance over fixed beliefs."[10] In Futoransky, however, the emphasis on voice and performance, the questioning of given forms, entirely predates her encounter with the East: these are rooted in her condition as the daughter of Jewish immigrants in a conservative society, growing up through the 1950s and 1960s when her desire to be a writer was shaped—and her urge to travel, the ultimate liberation—as well as her interest in opera with its extravagant gestures. Opera, for her, means melody and narration, means emotion, and she wants "to capture the emotion up to its ultimate consequences." Thus she feels closer to the poetic tradition of saying the emotion, as in Paul Eluard, than the philosophical current of poetry typified by Octavio Paz.[11] Indeed, through all her writing runs an undercurrent of the theatrical, a reflex to dramatize or make a diversion of each vicissitude, even to laugh at her own expectations. Her method, according to Masiello, is based not "on monumentality, but on the supplements of minor resistance," which "mocks the power of official myth and attacks its subjugating forces." It is a "contraband discourse" informed "by the practice of translation, an acknowledgment of the transformational magic of language that helps the foreigner negotiate difference."[12]

Still, Futoransky reminds us, the "absent language" is irreplaceable; depending on the circumstances and the person, its memory, its secret music, "permits or hinders the expatriate's most difficult acquisition: internal residence." Sooner or later, the ability to settle comes up against its limits. "Weakening, impotence arise when one wants to carry over the vast range of breathings that are indispensable for living within a language, because the tools do not respond, the voice is alien, and the spoken and written word are not up to the job." Her language as a writer, therefore, reflects the experience of such limits, "elaborated out of pure patchwork: phrases, scraps, vital harvests, palpitations from far and wide."[13] If within Western culture, as Saúl Sosnowski remarks, Jewish Latin Americans have inhabited a double marginality, Futoransky as a woman moving about alone through the world for some three decades may be considered thrice marginal.[14] Consequently, just as she has no secure ground to stand on, there is no authoritative discourse that will suffice for her. In this sense, what Rosa Sarabia has written about the use of a colloquial voice in her poetry holds true also for her fiction, that it is "above all an insolence before the given, the inherited. The inefficacy of the consecrated word, ready-made phrases, grammar and its rules as of eloquent poetic language . . . is thus laid bare."[15]

But the fragmentation is hardly of her making; rather, it is all about her in the wear and tear of such a life. The poems in *El diván de la puerta dorada* (The Couch of the Golden Door, 1984) examine this state first in her own body. "Wrinkles" briefly recounts how "the skin on my hands conceives intricate ideograms/that I decipher patiently." Finding the extremes of both joy and pain, she is left to accept that "I am what I am."[16] At moments, a recurring temptation in her books, she wants to imagine a perfect storybook love, knowing too well the romantic scenarios that end in tatters of disillusion. In one poem, she tries to cast herself in a traditional role, as a Portuguese woman dressed in black "whose sole occupation is waiting for the tides/that carry out and bring back my man," but the scene grows too complicated when she thinks of the man in question and she has to admit that "I'm rowing against the current and I'm getting tired."[17] Throughout the collection her main purpose is to situate herself in the present and to recognize her "flustered loves" in "the passionate shipwreck/that is [her] life."[18] Has she achieved any insight, she asks, after all her travels, or is it always the same battle? Twenty years "to open a window," she concludes in a poem written over two decades ("Cassandra: Twenty Years Later, Your Eyes Are Like Tigers"), commenting in part on the tango by Carlos Gardel, "Volver," where twenty years away are as nothing when the emotion remains fresh; Gardel's song, though, is about returning, whereas Futoransky had not yet gone back even for a visit. In her poem, therefore, it seems like no small advance to have gained at least a little light.

The stubbornness with which she tries to settle in Paris, to make new attachments, is taken up more fully in her novel *De Pe a Pa* (1986), a sequel to the China novel with the same protagonist. Subtitled *de Pekín a París* to underline the literal reference, the title is also a way of saying "from A to Z." In part, this is a narrative about how her language nearly did her in. The novel is structured like an alphabetical primer, reflecting the new language that she had to learn; yet in twelve chapters she only reaches the letter H, for hospital. The book starts out, however, with the double force of abracadabra and *amor*, and the implicit wish that the two terms were as one: the magic formula that might heal the sick, and Laura's need to believe in love against all odds, as the "only branch at the edge of the precipice," with her trust "in the repetition of a few phrases spoken by him."[19] Her Zairean prince, after Peking, had promised to arrange for a transfer to Madrid where she would join him, although even she, waiting in Paris, seems to have known better. Thus China enters in among her "zones of electrification," places in the world that still cause her pulse to race. She proceeds to consider the reasons that drew her to Paris—love's enchantments, literary destinies, and more—yet cannot forget that she remains an outsider, a *sale étranger* (dirty foreigner) like the rest, left to improvise her alternate existence there as best she can. The second chapter, therefore, is an act of defiance, a triumph of untranslatability, her language refusing to be assimilated as she playfully commands the most diverse words and references beginning with the letter B to heighten the theatricality of love lost, unrequited, transcended, complete with final curtain. Late in the novel, given her instinct to go against the grain, to work backward at the same time as forward, she performs the feat again, but on the letter A: she starts with *abracadabra* because of all it contains, like *abandonment* and *avarice* as well as to love (*amar*).

The narrative briefly takes on a semblance of linearity in the third chapter, C for *casa* (house), detailing the laborious search for an apartment with its false trails. Even among her compatriots, Laura discovers, few people can be trusted in the goods they pass on. When at last she finds a studio out in the 12th arrondissement, her chorus of friends tell her it will be like another exile, and all the paperwork required by the realtor proves yet one more trial. She realizes, meanwhile, that a line of demarcation exists between her exile friends in Paris: "those from before are connected with youth, the emotional freedom of choices and affinities; those met since arriving, with solitude and the ghetto."[20] At the letter D, *diván*, the psychiatrist's couch, her anxieties begin to pile up—about committing herself to her new home; guilt for not having shared the experience of compatriots who suffered the repression firsthand; her apartment is broken into, her very history in keepsakes stolen; on top of that, to have to go report the theft in her awful French. Later, after reflecting on the life of an artist, the difficulties of coming to Paris at forty instead of eighteen and looking for scraps of work, the arrival of two letters causes her to revisit sorrows from her past that intertwine now in Paris when they no longer hurt: these include her abortions long ago, the breakup of her marriage, and her next boyfriend, the Spaniard who ditched her; he resembled her beloved Uncle Iankel who has just died and whom her own quarreling parents dismissed as crazy and inept. She invokes the love and protection she felt as a child from her immigrant grandmother, and in turn is not surprised at the popularity of fortune-tellers in France.

As in her first novel, Futoransky here alternates between anthropological notes on the curious practices of the French and chronicling Laura's comic misadventures, like how she unexpectedly ended up with her first French lover, an act of mutual consolation, and the thankless friendship she endured with an older woman, a famous Latin American novelist. Try as she might to make her way, though, she still must face the periodic humiliations suffered from living in another language and misunderstanding French codes; at times it even seems hard to decipher her Latin American friends, each with their own fixed illusions, their ambitions and complaints.[21] As if in response to her predicament, she goes to seek work at UNESCO, as a translator, typist, anything. Again and again, she is told that she has come too late or too soon. In the final chapter, when she does land a temporary clerical job there, it coincides with a severe allergy that progressively breaks out all over her body, due in the end to Nivea cream. Narrated as a quasi-opera, the lowliness of her job contrasts with the grand mystery she represents in her sufferings, as each doctor proposes a new hypothesis about what ails her. At a gray hospital she is put through further tests in the humiliation of her body, and after a week she is released, handed a hefty bill and told at UNESCO that they will not pay it.

Her years of pilgrimage, Futoransky has said, have brought her "closer to being and less to seeming." If her experience abroad has entailed a certain mismatch with the cultures around her—be it the East or Israel or Paris—she has learned to inhabit her difference as a means to discovery and understanding. Moreover, being a foreigner has granted her a kind of defense mechanism, inseparable from the fact that her native tongue is transformed into a private language: the possibility to withdraw a while, to be "voluntarily autistic" as she puts it, so as to grow in her own way when the pain or pressures of the reigning milieu are too overpowering.[22] Despite the long separation, Argentina remains a fundamental reference for her, the anchor of specificity—in the rhythms of her speech, the character of her thought—to her wandering Jewishness. Since leaving, she has visited Argentina only twice: in 1984, after democracy was restored, and then eight years after. On the latter occasion she saw her return to the country as "an open wound that is healed and I know when I arrive that I never left."[23] In this she does at last echo Gardel.

The poems Futoransky was writing around the time of her Paris novel, however, tend still to concern a cataloguing of absences, moving from an emotion of place to the placing, or displacement, of emotion. The poem that opens *La sanguina* (The Sanguine Woman, 1987), "Probable Forgetting of Ithaca," first published in 1972 and slightly revised, reprises the theme of losses accumulated in exile by way of an unnamed Ulysses: "without flinching you carry the fate that fits you:/your place, you realize now,/left when you got there."[24] In a poem about her hometown, giving full resonance to its name, Santos Lugares (Holy Places), she notes that nothing remains as it was; all that exists is an old crumpled photograph of her mother as a girl alongside her grandmother. But the book soon focuses on the disenchantments of love: "The Queen never knew strategic skills/she believed that acting at emotion's own risk/a fine destiny awaited her."[25] In "Hammam," two middle-aged women recognize each other in a Parisian steam bath, each the other woman of their man. "Robotics" invokes figures of the living dead—Egyptian ushebti, Czech robot, Jewish golem—in order to "make him dream of me," only to tell herself to snap out of it. Such is the tenor of the final sequence of poems, often employing a Sappho-like brevity to sketch the pangs of her solitude, yet retaining a mordant gaze. As in "Body to Ground":

a stubborn
vocation for miracles
sustains me
I mean
sustained[26]

Or in the last poem, shortest of all, "He, Holofernes": "To watch him sleep—/ for the last time?"[27]

As a love poet, Futoransky reinscribes her experience of exile, because to sing of an absence is to mark that presence—of a person, a place, a time—that is life itself. Through language she reanimates the presence, to engage it once more. "Love," notes Guillermo Sucre, "is something more than a spiritual or bodily experience. Is it not equally a mythology and one which begins even by that of the word itself?"[28] But if, as Jorge Rodríguez Padrón insists, "the poetic experience in Spanish America is a form of vitalism, an affirmation of love as wisdom and center," Futoransky must challenge both the mythology and the wisdom, precisely because in spite of every setback she continues to believe.[29] Time and again, the received patterns by which love is imagined, made visible, have left her outside, dissatisfied, restless. Remarking in *Lunas de miel* (1996), her essay on honeymoons, that the glamour and glossy romanticism of marriage in Latin America was rooted largely in Catholic tradition, as a sort of compensation for the taboos and rigidity, she finds it no surprise that radio serials, *fotonovelas*, and soap operas should be so successful. That same atmosphere, in her view, helped give rise to the popularity of magical realism with its "cocktail of passions," like the fabulous weddings and incomparable couples found in Gabriel García Márquez, all of which condemned her, at her age and weight, "to gut countless love stories."[30] Her novel *Urracas* (Magpies, 1992) complicates matters further in that Julia, like previous protagonists, is involved with a married man. Although she doggedly keeps faith in love as if it were her true homeland, she is cast—inevitably, comically—into the eternal role of waiting.

Her most focused narrative, *Urracas* signals a new threshold in Futoransky's career as a writer in exile: it was her first book to be published in French translation before the Spanish original appeared.[31] Again a journey is at the heart of the tale, albeit less exotic, a train trip to Switzerland for a Christmas weekend; but here it serves as a framing device for the passions and preoccupations of two friends, Latin American women in Paris. Where Julia's specialty is waiting,

Cacha is a devotee of power—though she is never quite proper enough for her French in-laws—and as the magpies of the title they thus covet what others have. With much of the story situated in transit, the window of the train becomes a protagonist in itself for them "as a window on the past," on their "inner theater," the gateway to a stream of digressions.[32] Besides occasional thoughts of Argentina or her life in Paris, Julia's obsession is her absent lover Andrés, who had to spend the weekend with his wife and daughter. She ponders his habits and lies, their excursions together, his declarations of love—which God himself, principal interlocutor in her inner theater, witnessed. Cacha, for her part, so different in her ambitions and unaffected by such common concerns, cannot see why she puts up with him. For Julia every thought centered on Andrés only throws her off-balance. When she misses their connection in Lausanne (she keeps switching the names of Swiss cities and towns, all equally unreal to her), after each has gone off on her own, her first thought is to imagine what if he is calling her where she is due to be staying, to say he misses her, come back right away, he has the key to their new apartment?

She has a history of such torments from him: each time he would fantasize about divorcing his wife, to settle with Julia somewhere, only to grow anxious about his precious furniture. Andrés, it turns out, has again promised to divorce and to get an apartment for them in January. She just has to wait a little longer. But hardly has she left when the cad writes a letter that reaches her in Switzerland, declaring that he must renounce his desires for the sake of his daughter. Miserable, she heads out to a big party of Latin Americans where she keeps thinking she spots Andrés or his wife, until finally she phones him and gets the wife, a haughty Spanish conservative who insists on speaking French. As for Cacha, who took control of their house keys and claimed she didn't come to Switzerland to go partying with Latin Americans, she arrives there first and proceeds to dominate the festivities, while Julia goes and falls asleep in a kid's play room. The last brief chapter poses a counterweight to the whole preceding narrative by starting over where the book began, with Julia on line at the train station to buy her ticket, only this time she has forgotten her wallet. Running home, she catches the phone ringing. It is Andrés, who says he won't be available over the holidays. Then Cacha calls to cancel. When the dust settles, Julia realizes she is happy to stay home alone for the new year, ready at long last to write her adventure novel.

By opening the narrative at the end, Futoransky grants the value of adventure both to the unknown events that lie ahead for the protagonist in the alternate version as to the events just related, the trip to Switzerland along with the tribulations of a frustrated love, where her marginality—in relation to Europe, her lover, and her traveling companion—is reinforced at every turn. In a sense, this double vision signals an attitude beyond grappling with absences, found in her most recent books of poetry, *La Parca, enfrente* (Fate, before Us, 1995), and *Cortezas y fulgores* (Crusts and Radiance, 1997). Although she still tracks the losses and defeats, whether her own or of others, a certain acceptance takes precedence over lamentations—a result perhaps of getting older, of endurance. The many travel poems, localized almost entirely in Mediterranean settings, tend to celebrate the instances of life found there, to plumb the soulful particulars of a place, in which death, too, may figure in the landscape. Reflected through these in part, and directly in other poems, she sketches various self-portraits. "In Gerona I deciphered the names/on old Hebrew tombstones," she begins "Crema Catalana," about the surviving traces of the past in the medieval city, to end with a sort of surrender before language itself: "In my hands I am left with this swollen face, scabby and withered, where I am reflected/and with the aching and fragrant staff of the word/ *desconegut*, unknown, throbbing in my lap."[33] In "Self-Portrait 12/31/96" she follows an opposite movement inside out, from early ambitions and disappointments to the present where "in the galleys of useless and infinite jobs/dodging foremen/I smuggle poems like this one, in a hurry, torn out of me," concluding upon a wider perspective:

> it's raining inside and out
> we've got to buy roof tiles, plug up the leaks,
> before the ceiling and masonry cave in on us
>
> indispensable the repair of the temple and time:
>
> *if I don't do it myself, who,*
> *and if not now, when?*[34]

Given that Futoransky has often read her exile through the personal and historic framework of Jewishness, even as she sounds it for cracks to register her dissatisfactions, she makes it clear that Israel, despite her attachments, is not exactly her home either. A long poem she wrote after a trip to Jerusalem early in 1997, "Jerusa My Love," takes up the threads of love and sympathy, pain and recognition, belonging and independence, in one torrential sweep. Intersecting at each moment are the beauties of the desert landscape and the fervent human activity, "everyone armed and impatient." She offers tales of eccentric family relations who seem to have gone over the edge in that atmosphere, recalling that "in the dead sea scrolls the children of light do battle with the children of shadows/ . . . it would seem that the children of light won by a hair," only to be transformed "into the shadow of what we were, are and will be." Through her "ancient tears" for that deeply conflicted land, in which she sees herself, she knows she cannot stay:

> I look with
> horror at the havoc that so many bloody idols,
> so many thorns, so much shrapnel, wreak upon
> the land, the plants and the people
>
> and what to say of the concept of "chosen"
> **the spring that waters all the nonsense**
> the injustices

Amid the absurdities and futile human tenderness, and even the belated confirmation of parental love, "impregnated by intimate streetfood/by the mosaics/I pretend that I'm leaving."[35] Yet at the end of the poem, the exile's dilemma, she has bid farewell to all about her—and she is still there.

Living in Another Language: The Problem of Audience, Community

In the beginning, the writer stands alone. But not really alone, for there is the world around—the people known and encountered, the places and times traversed, and the thousands of other writers before and after echoing like gestures. Still, the writer's relation to a community is never simple. Nation, language, race, ethnicity, religion, gender, sexual orientation: these condition and may determine a writer's outlook, but they cannot contain it. Even in their distinction of a "minor literature," as that produced by a minority within a major language, Gilles Deleuze and Félix Guattari recognize the rebel impulse, the need not to belong entirely. Three characteristics mark such literature—deterritorialization of language, the connection to a political immediacy, and its innately collective value. Nonetheless, "if the writer is in the margins or completely outside his or her fragile community, this situation allows the writer all the more the possibility to express another possible community."[1] By way of some audience, as by the commerce of literary activity, the writer partakes in the creation of an open-ended community that cannot ever be fully typified, though it overlaps with other communities that may lay claim to him or her.

How, then, is the relation to community and to audience further complicated by the unpredictable effects of a writer's exile? From the circumstances of writing, to the opportunities to publish, to the circumstances of reading, each step of the process is likely transformed. Often, exile serves to reconfirm the writer's language community. Such was the case with Milan Kundera and other Czech writers who, leaving Czechoslovakia (and sometimes without leaving), had nowhere to publish in their native language until fellow-novelist Josef Skvorecky started his Czech publishing house, Sixty-Eight Publishers, in Toronto. More widespread, in this respect, are the many journals (*Linden Lane Magazine, Brújula*) and editorial imprints (Ediciones del Norte, The Latino Press, Ediciones Universal) created over the past two decades predominantly for Latin American writers living in the United States.

On the other hand, the writer's language itself can turn out to be the sign of exile well before the fact of physical exile. An ongoing debate in postcolonial societies has to do with distinguishing what is indigenous to a culture from what is the product of forced indoctrination, and how and when these might be separated. Where the terrain is literature, the issue of language makes this question particularly acute. In choosing to work in the local language or that of the former colonial power, the writer indicates what community or aspect of community will be his or her first concern. Those who opt for the local tongue clearly mark their commitment to the culture that most closely nourished them, yet those who work in the European language are not necessarily turning their backs on that culture. Rather, they may be trying to bridge cultures through their double perspective, the double distance created by their European-oriented university education. In postwar Africa, most writers chose the European languages, even though only a small percentage of the population could read those languages. "For whom were they writing?" asks Ngũgwa Thiong'o, who himself wrote in English for seventeen years. In 1977, he switched to G-kũyũ, gaining a new "sense of belonging" in his "attempt to reconnect [himself] to the community"; ever since, the English editions of his books have been translations from the original. "Whether I was based in Kenya or outside, my opting for English had already marked me as a writer in exile. . . . Thus the state of exile in the literary landscape reflects a larger state of alienation in the society as a whole, a clear case of colonial legacy which has left scars on the body, heart, and mind of the continent."[2]

Some writers, however, are formed in a sufficiently international context that their sense of community, even through language, is at best tenuous. Edmond Jabès, whose family had lived for generations amid the European colony in Cairo, was educated in France and published various books of poems there and in Paris, before and after the war. "I had only dreamed of one thing, to be integrated into French literature." Yet he also felt stifled by the close-knit social milieu he was part of and would periodically spend days at a time alone in the desert, "to depersonalize myself, to no longer be who I appeared to be to others in Cairo."[3] Then in 1957, at the age of 45, Jabès, as a Jew, was forced to leave Egypt after Gamal Abdel Nasser came to power. Though he settled with his family in Paris, France was a place of exile for him: it was there that his experience of the desert entered his books. A radical transformation came about in his writing, as his thought merged with Jewish tradition (despite his being an atheist) in the aphoristic intensity of the prose works that began with *The Book of Questions* in 1963. Of the many books that followed, he says: "I didn't understand the break I had made. I suffered terribly from it, because I didn't see where this adventure was going to lead me. Each time I felt myself a little more cut off from French literature . . . I felt I was losing my filiation with it, that I wouldn't find again the great writers whom I relied on."[4]

But something else may happen along the way when a writer lives in exile: after enough years or enough immersion in the dominant milieu, the writer occasionally passes over to the other side, temporarily or permanently, to write in the new language. For Vladimir Nabokov, the change was a way of responding to his new home and participating directly in the culture, to the point of writing one of the classic American novels; it is doubtful that his success with *Lolita*, given the American mass market, could have been achieved in a comparable way in another country. Samuel Beckett, too, knew success only after changing languages, as the French were particularly receptive to the plays he became known by; even so, his practice was rare in that he continued to alternate between English and French, according to the work he was writing. For most writers who undergo the metamorphosis, though, turning away from one's first language is a gradual process by which one prepares to confront the difficulties and risks. After twenty years in France, during which he attained considerable renown and wrote some of his essays directly in French, Kundera has now written his last two novels as well in French; due perhaps to the different formal properties of the language or to the effort of his task, these works are both shorter than his previous novels and structurally more contained. The philosopher E. M. Cioran, arriving in Paris as a young man in 1937, continued to write in his native Rumanian for ten years until translating Stéphane Mallarmé, he says, "all of a sudden it struck me that this made no sense. I'm in France . . . why am I doing this? I didn't want to go back to my own country. And that was a sort of illumination. I said, 'You have to renounce your native tongue.'" Still, his first book in French proved a trial by dictionaries, as he exhausted himself rewriting it four times.[5]

Changing or alternating languages for Spanish-American writers carries its own set of conditions according to the routes of cultural exchange that have marked the literature most. Carlos Fuentes, as the son of a diplomat, grew up completely fluent in English and French; over the years he has written occasional essays in these languages, and even wrote parts of his novel, *Christopher Unborn* (1987), in English. Rosario Ferré, the Puerto Rican writer, was largely educated in the United States and thus was thoroughly versed in both Latin and North American cultures. Although often her own translator, it was not until after many books that she wrote a novel, *The House on the Lagoon* (1995), directly in English. On the other hand, the Cuban exile Guillermo Cabrera Infante, living in London since 1965, has described himself as the only English writer working in Spanish; apart from some essays and film scripts, it took him two decades before he wrote a book in English, *Holy Smoke* (1985), a sort of history of cigars where his riotous linguistic playfulness resurfaces intact in the new language. But these examples seem to be one-time performances, not necessarily meant to signal a change, to prove rather that they can fully master, as writers, a language they have moved around in freely for so long.

The transition to French, by contrast, appears more fraught with implications. The writer who switches to French might sooner be viewed with suspicion by other Latin Americans, as if it were a betrayal or a pretension beyond reason. This reaction derives, no doubt, from the early fascination with French culture in Latin American countries and the later desire to transcend such an influence. In a sense, as though passing through a mirror, such a writer becomes lost to the body of Latin American literature: it is rare, for instance, that an anthology of Latin American literature ever includes any of the writers who have worked in French. Yet even if the switch does not elicit antagonism, it may be rather like the donning of a mask, but one whose expressions become identical with the writer's own particularities; the result is a removed presence, a kind of hide-and-seek via language, as it was for the surrealist poet César Moro. From his stay in Paris in the 1920s and 1930s, through his return to Peru and a decade in Mexico, to his final years back in Lima in the 1950s, Moro wrote most of his work in French, publishing only a few chapbooks in his lifetime. He was "not merely renouncing his native tongue," according to Julio Ortega, "but rather seeking his own language." His was a "profound revolt," marked by "an ethics of the marginal and radical artist," placing Eros at "the center of his work while not unaware of the dramas of solitude and abandonment."[6]

Where the use of French situated Moro in an alternate space, especially after his return to Latin America, reconfirming his poetry as a refuge for him from ordinary concerns, other writers are cast into a comparable margin simply by the difficulties of publishing in exile. Without a Spanish-language publisher for her last two books and her first two novels out of print in Spanish, Nivaria Tejera finds herself regarded almost as a historical figure, her work unavailable to the readers who would seem closest to her. And even without the screen of politics interfering, the Argentine writer Arnaldo Calveyra (b. 1929), residing in Paris since 1961, has seen far more of his work appear in French (published by Actes Sud) than in the original Spanish. In such circumstances the writer cannot help but straddle two worlds, hoping to communicate between them, although nothing is assured: what the exile risks is that he or she may be forgotten back home. In the present study, of those who write in French, two (Eduardo Manet, Silvia Baron Supervielle) have had little of their work published in Spanish, although they remain in contact with the Spanish-speaking world.

There is, however, an intermediate path in the confrontation between languages for a writer in exile, serving not just to enlarge one's potential audience but to open new possibilities for the work itself, both in what and how one writes. For Alicia Dujovne Ortiz (b. 1939), who moved to Paris in 1978 and survived mostly as a correspondent for Spanish-language newspapers, the fact of her being Latin American helped to interest French publishers in her first two novels and also enabled her to receive commissions for writing on Latin American subjects. One such opportunity was her book *Buenos Aires* (1984), written in French, for a collection on cities intended as personal accounts rather than tourist guides. Writing of her childhood there and the districts she lived in, it became clear to her that "Buenos Aires *is* loss, it *is* nostalgia, it's the sentiment of the past that won't return." Instead, she was able to return "by way of a mythical-nostalgic recreation."[7] Through exile she became interested in "the Argentina of popular myths," which had escaped her when she lived there. Years later, for another commission, she wrote a wild sort of biography, in first person, of the soccer star Diego Maradona. This, in effect, led the publisher Grasset to offer her a contract to write a real biography, *Eva Perón* (1995), which took far longer—in time and pages—than anticipated: as an Argentine woman, she recognized that she could not write it merely for a

French public. In the end, the book was so successful that it was translated into fifteen languages and, rare enough for a foreign writer, Grasset contracted her for two novels, paying a monthly stipend for her to write in her own language, Spanish. In the first of these, *Mireya* (1998), she treats the roots of tango and the career of Gardel in a story of French and Polish-Jewish prostitutes imported to Buenos Aires.

Writing the nonfiction books in French was a practical matter for Dujovne Ortiz. With the Eva Perón biography it was particularly helpful, in that the language restrained her, forcing her to maintain a certain seriousness and to leave aside the playful, associative, even hedonistic practice of her own language. For that reason she has not been inclined to write her fiction in French, and yet having written the other work left a lasting effect on her Spanish. "We allow ourselves all sorts of things in Spanish, with a lot of creativity and richness, but which is absolutely illogical. . . . The corset of French logical thought helped me curb my excesses in Spanish."[8] The Paraguayan writer Rubén Bareiro Saguier (b. 1930) derived a similar experience from his immersion in French critical thought after arriving in Paris in 1962 as a political exile. Though already a teacher and writer, devoting much attention to the suppressed bilingual culture of his native land (Guaraní and Spanish), the French system helped him frame his work with more rigor, to the point that he later rose through the French university ranks to become a researcher on Amerindian and Latin American culture at the Centre National de la Recherche Scientifique. His own linguistic and cultural thematics could be thus tied in, by way of French, to other bilingual practices throughout Latin America.

9

The Translated Self

(Edgardo Cozarinsky)

In the work of **Edgardo Cozarinsky** (b. 1939), the world is like a living palimpsest. Form, place, character, all inhabit a fertile uncertainty where other discourses, other voices, enter to construct an open dialogue. Both in his films and in his written narratives, the imaginative process readily blurs the distinction between fiction, essay, document, as the questioning of history merges with the questioning of self and the past bleeds through into the present. This instinct to cross cultures and disciplines was evident in his first film from 1971—whose title... was a "mere" ellipsis, to emphasize the discontinuities between cultural strata—a work suggesting, as Jonathan Rosenbaum notes, that "Argentina was already 'somewhere else' for Cozarinsky even before he became a literal exile."[1]

Arriving in Paris in 1974, he never consciously decided to stay. It was only by a series of steps—the effort to find European financing for a film, the worsening situation in Argentina—that he understood in retrospect the move he had made. From previous visits he was somewhat predisposed against Paris, both in response to the Argentine infatuation with the city and because, following Jorge Luis Borges, his sympathy lay rather with London; but as he discovered the diverse populations of Paris, he grew more enthusiastic about being there. It was during those first years, moreover, insofar as other people saw him as an exile, that he became interested in matters relating to the Jewish diaspora—though he was raised in a nonreligious household.[2] Yet he remained outside the reigning cultural fashions, for his work was neither dressed in a colorful exoticism nor did it preach a revolutionary politics, and not fitting such expectations was at times a hindrance for him.[3] Instead, exile became the route that led Cozarinsky to an extensive reflection on the displacements of cultures, the overlapping of experiences in a cosmopolitan space, and how one city may translate into another through any number of passageways or distorting mirrors. Often, a retrospective gesture guides these lines of thought, by which he has continued to read the city he came from and the city where he lives each through the perspective of the other.

Until recently his only book of fiction, *Urban Voodoo* (1985) presents a series of unsettling journeys made up of remembrances, nostalgia, piquant observations, crossed with sociohistorical analysis and borrowings from many sources. Divided into two parts, the book opens with a short story, "The Sentimental Journey"—the longest text and the one most like a conventional story, though it seems so close to the author's own situation that it feels more like a nightmare. Not surprisingly, it recalls the supernatural side of Henry James: Cozarinsky's first book, in 1964, was a study of James, *El laberinto de la apariencia* (The Labyrinth of Appearance). The story, written in the late 1970s during the dark days of Argentina's "dirty war" against its own people, treats the unwilling and unwitting return of the protagonist who goes out one evening to his local café in Paris's 20th arrondissement only to find—through details of the noise, the lights, the décor, the signs—that somehow he has ended up at a café he used to frequent in Buenos Aires. A sequence of encounters with old friends and acquaintances confirms his ghostly voyage, even as they cast doubt on what level it is really happening, challenging him at each turn as the one who left, who was too pure for such times. But these events are first preceded by a small incident: rummaging through old papers, he chances on the unused and now worthless return ticket from when he arrived in Paris; though curious "about the former person the ticket seemed to reveal," he sets it afire and flushes it down the toilet.[4] Cozarinsky himself did not go back to visit for over a decade, around the time his book came out.

The protagonist's journey, then, responds to that momentary curiosity, except it leaves him with an ambivalence that borders on terror. Like the markings by which he recognizes the transformation of his local café, he is confronted with staged effects, as if he has stumbled into a performance where he must represent himself. "The spectacle of the city is so hypnotic," it carries "the deceptive lifelikeness of a dream." Discovered by his friend Guillermo, who drives him home to see his wife, he "cannot even tell what part he is supposed to play," wary not to "step outside the chalk marks laid down for him." But no matter what he might say about his own difficulties, to them his part is fixed, for he is living "the life of an artist."[5] He notices new buildings, new freeways, that did not exist before he left, and each familiar face reminds him of others who disappeared. When he asks what happened to them, no one seems to hear him or remember. Rather, those who stayed are busy thriving, pursuing their practical careers, enjoying life. His old girlfriend Laura, an ex-Trotskyist now in public relations, rejects his useless memories and reproaches him for having always been a spectator and a skeptic. Repeatedly, the scenes of this enchanted night are couched in cinematic and literary terms, devices that test the suspension of his disbelief, as when he runs into the known police informer Felipeli, "shrewd stage manager" whose laughter "brings together murderers and the murdered." Everyone is an accomplice in turning a blind eye to past and present horrors, until he ends up playing "an uninvited Tiresias," cursed with "the most devaluated of currencies: memory." Soon all the characters crowd around him, taunting him to "take the plunge into reality," attacking him for having burned his ticket, and when he escapes from them he can no longer tell what terrain he is treading, whether the parks of Buenos Aires or Paris, though determined not to yield "to a terminal case of bad translation."[6]

In Cozarinsky's story, the temptation to nostalgia is at once unavoidable and fraught with peril. At the end, the protagonist closes his eyes, unsure if he is "afraid of seeing the last of Buenos Aires vanish or . . . of listening, once again, to its siren song."[7] The past, his idea of the past, lies just under the surface of his present reality, ready to rise again at the right provocation, like the unused ticket. Such is the exile's dilemma that the distant place, as first context in the world, though gone forever, remains quietly present somehow, just out of reach, responding to each new experience. Some writers thus choose to work with their nostalgia, to use its evocative force and even to outwit its potential for undermining them, while others try to keep it from interfering. Bareiro Saguier, who was imprisoned numerous times before leaving Paraguay for Paris, sees nostalgia as dangerous to writing because "it blurs the vision of our reality" with its "tendency to idealize."[8] Cozarinsky recognizes that yearning for an idealized past, and his story may be considered a warning, even to himself. In his case, moreover, this falls within a particular cultural matrix, as "a product of Argentina in Paris," in musician Kip Hanrahan's phrase referring to the music of *bandoneonista* Juan José Mosalini and its seductive "description of an Argentina that probably never existed," meant above all for fellow Argentines.[9]

Cozarinsky relates how certain antidotes helped offset his own nostalgia. In the early to mid–1980s, one friend visiting Paris each year would bring an annual miscellany on video, labeled "Chronicles of Everyday Horror," made up of "television advertisements, fragments of talk shows or *telenovelas*," for him to look at whenever a fit of nostalgia came on. Later, he began to make annual visits back to Buenos Aires: "I go there to suck the blood of my past," he says, "I recover the person I was many years ago. . . . There are always the equivalent of Proust's madeleines everywhere." At the same time, he would meet many younger people whose perspective on the city served as a correction. "So I get both, my own sentimental journey and other people's completely different, fresh look at things."[10]

The thirteen texts that comprise most of *Urban Voodoo*, grouped as "The Postcard Album of the Journey," were written between 1975 and 1980, thus from the outset of his exile. As postcards, these brief story-essays are about distances and correspondences, treating the secret connections between places, the quick illuminations cast back and forth in the juxtaposition or superimposing of motifs. As he notes in an afterword, they seek "to manufacture common, public images, a *déjà vu* that would dilute whatever is too subjective in an individual's sensibility and experience." Which does not mean that he is absent from the proceedings, on the contrary: his is the traveler's eye and he articulates a syntax of exile based on his trajectory, ever returning to Buenos Aires, ever departing. From his very approach he cultivates a method of absences and echoes, having written the pieces in what he calls a "foreigner's English," later translating them into Spanish; his purpose was "to erase the notion of an original," so that "the original itself becomes translation."[11] This in turn reflects the play between cultural elements, especially in the New World and the Old, as to question simple assumptions about influence, transference, copies.

Irrespective of their dates of composition, the texts are arranged with the focus shifting gradually from Argentina to Europe and beyond, though the traffic between places informs them all: even "(Star Quality)," about the unnamed Evita and the "selves she left behind," is set into motion by a dream the faraway narrator had about her and how he knew, on waking, he "would never make a film about her."[12] The last piece, "(One for the Road)," proposes a fleeting return of sorts, while marking the most geographical transitions in barely three pages, as it begins and ends with a line that is never followed up directly, "Today I feel like writing about Buenos Aires." Instead, it proceeds, "The saga of vanished wealth feeds on the swindles of History." He considers the ornate Alexandre III bridge in Paris, which recalls "a ghostly assembly of Russian bond holders" from the turn of the century, whose engagements were never honored by the Soviets: the original bonds he found papering the walls of a children's room in a dilapidated apartment in Passy. The "run-down mansions" and "haughty Opera Theater" in Manaus are next, abandoned to the jungle by the ruined Brazilian rubber barons, as seen by his father in the 1930s, who also recounted the forlorn opulence of Punta Arenas, at the bottom of Chile, after the Panama Canal opened. From there he reflects on Trieste, "left quivering between blurred borders," and Alexandria, "its polyglot miscegenation of greedy minorities," which remain as "cities of the mind." It is a unique itinerary he follows here: "behind the splendor of great capitals I enjoy detecting a ghost town struggling to be released." And only through affirming his "resilient allegiance to ports," with their evocative magic of imported goods, does he manage in the end to pronounce once more the city of his own departure.[13]

What propels him in these texts is the tension between the image and reality of places, which for the exile, for the traveler, can never be resolved. Every image, of course, is made up of other images that do not dissipate so much as become modified on contact with a place or in the contrast with other places. He is particularly drawn by the tricks of illusion laid bare, the twilight moment when a city like Paris "seems to accept its destiny of stage decor, painted backdrop."[14] True to form, the postcards are laced with preestablished images drawn from literature, movies, and popular culture, but Cozarinsky layers in another element: quotations from a wide array of other texts, "residues of reading," that precede and follow these pieces like so many revolving mirrors.[15] Thus, at the start of the series, only a page after "The Sentimental Journey" ends, a quote from Ross MacDonald's novel *The Chill* recalls: "The city where I was born and raised. The city where everything happened. I ran away, but you can't run away from the landscape of your dreams."[16] The first postcard, "(Early Nothing)," begins with the notion that children watching a slide show, when they become aware of the screen in the intervals, experience "a thrilled admission into the realm of knowledge." For the children of Buenos Aires like himself, the various historical fictions projected onto the Argentine screen over two centuries shared only "the brittle nature of an optical illusion." Discovering the intervals, however, left them not with a sense of knowledge but rather "a resilient taste of nothingness." So that when they wandered from

Plato's cave, "the realm of originals" produced "shocks of recognition and disillusion" and in the end reminded them "less of [the] reproduced, debased image, than of the impending catastrophe that was to smash that image."[17]

It is precisely midway through the thirteen postcards, "(Cheap Thrills)," that Buenos Aires and Paris fold in and out of each other most for the narrator. Again, he arrives at his insights as a spectator before a frame, yet here the experience is multiplied. From the window of the métro coming in to the elevated Barbès-Rochechouart station, his gaze is attracted by the "templelike" Luxor-Pathé cinema, and one evening he ventures out into the Arab neighborhood curious for whatever exotic movie the theater might offer. He finds instead an Egyptian tearjerker wrapped in cheap patriotism and wonders how he manages to watch it, seated between "the loukoum-eating mother and daughter" on one side and "the young, heavily cologned couple" on the other, without his usual skepticism. It must be because he is "a cultural tourist," which he no longer could afford to be in his own country. He is reminded of comparable singing idols in Spanish, and how the same lower middle-class public was really quite familiar to him in Buenos Aires, where such mass sentiments sooner frightened him. Emerging from the theater he has a mild shock to find himself in France, feeling he has just spent "a last, posthumous evening at the Armonia." This was a "shabby palace" by the early 1960s when he used to go, as a displaced film buff studying Hollywood *auteurs* amid an audience of groping teenagers and "heterodox couplings." Years later the theater was closed down after a construction worker accidentally killed a boy he was raping in the men's room, which was entered through the "occasional rectangle of light" to the side of the screen. The narrator walks away then, through the Paris night, and onto his regular métro line, which accepts him "with a semblance of direction."[18]

Besides the historical moment in which Cozarinsky came to Paris, the city has been the most propitious location for him to pursue his main activity, writing and directing films. As with *Urban Voodoo*, he might be speaking of his own hard-to-classify documentaries and features when he writes of Borges' stories: "The less those texts respond to the accepted statutes of fiction, the more strongly they display the narrative process, which directs a *mise-en-scène* whose purpose is neither mimetic nor representational but intellectual: to arouse pleasure in the recognition of [the] 'overall form.'"[19] Being an outsider —and mostly writing his scripts in French—has provided the distinct vantage point that enables him to treat the German occupation in Paris (*One Man's War*), the need for escape of a Swiss insurance salesman in Rotterdam (*High*

Seas), and the advance of European "civilization" into Argentina's "Wild West" of a century ago (*Warriors and Captives*). But in *Sunset Boulevards* (1992), he implicates himself, merging personal essay with historical research to focus on the land of his childhood and the incipient crossing of two roads on the day Argentine crowds in Buenos Aires celebrated the liberation of Paris. From the start he establishes a dialogue between the time of making the film and that time almost fifty years earlier, exploring by interviews (with the writers Adolfo Bioy Casares and Gloria Alcorta, another Argentine in Paris) what the liberation meant to his compatriots.

However, he soon veers onto what seems a side path but is really the central concern of his film, with the discovery that the theater actress Falconetti, best known for her only film role as the lead in Carl Theodor Dreyer's *La Passion de Jeanne d'Arc* (1928), was also in Buenos Aires then, her career in decline, dying there not long after the war. He seeks out those who knew her, and declaring that she was also present that day singing "La Marseillaise," he reveals another piece of his puzzle: he as a child was there too in the Plaza Francia, holding his parents' hands, not understanding either the people's joy nor the language they were singing. Questioning the fate of others after the war, sinister figures who may have found refuge in Argentina, he lands on another actor he only became aware of later as a film buff, Robert Le Vigan, seen in French classics of the 1930s, who fled to Argentina as a defeated Nazi collaborator and lived another two decades far away from the capital. But, Cozarinsky the narrator concludes:

> There is no innocent investigation. The detective always ends up learning something about himself. . . . I set out on the trail of Falconetti and Le Vigan. What had they gone to look for there? Perhaps, quite simply, the most stubborn of mirages, to start over from zero. The same that impelled me to make the opposite voyage. In my youth, I dreamed of living in Paris. Today, in Paris, I think of the city of my adolescence. . . . The movie theaters now gone where I learned to recognize elsewheres full of promise. . . . Today the only films that make me dream are the films still to be made.[20]

Even when writing those lines, he had in mind a project that was to take six years to realize, from the first seed planted in him on hearing a broadcast from France Musique on the composer Dimitri Shostakovich. In *Rothschild's Violin* (1996), Cozarinsky seeks as ever to "set disparate materials into conversation," mixing fiction and documentary, past and present, original and archival footage.[21] Remarkably, his film welds a far-reaching narrative out of the several layers of its development, each marking an in-between space for the transmission and renewal of life. At the center of its three-part structure is the story by Anton Chekhov about a bitter, old coffin-maker, Bronza, who supplements his meager income playing violin in the local Jewish orchestra for weddings; an anti-Semite, he always berates Rothschild the flautist for his plaintive style until the day Bronza realizes he is dying and in a gesture of repentance gives his violin to him, which is a sort of liberation for Rothschild. Chosen by Benjamin Fleischmann, favored pupil of Shostakovich on the eve of the war, this story was the subject of a one-act opera fated to be his only work. Fleischmann died, a Jew, defending Leningrad against the Germans. Through the war and after, Shostakovich completed the orchestration but despite his own official favor, it was performed only once, twenty years later. The first part of the film, then, places the teacher-student relationship in its historical context, up until the student enlists and the teacher is evacuated from the city; the second part presents the opera, and the third rejoins Shostakovich after the war with his growing disillusionment. Just as Cozarinsky wanted "to recreate a diaspora idealized through music and song . . . in conflict with the grotesque 'realities' of the Stalinist period," he explores the mutual influence of teacher and student and carries that spark across an unexpected transition in the end.[22] Emerging from a cinema, Shostakovich finds a small book of popular Jewish poetry at a kiosk and crossing the plaza he is suddenly in the modern city fifty years later, after the fall of the Soviet Union, amid a teeming crowd indifferent to the towering capitalist billboards. Inasmuch as Yiddish motifs began to influence the composer's work during the postwar decades, music becomes the ultimate bearer of memory: in the way that diverse layers of experience may be embedded into music, the process seems reminiscent of Cozarinsky's own hybrid texts.

10

New World Transplants: Foreigners in French

(Eduardo Manet, Silvia Baron Supervielle)

In the many plays and novels of the Cuban writer **Eduardo Manet** (b. 1930), the dynamic force, the agent of change, inevitably comes from outside. By way of the outsider's perspective, new possibilities for growth open up; conversely, the threat or promise of what lies beyond may hasten the ultimate dissolution of certain characters. Rooted in his own experience, a cross-cultural matrix informs his work whose stereoscopic vision accounts for fertile ambiguities, a frequent use of irony and a constant questioning of absolute truths.

For some four decades Manet has written nearly all his texts in French, yet when he first arrived in Paris in 1952 he did not speak the language. His decision to write in French, he says, was both "a practical choice and an angry choice." Back in Cuba he had had a precocious start as a cultural journalist and poet in his mid-teens and as the author of several plays that gained some attention.[1] But frustrated by the situation in Cuba at the time of Fulgencio Batista's coup d'état, he left for Paris where he studied theater and mime for three years; in Italy he studied language and literature for two more years, then returned to Paris to join Jacques Lecoq's mime troupe. In response to the dim prospects for a writer in

Cuba, he was determined to write in another language, trying English, Portuguese, and Italian, before a fiction competition from the French publisher Julliard accepted his story, thus confirming that he could write in French.[2] Later, Julliard published his first novel, *Les Etrangers dans la ville* (Strangers in the City, 1960), based on his years living at the Cité Universitaire in Paris.

Meanwhile, Fidel Castro and his brother Raúl, whom Manet had known as a university student, invited him back to Cuba in 1960 to work for the revolution. There he became general director at the national theater and established ties with many international troupes—Brechtians, Jerzy Grotowski, and various Latin Americans. Given his lifelong interest in film, he also wrote and directed six documentary shorts and four features for the national film institute. Amid such activity, he managed to write his second novel, *Un cri sur le rivage* (A Cry from the Shore, 1963), billed by his publisher as the first novel of the Cuban Revolution. Curiously, he wrote that book, too, in French, perhaps from the momentum of his previous work. In that way, as Phyllis Zatlin points out, the novel's balanced view of the revolution, including some negative aspects, was published at a safe distance from Cuban readers and the state, as well.[3] But just as in the 1950s when he wrote a few plays in Spanish, he did not abandon his native tongue. Indeed, *The Nuns* (1967), the play that made him internationally famous, though written in Spanish, was to be pivotal for him and facilitated his permanent return to Paris.

Unable to get his macabre farce staged in Cuba, he wrote a French version that a friend ended up giving to Roger Blin, the director of Samuel Beckett and Jean Genet. When Blin wrote him in Cuba in 1968 saying he wanted to do the play, Manet was able to get leave from the Institute of Cinema to go to Paris. By then, Castro's support for the Soviet invasion of Czechoslovakia convinced Manet it was time to make the break. The production, at the Poche-Montparnasse, ran for a year and launched his career as a playwright in French. Still, he sometimes lamented the separation from Spanish and the fact that in Latin America and France people tended to forget him when speaking of Latin American writers, though much of his work is set there. Certainly, in those years his choices were viewed as a betrayal by some people on the left, but for him as an artist it was a matter of survival. Zatlin notes that a Cuban playwright in the United States can write in Spanish and still have an audience, whereas in France no such option exists.[4] "I write in French, because French editors and French directors wanted my novels and plays. Nobody ever asks me for them in Spain, Venezuela, Mexico, and of course never in Cuba." He relates that one day Beckett himself consoled him, "'Eduardo, don't worry. I wrote in French because I wanted to forget Joyce.' And I wanted to forget Lorca's influence on me, and Valle-Inclán. He said to me, 'Anyhow, writers are always exiles and you write in the language that you're published.'" Paradoxically, despite his later campaigns against Castro with French intellectuals of the left, it was Manet's new status—plus becoming a French citizen in 1979—that opened the recent possibility of a return visit. When he wrote the script, in Spanish, for a friend to make a film in Cuba, the embassy did not object to the idea that he might work there: "We have nothing against Mr. Manet, he is a French writer."[5]

The Nuns, set in an abandoned cellar in Haiti during the first slave revolts before independence in 1804, features three nuns and a wealthy *señora* as the characters. The nuns have convinced her that they can get her off the island via a friend with a boat if only she brings her jewels as payment. Except for their habits, however, the nuns hardly look like sisters of mercy: rather they are cigar-smoking men, though the *señora* doesn't seem to notice given her limited experience. Their plan, duly carried out, is to kill the lady when she arrives and to rob her of the treasure. But the trap snares them in turn. The meek and nervous mute Sister Ines, little more than a servant to the Mother Superior, tries to save the *señora*, grateful for her gift, even to protect her corpse later, offering such resistance that she must ultimately be killed as well. Worse for them, though, is the threat without: the Mother Superior has lured the *señora* by exaggerating the dangers they faced, only to find that it has all come true, with the rising of the drums and the mayhem in the streets. Time and again the pounding on their door puts them in a panic, so they dig up the lady's corpse and deck her out with the jewelry, tailoring their story according to who shall emerge victorious, the slaves or the landowners. In the end, fighting among themselves, the Mother Superior and Sister Angela struggle desperately to escape as their barricades collapse before the unknown invaders.

Like most of Manet's theatre, the play sets in motion many layers of illusion and operates chiefly on a poetic level, weaving a network of resonances that sooner frustrate those who would seek a simple message. If those who read it in Cuba at the time found its stance on the revolution unclear, in France it was celebrated by leftist critics who could see it as a satire on counterrevolution and opportunists in general, while conservatives attacked it as sacrilegious. Blin remarks that some perceived it as a play about homosexuality, and that it was quite popular among the gay community in Paris.[6] Yet, despite the cross-dressing, the text always speaks of the nuns as women—even as it emphasizes that the actors playing them should remain natural and masculine in their voices and gestures. It is this tension regarding the nature of the characters, mixed with their constant bickering and the complications of their plan, that generates much of the piece's humor. At any rate, the play was inspired by a true event, in which the nuns were women in disguise, but two actor-friends convinced him to use cross-gender casting in the tradition of Kabuki.

Over the next decade, Manet wrote several plays in what Zatlin terms his "early exile theatre of enclosure."[7] *Eux ou La prise du pouvoir* (Them, or Taking Power, 1969) portrays the more personal entrapment of a couple struggling against their mutual estrangement and the disintegration of their identity, yet unable really to leave. Grabbing at the shreds of cultures that have formed them, scavenging among past dreams and disappointments, husband and wife proceed through an intricate series of role-playing in a vain effort to start over. The deception and false hopes are more insidious still in *Holocaustum ou le Borgne* (Holocaustum, or The One-Eyed Man, 1972), set in another cell-like confine where three Roman prisoners must decide which of them will be the last man thrown to the lions to appease the waiting crowd, since the emperor has just converted to the new religion. Learning that he may first have his desires satisfied, Tibulus volunteers and so much enjoys his sumptuous meal, and a beautiful maiden too, that he reneges on his offer; before his friends tear him apart, the One-Eyed Man enters their cell and announces he will go in their place. The comic ruffians are all ready to claim their freedom, but can't help questioning the stranger about his motives, to the point that they physically mistreat him for their suspicions. After he convinces them that his sacrifice will gain him entry to the eternal paradise, they hurry to preempt him and all three go out to meet the lions. Alone onstage in the end, the man takes off his eye patch and just smiles.

As in *The Nuns*, revolution provides the background for two subsequent plays where characters who are remnants of the old order desperately seek refuge from a changed world. To all these works Zatlin applies the criteria that Diana Taylor uses in describing the "theatre of crisis" in Latin America, "internal decomposition and external chaos."[8] Both in *Madras, la nuit où . . .* (That Night in Madras, 1974), with its unspecified locale, and *Lady Strass* (1977), set in Belize, the central figure is a British widow trying to hold on to the lost glory of colonial times in ruined and pitiful mansions. In each, the lady mourns a youthful romantic love with someone from the other side, one of the colonial subjects, as she forces those within her space to reenact her version of the past. While the household in the first play, except for the young servant, remains closed upon itself at the end when the revolution triumphs, the character in *Lady Strass* inhabits a newly independent country from the start; her barricades are meant to protect not only herself but English territory as well. When two hungry adventurers, a Guatemalan and a Frenchman, break into her house where she lives alone, she subdues them with her rifle. As the role-playing intensifies, the Guatemalan gains the upper hand by forcing her to confront the truth about her past, her own collusions and betrayals. With her descent into madness the Frenchman, a fellow European, decides to stay and take care of her, his room and board secure; the other man opts for his freedom instead. As Zatlin makes clear, it is only the representatives of the people, of the new order, who are able to break out in these plays. Such metaphorical enclosures were common to many theatrical texts that grew out of both the Spanish Civil War and the Cuban Revolution, but for Manet, she suggests, it may have also responded to his own alienation from Cuba and his status as an exile in France.[9]

In later plays, the theatrical space is more porous and expansive, allowing for fluid changes of scene. The outside that is at issue tends less to be represented physically as it concerns more a confrontation of cultures. As in Manet's own life, the linguistic overlap is reflected in his plays with words or phrases of Spanish—though other languages too—sprinkled throughout the French text. These are used not for mere effect, but rather for their particular expressive value and to indicate the interpenetration of cultural experiences, in the same way that he employs a wide range of music, filmic syntax, and diverse theatrical traditions: each resource, directly or as counterpoint, thus comments on the theatrical enterprise and on the cumulative perception brought to bear. *Un balcon sur les Andes* (A Balcony onto the Andes, 1979) perhaps goes furthest in that it follows the changing fortunes of a small French theater troupe in South America during the mid-nineteenth century. As their Spanish improves, the players' speech becomes so intertwined with the two languages that they often lose track of which they're speaking in the heat of argument. But one of the central motifs is how a timeworn story can elicit different responses according to context. At the beginning, in France, Blaise and Tarrasin, tired of performing their usual story about a cuckold, his wife, and her lover, put on a little play in the republican spirit where even the deposed king sees the light, but just then, the revolution of 1848 is suppressed and they are thrown in jail. Escaping, they sail to Peru and resume their métier, avoiding politics with the story of the cuckold and his wife. Their first surprise: the public roots not for the husband but for the woman and her freedom to love whom she chooses. The company takes their show on tour—Peru, Bolivia, Paraguay, Brazil—seeking their own Eldorado as in the play's title. Among border disputes and contending factions, the actors' status as foreigners works alternately for and against them. Brought before the outlaw General Palomares, who would annex disputed lands to form his own country, they discover a great admirer of France and Napoleon. Their play of the cuckold, who is also a soldier, pleases him since he detests all regular armies. He insists that, like Louis XIV, he will help the arts flourish in European style and—Manet tweaking his French public—he will even impose the French language: "Our Indians will speak French and so perhaps they will cease to be Indians."[10] But their protector is overthrown, and faced with a series of replacements the players keep shifting their allegiance and the nuances of their work until they end up siding with opposite armies, finally outsiders to each other.

Despite the poetic freedom which Manet invests in his plays, they are usually situated at historically precise moments when the cultural forces in contention are most clearly defined. In this manner, two tragedies from the early 1980s explore issues set off by interventions from outside. *Mendoza, en Argentine . . .* (1983) takes place in the provincial Argentine city of Mendoza in 1933 as an increasingly powerful army is evicting Indians from unused government lands. In brief recurring scenes in the present, the schoolteacher Baptiste undergoes torture by the ambitious Colonel Sanchez, his brother-in-law, who is obsessed with catching the revolutionary Emilio Laguardia, arrived from afar to help the Indians defend their rights. The fate of these men, each an outsider in his way, is intertwined with the three Montalvo sisters: Asunción, the illegitimate *mestiza* half-sister who oversees the estate and defends the status quo, marrying off Raquel to Sanchez while Lorna chooses Baptiste. But when Asunción takes in a clandestine and wounded Laguardia, she becomes his lover until he takes up with the unhappy Raquel, who joins the revolutionaries to spite her husband. In the end, there remain nothing but absences—Baptiste killed under custody; Lorna, who takes to the open road with her infant child; and Asunción, left alone with her ghosts. *Ma'Déa* (1984), a play for three actresses, updates the Medea story to Haiti, 1946, where the title character must exorcise her despair since her husband, a white American who arrived with the marines as a presidential adviser, has left her. As a mulatta, in the view of her mother and her aunt, it was well-regarded to marry white, to "improve the race" and even escape, but they question the choice of an American, who is the enemy.[11] On a trip to Marseilles he fell for an Algerian chambermaid who becomes the target of Ma'Déa's revenge on him. But before that is achieved, the two women, like their "two exploited lands," measure their differences from each other and from him: Jasmine suggests that it is not a betrayal after all, since they look quite alike with her as the younger version. Yet Ma'Déa points out that he never wanted to bring her home to his family, whereas he would the Arab woman, who would make them think of a Hollywood Cleopatra.[12]

With *Monsieur Lovestar et son voisin de palier* (Monsieur Lovestar and His Neighbor across the Hall, 1987), Manet achieves what may be the purest and most economical expression of his ongoing concerns. The two-character play is set in the present for a change, in France, in Lovestar's apartment. An effete and famous literary translator, he is enjoying a lavish dinner and proudly listening to a tape of his recent lecture on T. S. Eliot when his neighbor Salcedo, a Portuguese repairman and shopkeeper whose existence had long escaped his notice, enters the open door unannounced. Salcedo wants him to translate a fifty-two-page love letter and will pay any price, but Lovestar dismisses the task, rejecting the first lines as sentimental. From the dueling mispronunciations of each other's foreign names and their clashing assumptions about the other's cultural viewpoint—complicated by Lovestar's English surname—they couldn't be more different. Salcedo, in anguish since his wife left him, hopes to publish the letter so that she will see her name and maybe, someday, come back to him. Slowly, over wine and the memory-inducing effects of good food, Lovestar lets his unsympathetic shell gradually crack open, hearing the depths of his neighbor's loss, and he tells of his own broken heart over his youthful lover who wasted away from AIDS, until he was unable to bear the gaze of those ghostly eyes and abandoned him to die alone. He, the translator, did not believe in an afterlife, so had no hope of an ultimate reunion, unlike Salcedo whose hope remains alive. Thus, the neighbors come to an understanding finally. Despite his earlier resistance, Lovestar assures his neighbor the night is young, they should start to work, and reading the first lines of the letter again, with renewed feeling he is able to pronounce the last words of the play: "*Mon amour.*"[13]

In that he often treats an outsider's perspective, Manet echoes Edgardo Cozarinsky's conclusions about working in France, who accepts his "official role" as "a foreign artist in Paris," where "like it or not there is no assimilation possible."[14] There may be a merging of elements as in music, like the Franco-Argentine tango orchestra led by Juan José Mosalini or the numerous American jazz musicians like Steve Lacy whose bands may include French musicians, but after many years' residence they still remain foreigners. For Manet and others who write in French, describing them as French writers or even as hyphenates, such as Cuban-French, may place too much emphasis on defining them by their chosen language at the expense of who they are and what they bring to the language. "France is going through an identity crisis," says Manet. "So it appeals to their vanity and sense of national glory that foreigners should come and write in French. And we benefit from this."[15] While most of his fiction concerns Cuba, writing in his adopted tongue establishes a distance that is different from physical exile, since his primary audience is even further removed than he is from the place and the culture. "I'm a sort of liaison," he explains, "a dangerous liaison between Cuba and France."[16]

After his early books of fiction, which Manet has dismissed as student works, he did not publish another novel until two decades later. *La Mauresque* (The Moorish Woman, 1982), the first of what became a trilogy, is based largely on his mother's memories of his childhood in Cuba in the 1930s. A lyrical narrative, it traces the close bond between mother and son from their years in Santiago de Cuba, in the eastern province of Oriente where Manet was born, to their move to Havana and life in the capital after the dictator Gerardo Machado was overthrown in 1933. The protagonist of the title had always told her son she was of Moorish or Gypsy extraction, so as to explain her rebellious spirit, how she ran off to Cuba with a married man, his father, and was disowned by her family in Córdoba, Spain. Though she is but one of several *queridas* (mistresses) that he keeps around Cuba as an active lawyer and political man, her emotional well-being constantly hinges on him, as she endures repeated disappointments only to forget them with the next turn in her favor. But even at the end, crushed by an especially painful betrayal on his part, she is able to set aside her sorrows when she receives a letter from her brothers in Spain, whom the boy never knew existed, who turn to her for help: with Franco's victory they fear that Hitler will arrive and so they must flee. Only then, on the last page—confirming sporadic signs earlier in the story—does she reveal to him that she descends from *marranos*, converted Jews, and although he doesn't entirely understand, he knows that his childhood is over.[17] Manet himself, because of his parents, grew up with "the nostalgia for Spain without knowing Spain," but when he received that same revelation at thirteen, he was marked ever after by a nostalgia for the Jewish upbringing that he never had.[18]

The unnamed child, therefore, is granted a particularly rich perspective on the world by the complexities of his situation, which hinge on experiences outside the mainstream of society. In effect, the novel is an itinerary of such experiences. Not only are his parents immigrants, but he is illegitimate as well—his father a distant figure who mostly shows up at intervals just to stay the night, chasing the child from his mother's bed. Raised like a prince despite all the uncertainties of their situation, he is also brought up by a Haitian nanny who invites him to be the guest of honor at a voodoo ceremony. This privileged glimpse into the African depths of Cuban society, which recurs later in the trilogy, had a lasting effect on Manet's own sensitivity for New World cultures. Although the child's mother is an avowed Christian, she neither likes the church nor the pope, and appreciates other sources of mystical knowledge such as voodoo and tarot. Still, although he witnesses student confrontations with police in the street before his window, the boy remains sheltered in the maternal environment: when he takes cover from a rainstorm—in the provincial city where the bus stops on their long trip to Havana—it comes as a shock to find the poor peasant family with him in the doorway, who must surely see him as a foreigner in his elegant imported clothes. His entry into public school is delayed, moreover, due to the women at home, his own curiosity, and the young women students his mother takes in as boarders. Havana in turn becomes like a first exile for him, although he discovers there yet another fantastic world, the Chinese district, as his family, too, grows larger: Senta the nanny eventually marries the enterprising grocer Charly Wong. These all serve as points on the compass for the child in counterpoint to the enigma of his father, who tries to navigate an honorable path among changing political fortunes.

Though Manet bends historical and personal details a bit, his Cuban novels are intricately related to a specific time and place, but in his next novel he took a departure in quite the opposite direction. In *Zone interdite* (Forbidden Zone, 1984) he imagines a nameless totalitarian state devoid of history where the only human warmth, at least for the narrator, comes from his relations with foreigners. By turns evoking the state apparatus of Cuba, the sterile modern labyrinths of Paris suburbs, and the massive lunacy of the autocratic vision perpetrated in Rumania, the story follows the narrator's almost unwitting climb through the ranks of power. A freelance multilingual translator, he is recommended for entry into the Center for Information and Surveillance, the seat of control known as the House, where every post is precarious and it is easy to fall out of favor. Employed to detect antigovernment activity, he proves rather effective, though with no special fervor or patriotism. Eventually, he grows too uncomfortable with his pernicious role of inducing children to inform on their elders, and this due to the humanizing influence of two immigrants who have each fled worse horrors. Lin-Ah, who arrives with her two children as boat people, gets a job as the concierge in his building, thanks to him, and becomes his lover. He knows he can only protect them by remaining on good terms at the center. In a clear critique of France, Manet has the narrator confront the hypocrisy of the populace on such matters: "On the one hand, they scorned and hated the foreigners who took their places and ate their bread; on the other, for reasons of international prestige, they were eager to be seen as an open and generous land of asylum."[19]

The narrator's friendship with Pablo, whose bar in town welcomes both the center's bosses and sundry misfits, is launched when he speaks to him in his native tongue. Pablo tells of his country and later of his wife, hideously maimed from the terrible civil war back home and kept upstairs under constant care. But Pablo has a secret connection, having known the reclusive and dying ruler years ago as an ordinary man, so he is able to help guide the narrator with occasional advice. At length, despite the patronage of a section chief who goes on to become director of the center, the narrator joins Pablo in leaving everything behind to go work on the Project, a utopian undertaking about which everyone speculates—a great collective purpose to usher in a new age—but no one knows. Along with other volunteers, they discover a diabolically absurd mixture of futile labor camps and sinister paradise: the Project turns out to be a mad dream of national isolation in the form of a long wall parallel to the coast, slowly built of marble blocks, to close the land against the sea; for relief, at regular intervals, the workers are housed in a luxurious mansion, unable to leave but with every sort of pleasure at their disposal. The country thus poised at its self-destructive limits, his friendship with Pablo impels the narrator to go collect on an old offer from his former mentor, now the new ruler, and he returns in charge of the cursed Project. At the press of a button, in the end, the wall comes crumbling down.

Manet the outsider, writing in his adopted tongue, perhaps has no choice but to combat the isolationist mentality. But as a born islander, he cannot ignore a related impulse: departure. When the world gets too small, it is time to go elsewhere, and in his novels the characters who go leave everything behind. Yet, inevitably, memory restores what was abandoned and the departure turns out to be just the beginning of a long circuitous return. For the narrator-protagonist of *L'île du lézard vert* (Green Lizard Island, 1992), the second in Manet's Cuban trilogy, departure comes only after a long accumulation of experiences on the island, with his promise in the last line, "I'm going away. I'm going to leave this prison forever."[20] Set over the course of three summers from 1948 to 1950, during his adolescence in Havana, the novel opens with the narrator's fifteenth birthday party—a disaster for his mother due to his father's absence—where Luis Wong blesses the mixture of races in Cuba, like the family and friends assembled. Again, he is initiated into the world under the guidance of foreigners, and a central concern is what to make of his Jewish identity: the story of his mother's background is developed here more than in the earlier novel. With his father's anti-German bias, he first avoids the German-born classmate whom he nicknames Lohengrin, to become his best friend after learning that the boy is Jewish. Lohengrin makes him discover the richness of Havana's districts, and introduces him to politics, the Communist Party, as an alternative to the old choice between being a traditional Jew and becoming a *converso*. Meanwhile, the narrator's lover, Gipsie—an eclectic patron of the arts, a wealthy older woman of a Mexican father—warns against all inquisitors and dogmatists, cultural or political.

Later, attending a *santería* ceremony for his mother—to get over the latest shock of his father's infidelity, that he has a half-brother nearly his age—the narrator questions whether it is possible "to live without believing in something? A god, a party, an art, the Other?"[21] At the bar mitzvah of Lohengrin's neighbor, he feels lost, not having been brought up within the Jewish community, but his skeptical friend notes that in Cuba the Jews are viewed simply as rich people or, if they are poor, as Polacks. For his mother, by contrast, being Jewish is a curse, the sign of her suffering by his father and of the loss of her home in Spain. She warns him, moreover, in her unique theory about Cuba, how precisely because of its geographical situation it is predestined to serve as a test tube for the confrontation between two continents, north and south. But the narrator's own problem of identity, ultimately, is reflected by his two Jewish friends: Lohengrin, who would replace Jewishness with politics to make common cause with fellow Cubans, and Levy Stern, who is emigrating to Israel to work on a kibbutz. Although the option of Israel tempts the narrator for a mad romantic moment, it is the convoluted, pointless intrigues of politics that sweep him up in spite of his doubts and, after much damage to those around him, spit him out the other end.

Writing such novels for a French reading public, Manet sometimes makes use of his position to inject his own commentary. In *La Mauresque*, he puts in perspective a general Latin American tendency to exaggerate the truth, as a trait inherited from the Spanish, in order to humanize the dictator Machado, to understand him as a politician of his era imitating the strongmen of Europe. In *L'île du lézard vert*, he explains the Cuban style of driving, their way of brutalizing automobiles, as an influence of American consumer culture where everything is replaceable. *Habanera* (1994), set in the early 1950s to close the trilogy, takes the outsider's angle as part of his narrative method: Mario the protagonist, a young Italian count whose father was a fascist, vows never to return to Italy when he leaves for Cuba where his maternal uncle has lived for thirty years. His wealthy uncle, long out of touch with the family that disowned him for going off with a mulatta, had made a similar vow, cutting his ties to "that aristocracy fossilized in its pride and its superiority complex. The foreign elites in Cuba," he warns Mario, "be they Jewish, English, American, or Italian, live in a closed circle, in order to perpetuate their sense of belonging to an elite."[22] Instead, although avoiding politics, the uncle engages in business ventures with many of Batista's cronies, while Mario, preserving his own safe distance, falls in with friends on the left. Stopping through New York on his way to Havana, he had befriended a young doctor returning home, a rebel against his class.

Poised between his friends and his uncle, who sets him up in luxurious offices to direct a new culture magazine, Mario thus serves as a guide to different levels of society as well as to famous nightspots of the time. He enjoys the best vantage point to see what everyone is up to, yet he cannot help being implicated in events. He becomes the lover of Sonia Suez, celebrated singer and star of popular Mexican films who has had dealings with everyone. And his willingness to look the other way, to play the innocent, helps his friends and even his secretary pursue their clandestine activities. To underscore his remove, various editions of Petrarch's *Canzoniere* accompany Mario throughout the story as his literary or spiritual base, an obsession for another time and place, for an idealized version of home. But when comrades of Ruben the doctor, thanks to Mario, gain entry to Sonia's annual soirée and then assassinate a senator who is close to both Batista and Mario's uncle, it is clear that he has stepped over the line: barely has he expressed his newfound sense of belonging than his sort of passive militancy earns him expulsion. It has become impossible, his uncle tells him, even to be an observer. Yet before he leaves for Mexico at the end, where Sonia will join him, he needs to bear witness and not be protected for once: told of Ruben's murder in retribution, he insists on being taken to the morgue to see firsthand his friend's tortured corpse.

Manet further marks his own distance from Cuba in *Rhapsodie cubaine* (1996), which treats the Cuban Revolution over three and a half decades among Cuban exiles in Miami. The wedge dividing the characters in the novel, especially the couple at its center, is the obsession with Castro. Julian, the protagonist, thirteen when he leaves Cuba with his parents at the beginning of 1960, will always feel himself divided by his double culture, belonging not entirely to either. His parents, as well, are divided, first of all by the difference in their Spanish origins: his austere father from Aragon in the north, his fiery maternal grandmother from Sevilla. The father, a successful businessman who depletes his wealth supporting anti-Castro activists, views the move not as exile but "a prolonged departure."[23] The mother, an alcoholic who endures repeated health cures and gradually vanishes in the service of her guru, like her son will long resent being forced by the father to leave Cuba. Julian does not share the Cubans' preoccupation with exile, and feels malaise each time he returns from college to his dysfunctional family and the fake modernity of Florida, which seems to shed all history. After graduating from Harvard, he almost accepts an offer to join his best friend's family-owned publicity agency, but on a summer visit home he is enchanted by the teenage Emma who appears at a rally to tell of her father imprisoned in Cuba. Unable to forget her, he takes a job teaching in a local private school.

Though he eventually marries her, Julian recognizes that Emma, in her lifelong crusade to defeat Castro, struggles for a nonexistent place, the island of her imagination, while he wants only to integrate himself into his adopted home. His college friend Louis, the Boston brahmin, has gone off to Japan meanwhile and married a Japanese woman, gaining a new perspective on his native land; when he later visits with his wife and children, he explains how he wants them to see a multiethnic America, convinced that the future of the world is in hybrids—a familiar theme in Manet's work. Emma, who postpones raising a family for the sake of her crusade, finds at last that she cannot have children, but the crushing disappointment comes when her father is released after twenty years in a Cuban prison: arriving in Miami, he reveals that he has not come to lead the fight against Castro but rather to live and work for peace. One after another, the characters who persist in their ghetto instinct of exile, their suffocating and nostalgic quest to erase the recent past of Cuba, end up, in effect, defeated themselves. But even when Julian and Emma separate finally, the bond remains stubborn in spite of all and resolution will not come easily: he knows that only with his own return to Cuba will he manage to free himself of her.

• •

Precisely due to her experience of the foreign, and to changing languages, **Silvia Baron Supervielle** (b. 1934) in her writing stalks the edges of silence for the cadence of a hidden voice, listening to the music of a text unfold. With the barest of elements—wind, sea, sky, a window, a stretch of land, and the perpetual yearning to cross beyond, to make the journey, to set out toward an elsewhere—her poems and prose trace the wellspring of desire in its most spiritual guise. Quotidian details, names, historical time seldom surface in the choreography of gestures by which her solitary characters, ever strangers, seek their resonance in the world, with other figures, other presences. The practice of literature thus becomes both a quest for and articulation of that "enigmatic language" that rises from the depths. As she asks in a recent essay, "How can we be sure that the language received at birth will be in harmony with the enigma of our being, with the sensibility of our spirit, with the secret desire of our imagination?"[24]

Like many of her generation who grew up in the immigrant culture of Buenos Aires, she was early aware of "the horizon and its promise."[25] Her mother, born in Uruguay of Spanish and Basque lineage, died when she was two, so that she was raised largely by her paternal grandmother, who was of French origin and first cousin to Jules Supervielle; in part, the grandmother's nostalgia for French culture became her own. Nonetheless, Spanish was her first language, spoken at home and at school, and in which she wrote her early poems and stories with no particular ambition to be a writer. In the 1950s, she visited Europe twice, as well as the United States, but it was not until she returned to Paris in 1961 that she sought to prolong her stay. Four decades later she still lives in Paris, on the Ile Saint-Louis where she moved that first year, but even after some dozen books written in French she insists on being identified with her native land—not as French, and certainly not Franco-Argentine, but simply as Argentine, "an Argentine who went away." That, she explains, is the country of her beginnings, her memories, where many of her closest friends remain, and where her open and affectionate way of being that is so different from the French was formed. These deep ties to Argentina she distinguishes from the sense of *patria*, fatherland, which she does not feel at all. Rather, she claims the more universal heritage of the Argentine melting pot: "In reality, Argentines have been non-local from the start, because we were told we had to read French, English, Italian." Thus, one is "from everywhere and nowhere."[26]

In effect, Baron Supervielle has always felt herself "a foreigner on both sides" of the ocean, "a total exile," but she also derives a certain unity from that condition. For her, coming to Paris, deciding to stay, was a mysterious process, part of a long gestation that led to her becoming a serious writer.[27] As she says in an essay about the impulse to set out across the sea, "To leave is to be reborn from one's personal mystery."[28] It helped that work and housing came easily in Paris, confirming her newfound independence from her native milieu: alone and anonymous, comforted by the village ambience of the Ile Saint-Louis with its many artists, she was able to plunge into the life that was opening before her. The spirit of Paris, she recalls, "shed light on who one was," it gave her "the key to what one could be," providing an experience that "was very constructive inside and that clarified many questions."[29] There was still, however, the matter of language. "The leap across the ocean left me as if in suspense, midway between one place, one language, and another."[30] She felt unable to find "a harmony between myself and where I was. It seemed I would never achieve any wholeness if I kept writing in Spanish." As her texts accumulated, writer friends who didn't read Spanish asked to see her work. So she translated some poems for them, until at last, in the late 1960s, she began to write directly in French, which initiated a new type of writing for her, one that she recognized as quite her own.[31]

If in Spanish she wrote longer, more elaborate poems, in French her poems ended up greatly reduced, stripped to the barest essentials, where silence too sounded differently. "I saw myself" in the new work. "I said that is exactly what I am, this sort of poverty of words, this fear of the language." But her discovery, she feels, had nothing to do with her early background in French culture and might equally have occurred elsewhere. On the contrary, it was a result of the distances in which she lived, from her native land as well as her new tongue, which remains distant for her.[32] That quality of obstacle, of resistance, in the adopted language forced her to develop new solutions. Like her new life, she had found the path of "a writing without preexisting form, an unexpected music."[33] In her essay "El cambio de lengua para un escritor" (The change of language for a writer), written for a series of talks in Buenos Aires in 1997—though she has returned about every two years, this was her first visit professionally, invited as a French writer by the Alliance Française—she believes it is not necessary for a transplanted writer to forget one's maternal tongue nor to enter completely into the new one, but rather "to stay on its shore in order to have the possibility of glimpsing the reflection of the universe. A writer's language is brought into existence on the shore."[34] As happened for her, "the passage from one language to the other becomes a magical, blind, impassioned movement that forms part of the creative act."[35]

In 1970, *Les Lettres Nouvelles*, edited by Maurice Nadeau, was the first journal to publish her poems, which Hector Bianciotti brought to him. A chapbook appeared in 1977, followed by two others, but only in 1983 did her first full-length volume of poetry come out, *La distance de sable* (The Distance of Sand). Writing in *Le Nouvel Observateur* on the occasion, Bianciotti appreciated "her way of drawing from the real what she feels as unique and primordial, of depositing onto the page nothing but allusive silhouettes." Her poetry, he said, "culls vestiges, follows after traces on the shadow line between oblivion and memory."[36] José Corti was the publisher of nearly all her books over the subsequent decade, a period in which her writing gained intensity, starting with *Lectures du vent* (Readings of the Wind, 1988). As the title suggests, she remains alert to hidden currents, whose force is revealed in the encounter with the solid present: the creeping ivy that could strangle the tree, the silent voice that would rend the paper. Her quiet lyrics—always untitled, punctuated simply by linebreaks—seem almost frail, tenuous, yet engraved into the muteness of stone, gestures finely tuned in their equilibrium:

> it all goes away
>
> even absence
>
> no flower
> or thought
> that is not
> in the emptiness[37]

But every form of absence recalls something of the life past or to come, like a frame to its very passage, "the channel of the alley/that invites the wind/to lift the tree."[38] The space between is where she finds her true place, which offers not so much an occasion for longing as reflection, animating the apparent emptiness in the hushed dialogue of an unlocated here and there. "I imitate the shore/to tell the distance/returned at a gallop/over the sand."[39] Though her writing is largely devoid of particularities—the realm of proper nouns and history in numbers—such lines do signal a key vector that recurs even more in the prose. The reference to horses, in her trajectory, denotes Argentina, the wide expanses, an incessant going toward the horizon, and a certain rhythm or breathing left behind in her youth there. The quality of witness that prevails in these poems attests to a transient breath, a movement, that might otherwise go unnoticed, "this body [that could] disappear/in a different dream/as though nothing were/capable of seeing it."[40] What is lost may come back, or is not altogether lost, but the search in turn may require a practice of total abandonment:

> and [if] we emptied the room
> and smashed the mirrors
> and untied the rope

> from ports and boats
> and . . .
> we declare ourselves
> dust undone at the sill
> of a word from nowhere
> the smallest stolen breath
> will be restored[41]

Subjunctive tenses occur often in her poetry, lending a tone of suspension; it would take little, she knows, for life to come out another way. Writing is like a sacred act for her, a delicate engagement with the most basic elements. In a short essay she describes the struggle: "To intercept silence. Poetry is silence, a silence comparable to an underlying light around me, in me, on the paper. I know that if I lean over my desk, this silence will be summoned to spill forth drop by drop and that, subtly, the sharpened point of the pen will break free of my heart and spread across the expanse the brief trembling of a drawing. Poetry is a drawing that expresses the silence. A drawing devoid of figures."[42]

That silence is a product of distance traversed, of difficult separations: an exile's silence in which language has lost its innocence, at the threshold of metamorphosis. And it is a silence, a distance, that makes a certain kind of hearing possible. She would thus devise a way of speaking that can "rejoin/ what was long ago detached." Inevitably, to do so entails

> this returning to the windows
> of inextinguishable space
> to regain an abandoned
> coast . . .
> as an illegible word
> gathers up its message
> shattered faraway[43]

But if the wake of departures may be read in the trace and echo carried on the wind, her next book, *L'eau étrangère* (Foreign Water, 1993), follows the process of voyage and transformation in the land beyond. Here the silence is also imminence:

> the window of distance
> closed in the chest

> like the once a time word
> buried in the memory
> the gaze of someone
> getting ready to leave[44]

The book opens, however, with "A Voice," the first of five sequences of poems. Like the other side of the silence, "a voice by distances/arises at the horizon/and by clouds grazes/the current of the plain."[45] Whatever the medium, it is the way by which natural forces—including the writer—may speak to or through each other and communicate. Indeed, the poet merges with such forces in their transfigured movement, until she is their voice and they are hers:

> dreaming in the tide
> that brings back the tumult
> of abandoned shores
> ... am I the sign
> left at the edge of the sea
> ... the interpreter of distant
> insatiable waves
> that write the forgotten
> voice of destiny[46]

Yet to write, to journey, to venture with the skill of an acrobat across an internal or external space, requires patience and even faith, for there is no final attainment when one quests after the ineffable, there is only the path itself, for each to discover on his or her own. As she writes further on,

> whether I go by the north
> where my steps advance
> or I remain in the south
> held by my thoughts
> whether I voyage elsewhere
> ... whether I inhabit the realms
> of dream or the empires
> of love it will all be
> equidistant from the same
> impregnable center[47]

For Baron Supervielle, crossing the sea that leads to the foreign, the opposite shores also comprise the relation between north and south. These poles are fundamental to her writing, less as opposites than in the potential they pose for each other of other worlds, other existences—beyond the specificity of France and Argentina, beyond all the intervening history between those countries and continents. As for the original explorers, but in both directions, there still remains a substantial element of the unknown for one who sets out; as in the poet's own voyage, the tide of changes even in oneself cannot be foretold. The latter parts of *L'eau étrangère* focus on this mystery, like the title section, which begins with one of her shortest poems:

> there beyond
> blind
> oblivion and
> the strange
> ocean[48]

Like a spiritual apprentice before an undisclosed deity, the voyager sees his or her self-image deformed and negated in the process. Thus, "a sea lifts away/my eyes and a dream/gradually erases/my face."[49] Once undertaken, the passage turns out to be constant, the movement a perpetual going toward, beyond time or place. Remarkably, in such work, she manages to preserve the anonymity of one newly arrived in a strange land, for whom new beginnings become almost routine, until the subject slowly slips away, unable to occupy its own space. As in the final poem:

> here remains
> forever
> outside
> of me[50]

Her latest book of poems, *Après le pas* (After the Step, 1997), while exploring similar themes, shows a greater emphasis on the connections between things. A word or phrase may set up a rhythm, by its sound launching an unexpected correspondence that takes the poet further. Indeed, the first poem offers some continuity with the last page of the previous book—

> here the time
> neither keeps
> nor misleads

> here the grass
> rests
> from the ruins[51]

To speak of a *here*, like present time as well, slippage seems inevitable; for the exile at least, and for the voyager, it is not possible except in terms of *there* and *elsewhere*. But the connectedness in this book can be physical, too, a simple sequence of movements that yield an unintended result:

> without respite
> I erect
> a scaffolding
>
> whose board
> collapses
> after the step[52]

Most often, though, what begins as the semblance of a physical act soon turns figurative, for every gesture may serve to illuminate the mystery of the world. There is the motif of walking as meditative practice, where

> he would talk to himself in order to know
> his voice . . .
> he would lose his way in order to follow
> the rivers' reflections
>   . . . and to be transfigured
> like the ghost
> discovered by the night[53]

Only writing is capable of moving among these levels, in its fluid and supple discourse, a mirror of the spirit that would transcend its unknowable limits. It is part of writing's nature, that it seeks to intrude upon another space:

> as much as the breaking
> of the sea and the flashes
> from the lighthouse that profane it
>   . . . as the suburban streets
> and the leaning balconies

> and the pen that pursues
> its figures without support
> I try to leap through
> the masked impasse[54]

It cannot be helped, therefore, that such yearning should also be marked by a measure of disappointment, by the temptation to silence or resignation, even as the poet recognizes she cannot turn back, she must persist in her stubborn pursuit, let language make its own pacts.

> it's not this dream
> that I wanted
> to have nor this reality
> pretend nor translate
> these notes detached
> from the voyage of my eyes
> what I recompose
> from a murmur withheld
> while another
> register consumes
> the separation[55]

The connections, of course, may arise from the very language, which she seizes upon and elaborates through syntax; often her poems hinge on parallel gestures, interlocking grammatical figures that amplify a moment of insight. Yet even for the poet, writing escapes, resists containment, resonates beyond intended meanings. Perhaps she will have no choice then but to set language free, as it were,

> to abandon words
> by the side of the road
> ... so that the juice of another
> solitude may penetrate them
> ... so that a new signal
> vain and without reason
> may signify them[56]

Rather, writing itself is the voyage beyond, and if she cannot abandon language, it may be that she must continually set herself free, become almost selfless, in that most intimate practice whose reading is never final:

> with the help of the pen
> of the pencil and erasures
> that graze the copies
> thanks to the ink soaked
> in ocean and distance
>   ... I raise a trace
> rubbed out alive[57]

Baron Supervielle had been writing poetry in French for some two decades before she undertook the adventure of prose. In doing so, she explains: "I really wanted to lengthen my phrases, because I had spent so much time writing these poems that were very pared down. So it was like playing with the language a bit, letting myself go ... I had no idea what would come out when I started. I was curious to go a little further in the language, which was always beyond me."[58] The three works of fiction produced to date, made up of an intensely poetic prose where a sort of shadow narrative unfolds in dreamlike sequences, explore each in their way the fertile tension between *page* and *plage* (beach). Before the expanse of the shore, as of the page, one may contemplate the border to the beyond, the beckoning horizon, from either side of the Atlantic. The first of these books, *L'or de l'incertitude* (The Gold of Uncertainty, 1990), marks the only instance where she employs specific historical material, concerning the young chronicler Antonio Pigafetta and his written account aboard Magellan's voyage around the globe; unlike the captain, he was one of the small number of survivors to complete the journey in 1522.

Dispersed through the novel are some two dozen excerpts from Pigafetta's account that describes the explorers' entry into the Río de la Plata, their encounters with natives, the flora and fauna, some basic vocabulary in the local language, and on down the coast to the tip of the continent where they discover the passage to the Pacific through the Straits of Magellan. But more than the mere counterpoint of archival material, Pigafetta's text poses the generative possibilities of reading, in its aspect of a pre-text or a first layer, and occasions ample reflections for both the writer and her protagonist. It is the craft, the use of language, that seems to most interest the writer. Pigafetta apparently wrote his story in a mixture of languages—his native Venetian dialect and French, plus occasional Spanish terms. For Baron Supervielle, this perfectly illustrates the situation in Europe at that time with the shifting sovereignties of languages, from the decline of Latin for official purposes to the contributions of vernacular tongues in emerging literatures.[59] Further, the way in which the fantastic new world is presented in his journal links it "above all to the imaginary adventures of childhood."[60] That quality, in turn, makes it the protagonist's favorite book as a boy, such that it inspires him not just to make the reverse journey—crossing by boat in the present century from south to north—but embarking at the same age of nineteen, he also decides to call himself by the only name he is given in the novel, like the chronicler, Antonio.

The narrative opens, however, at a third point, roughly akin to our own time in an unnamed Paris, with the shadowy figure of a man who alternately watches from his high window and descends to the streets to go walking contemplatively along the river. It becomes clear that he is Antonio later in life, his journey long in the past, settled in his adopted home yet ever elsewhere in his thoughts. Nowhere is he referred to as Antonio: the name, he realizes, belonged to the boy when he set out on his adventure, but after that it no longer applied. This, then, constitutes the essential structure of relationships common to all three of Baron Supervielle's prose works, between one who watches and one who engages upon a sequence of actions, both dreamers, prefigured by a third element that is textual and more or less sets the terms. Indeed, the state of reverie, like a junction between memory and imagination, unites man and boy in a contemporaneous time, just as it joins the boy with the scribe of four centuries earlier in whose chronicle he loves to lose himself. The proximity of the literary to dreaming is underlined, moreover, by the fact that both the scribe writing and the boy reading resume such activity only at the end of each day, at night. But the book is made up of multiple crossings that sketch a history of distances assimilated; in the ensuing loss, each figure finds its counterparts, its reciprocal measure to connect it again with others. Thus, the elusive presence of the watcher peers out as though protectively to the faraway sea where the boat in another time, with his earlier self, approaches the northern shore. That voyage, he understands, responds to other voyages, not just that of Pigafetta, but in his own family.

Into such details the author weaves strands from her own biography. Like her, the boy was orphaned at a young age when his mother died; his paternal grandmother would likewise enchant him with tales of the land across the sea, and when she spoke in the language of that place it seemed to transform her dream into reality. From there the old lady's father first set out, another adolescent, only to reach the southern shore shipwrecked. The boy's journey, therefore, is like a return, the mirror of his ancestor, as it fulfills the yearning of his grandmother, who could not go. But there is yet another in whose name he travels, his beloved nanny Lina, who came from that same continent where he is headed, whose protective care finds an echo in the grown man watching over these scenes from his window; when she set foot in the new land, the trembling immigrant alone, it was clear that "arriving signified another voyage."[61] For the watcher, these women who died far away from him continue to live in images. "Nothing disappeared totally," he knows; "everything had a double aspect, and images too could awaken differently."[62] Like the framed photo of his mother, which in its way stopped time: "It was part of the distance like everything worthy of beauty, that which we were destined to rejoin, to which we were attached, for which we remained in silence: it was part of the things sworn to be loved without seeing, or touching, or understanding, like the sky strewn with stars. This face was a word . . . it professed a teaching."[63]

Hardly linear, the narrative moves rather amid a network of correspondences, even as the boy in his northward journey and the scribe in his voyage south slowly advance, intermittently, both seeking that "passage missing on maps and in the alphabet . . . joining one sea to another . . . one language to another."[64] Like the recurring image of the horseman, silent messenger across the wide pampa, each increment of passage intuitively links to others. When the man at his window reflects upon Lina's death, who was moved in the event into the family quarters of the house, the scribe in his journal, as the ship searches for the southern straits, has for the first time switched to French. Later, the man gets up, transported by the thought of how old his mother would be, had she lived. He imagines seeing her one day, she would recognize him by his eyes; unreachable as she is, he feels certain that his tears were always for her. Then, as the ship struggles to find its way through the straits, the scribe recalls their earlier entry upriver, how, instead of the discovery of gold, it was the uncertainty that won out, their fear of what might be calling from the riverbanks. The watcher, walking along the river in the modern city at night, perceives the apparition of an Angel bent over a Young Woman whose gaze will not meet his even as the phrase escapes from his lips, *Be not afraid*. This, devoid of specific religious reference, is but the ultimate invitation to the voyage, to let go of both shores, taking nothing, "as though suddenly called by something, someone."[65]

In *Le Livre du retour* (The Book of Return, 1993), Baron Supervielle focuses not on the return to an origin, but rather to the points of departure and especially of arrival. If the previous book dwelled in the suspended time of the voyage, here she takes up those moments, at opposite shores, where the mystery is most resonant, as corresponding instances of greatest possibility. Even so, a voyage is required to get there, for the woman in the capital of her adopted land who takes a long train ride west to revisit that coast, as for the girl in that southern land who would set out before dawn on her horse Adiós, each day riding further, pushing toward the horizon. Here too a book fuels the girl's dreams, read at night, about another girl brought up on an island by her father, the keeper of the lighthouse. That island—its name, Longstone, in a language foreign to both the girl in the south and the woman—turns out to be the same place along the coast where the woman arrived after crossing the ocean. At first, the storybook with its engravings lies just beyond recall, a vague memory, but as the narrative advances along with the respective journeys to the coast, the girl in the lighthouse rises into view, her story and its implications taking greater presence until it becomes like a beacon illuminating the traveler's tale.

But outside these narrative threads remains the first-person narrator. In the earlier novel, the narrator maintained some distance, like an independent shadow to the fleeting silhouette of the man at his window. This time, though the narrator again moves about like a shadow, she is intimately bound up with the characters due to her direct use of first-person in speaking for them: for the girl with her departures on horseback and for the woman in the capital bent over her desk with pen and paper. Only the woman as traveler, lost in reverie before the passing landscape outside her train window, and Gloria in her lighthouse, are rendered in third-person—until the train approaches its destination and the narrator speaks in the first-person plural.

> Soon we'll arrive at that shore . . . where I disembarked one day. . . . Me and who?
> Everything leads one to believe that *we* is now she who travels and she who remains leaning over her papers. She who undertook the voyage of return and she who hasn't stopped leaving without moving from her table.[66]

So that, near the end of the novel, as the woman gets off the train, exits the station, walks downhill to the beach, the narrator has regained the first-person singular. Yet from the start the narrator shifts back and forth, the meaning of *we* ever uncertain. "I address myself to someone who is familiar with invisibility," she says, whose nature might be like an angel, a word, a star; or else, an accompanying absence, one who was left behind, who did not make the journey.[67]

In mapping the process of separation, the narrative insists on another way of reckoning the season and a sense of place, on communicating through the silence and shadow of the interval. "It may be that the sea is the consequence of a departure," born of the tears yet offering a substitution: "since we are no longer allowed to see each other, a mirror was spread out at our feet."[68] She recalls the endless plain where she used to ride on her horse, the feeling of wildness, that they too might take off like the birds in the sky. One day she commits "an imprudence" in trying to verify the reality of those lands beyond the sea—a precise location, even to go there—and learns that the one who leaves will never be granted permission to return. "The papers pushed me out . . . you're no longer part of this side of the sea, of the land . . . stay where you are on the other side, in that language you counterfeit and that you'll never manage to inhabit."[69] For the girl on horseback, the pages of her book merge with the open expanse where she rides, as over waves, heading toward the image of the sea and the lighthouse gathered from the book. Gloria, by contrast, in the book, doesn't know the land, has never seen things ripen. The supreme event in her story is sudden: the shipwreck she witnesses one night upon a nearby rock, which will lead to her own departure.

In Bianciotti's phrase, this book functions "by a play of delicate modulations . . . like the echo of a conference of dreams."[70] Gloria, in rescuing survivors from the wreck with the help of her father, becomes a heroine to the outside world, which besieges her with attention; at first she withdraws into the ascetic purity of her sea-bound silence, but a spark grows within and she knows it is time to leave her island. The girl as well, riding in the south, recognizes that her time has come and that her horse Adiós, perhaps her only real tie to the locale, will take her on the inevitable path away. But "abandoning Adiós on the beach, I was forever torn away from myself. And since then I have pretended to live." Because her "nonappearance, nonbelonging" would eventually be found out, she decided, like Gloria, to take the first step.[71] At the end when the narrator returns to the sea, though unable to make the crossing, she knows that her eyes upon the sea will complete the return and reunite her with the others "on that shore of departure which, more than to me, belonged to Adiós, to Gloria, and to our dreams."[72] Like the curiosity first awakened by what lay beyond, the voyage of return is dependent upon the gaze, but even more so: it may be that the only return possible for those who leave, like the interwoven practices of reading and writing, lies in tracing back the lines that led them away.

Around the same time that she switched to writing in French, Baron Supervielle also began translating poems by Argentine authors, at the request of friends. "It accompanied my own work. It brought me closer to the other shore in my memory, and little by little I became a translator as I became a writer. Mysteriously as well, since it formed part of the same movement of writing, of carrying near me the writers I loved."[73] Since her own books first appeared, she has published some dozen books of translations, notably Marguerite Yourcenar's poems and plays into Spanish and a number of Argentine writers into French: Alejandra Pizarnik, Jorge Luis Borges, Macedonio Fernández, Roberto Juarroz, Juan Rodolfo Wilcock, and Silvina Ocampo. "When you translate, you are two instead of one. You take a rest from yourself and become the other a little." But after she finished translating Juarroz's *Fragments verticaux* (1993), she says, "I wasn't able to come back to myself. I remained in a somewhat exalted world and so quite naturally I took up the Bible again."[74] The result was *Nouvelles Cantates* (1995), a different kind of translation, her own selections from the Old and New Testaments. As her way of approaching a knowledge of God, this too was a measure of exile, like her lapsed relation to the church: in her foreword she relates her feeling that the stories "were inspired by another earlier, mysterious volume that was the key to knowledge and life," its contents destined "to be repeated and completed in the subsequent books."[75] Above all, she was struck by the marvelous strangeness of the writing, which she recasts in a series of fragments from each book, sometimes as verse, like a rapid gleaning of mysterious or intimate turnings. Biblical stories (Samson, Ruth, Judith) are told against the grain of narrative, by moments that let the discontinuities shine through; as in her own narratives, the stories are often rendered as subtexts.

During the same period she was also writing her third book of prose, *La Frontière* (The Border, 1995), the sparest of her narratives. Along a strand of beach a boy goes dancing, leaping into the air as if trying to take off, while from her garden window a woman watches him. The boy "has never met anyone," the text begins. He has always been alone, yet he feels he once knew someone long ago who resembled him. Half-naked, he knows neither his own physiognomy, nor his age—about thirteen—nor the names of things around him. Even his shadow, which he plays with at the edge of the sea, is foreign to him.[76] Though he senses a place beyond the sea, he lacks the memory to decipher appearances and disappearances. As for the woman, since he first showed up, she waits only to see him again each day. She does not know how to dream, but through him she feels she belongs "to the earth, the sky, her own breathing." Like her, the local denizens seldom go out, and do so with lowered gaze, unseeing. On Sundays after mass, the men lingering in the café prefer silence, never alluding to their seafaring days in the past, their tradition as sailors.[77] What ails them deeply is the complete absence of children, who deserted the village to fill the boats and depart triumphantly for the South, gone forever. In this story, the South is barely a reference, the glimmer of past and future adventures that either way signals loss.

Clearly the framework of loss, of absence, is where Baron Supervielle's poetic narratives flourish. She seeks out solitary characters amid empty spaces, she says, "because through them I myself might find or touch something essential, something of life, the world, the beyond. . . . It's a place outside the present and past, where there is no time. A bit as if it were a place of devastation, where one had to start over with everything, and in this rebirth one could touch the essential."[78] Among the children who went away is the woman's own son—not revealed until near the end of the book—but unlike her neighbors, from whom she remains apart, she did not experience the exodus as abandonment; rather, she shared the children's joy in departure, as if she had wished it upon them, even as she hoped to see them again. Once the dancer appeared, her thoughts went to him and she "came aboard as well," an "initiate to the dream." In watching him, in her waiting, she knows that "it is not necessary to make a voyage in order to be the voyage."[79] He could be imaginary, it wouldn't matter: "more than anything, for her, he signified a return."[80] Like a distillation of the children who have gone beyond, he has come to perform a perpetual going, as though to accompany her, until he, too, goes away.

The boy's own yearning, like the sea, is to pass beyond the difference that marks him, "writing and rewriting in the sky the stir at the border."[81] He wants first to see himself, find a mirror, a friend, to break his solitude. Parallel to the shoreline grows a wall of trees where he has not strayed due to uncertainty; at night he enters the forest and gains direction, a sense of company, marveling at his own voice among the trees. He dreams of a luminous presence there, and far away the friend grows visible, angelic silhouette advancing; the friend resembles him. The boy fears exiting the forest, limitless opening, "dissolution of that new form that is the other and him," for he has grown used to the forest that gave him a voice.[82] Back on the shore, he sees the silhouette at last, and the Angel slowly comes toward him until they join hands, "the fabulous junction: to be one and the other."[83] Opening their fingers, the friend smoothes the sand, writes in it the sea's confession, erasing and writing further along. Waking, the boy reads the message, and moves off reading and rewriting with his steps. Suddenly he leaps into flight, writing his figures in the dawn sky.

Through her narratives and poems, Silvia Baron Supervielle has evolved a poetics of departure that hovers at the edge of presence, sounding an absence: music of trace and imminence, born of her own voyage and crossing.

> I abandoned
> my tongue
> and walked
> a long time
>
> even the rhythm
> of my steps
> I gave up[84]

11

Académicien

(Hector Bianciotti)

Far less than for most Argentine writers, it seems, there was little in the early formation of **Hector Bianciotti** (b. 1930) to set him on a path to Paris. Born in Córdoba, the son of Italian immigrant farmers from the Piedmont region, he grew up on the vast pampa—often described in his fiction as a landscape of desolation, a limitless expanse where escape appears impossible. Like other children there, he was seen as a source of labor, valued to the degree that he contributed to the work at hand. And as happens with many children of immigrants in the New World, all perspective of the past was cut off, at least in the guise of language: his parents spoke the Piedmontese dialect among themselves but not with him, in order that he fit in better. So that, by the time he left for Europe in 1955, on a ship bound for Naples, after the insidious terror of the Perón era, the voyage was not just a leap for survival but also a kind of return.

Throughout his childhood, in the strange exile he was born to, he had been avid for signals of other possibilities. In his fourth novel, *La busca del jardín* (The Search for the Garden, 1977), an incident from Bianciotti's own life, the protagonist as a boy has a revelation glancing over his aunt's shoulder at her monthly women's magazine as he views the photo of a woman unlike any he knows: elegantly dressed in red, amid stylish furnishings, she represents for him a "message from that vague other world that his imagination situated beyond the plains." The women around him are worn down by the rigors of their existence, his mother resigned to her lack of real choices, whereas the woman in the photo commands the space around her, conscious of her body, and emanates "a decanting of life, a certain order imposed on nature."[1] Earlier, at the start of the novel, he makes a related though more essential discovery when the family moves to another house on the plains and he finds refuge from the endless monotony of the land in "the geometry of a garden," with its diversity of trees and bushes. Amid the play and symmetry of forms he feels exaltation, even happiness, and there he will return to read and think, until the day his father chases him out in favor of more useful occupations.[2] From then on, the itinerary of the boy's life is determined in the search for that garden.

In effect, Bianciotti the writer traces to such moments his appreciation of form, order, limits, style, as an antidote to the dizzying emptiness of the plains; not for the sake of an external set of rules, but rather in the ever-renewed practice of divining what the material itself will allow, the material being first of all language. Much as he derives a sense of structure from music —his way of varying the rhythms of his sentences, of building atmosphere, establishing symmetries in the overall dynamics of a narrative—so he remains sensitive to the cadences and melody of syntax, to the "secret metrics in prose." This process is fundamental to the resultant text: "I've found the phrase, but the last word has three syllables, I need a word with two. I sacrifice a word, I change the meaning. An idea is modified because a word that we weren't expecting has entered the phrase."[3] In large part, his attention to the evocative nuances of words, the shape and qualities of their sounds, springs from the tension between languages that he experienced—both in childhood with the suppression of Piedmontese that he nonetheless was hearing, and as an adult settled in Paris since 1961.

With Spanish and later French, he underwent the conscious imposition of a language by force of circumstance. His first job, after arriving in Paris, was as a reader at Gallimard, writing reports in French; by the end of the decade, Maurice Nadeau, who had published his first books in French translation, invited him to write for La Quinzaine littéraire; in 1972, Bianciotti became a literary critic for Le Nouvel Observateur, until joining Le Monde in 1986. Meanwhile, he surrounded himself with dictionaries: on the one hand, to help him rise to the occasion in his new language, and on the other, he says, "in the hope of safeguarding the language of my childhood."[4] For the first two decades, at the same time as his articles and reader's reports, he was writing his novels in Spanish, starting with *Los desiertos dorados* (The Golden Deserts, 1967). But *La busca del jardín* marks the beginning of a turn in his trajectory. His previous books, confined to the stagelike settings of meticulously detailed houses and their environs, far from his native terrain, corresponded to a "need to feel invulnerable before nature.... Although I lived in Europe, through those first books I was still fleeing the pampa. Then the moment came when I felt rooted here. So I was able to recuperate the essential part of the past ... and everything that provoked my vocation for escape."[5] *La busca del jardín* returns to the open plains of Argentina—yet in counterpoint with the act of memory, across the distance of time and space, of the man whom the boy became. Through the "incurable nostalgia" for his origins, he is convinced that "only childhood, happy or disastrous, is real ... there is no other country, one is not from another country."[6] The first of many such returns in Bianciotti's fiction, this proves to be the necessary counterpart to his initial return, to the continent of his ancestors, and reinforces the dual perspective by which he will always be a man from elsewhere.

Still, the novel in its French title, *Le traité des saisons* (The Treatise on the Seasons), and the means it employs to make the journey back, also seem to point ahead.[7] Not only does the title suggest a method of discourse more common to the reasoned practices of his adopted home, he constructs the book by elaborating a sort of personal dictionary. The twenty-nine chapters are preceded by a word, like the key to each text and the resonances or associations it sounds, forming "a small constellation" of significant moments from a life.[8] His research, as it were, into such ramifications of meaning of a word, came at a curious point in his production, a resident of Paris for some fifteen years by then. Linguistically isolated by living in France, he had developed a style in his books, partly through reading, where the Spanish was not identifiable as the usage of an Argentine or a Spaniard (before Paris he had spent five years in Spain). As will happen after enough time in a foreign country, becoming more comfortable with the language, sometimes French words or phrases would come to mind when he wrote before he found the term in Spanish, which he might translate. Eventually, around the time he was writing the novel, or not long after, this process of interpenetration led to a certain insecurity in the use of his native tongue.[9] His Spanish was becoming uprooted, destroyed by French syntax. By the end of working on his next book, *El amor no es amado* (Love Is Not Beloved, 1982), suddenly he found the courage to make the switch. He had written ten stories and wanted one more to complete the collection: he found himself starting the story in French with what seemed a typical turn of phrase, "Aussi loin qu'il m'en souvient" (as far back as I can remember).[10] When he embarked on his first novel written in French, *Sans la miséricorde du Christ* (Without Christ's Mercy, 1985), the practice soon became reversed—if sometimes he couldn't find the word in French, it was Spanish, or even Italian, that came to his aid.[11]

Dictionaries, one might say, became his destiny. The first Latin American writer elected to the Académie Française, at the beginning of 1997, after four novels and countless articles written in French, he has come well prepared for partaking in the eternal task of revising the dictionary of the French language. Not only has he drawn on the tradition of his adopted tongue as a writer—his narratives often crystallize or turn about on a phrase, an aphorism worthy of the French moralists—but he also seeks to revive lost words and shadings. "The language is a shared tradition," he says, "and each word is a shared symbol. What the writer can do is share the meaning of the word, make it richer than the meanings in the dictionary, to make a word more potent, more evocative."[12] Having come from outside and chosen the language, he has thus maintained an attitude of permanent apprenticeship, always curious, even in his reading of modern stylists like Paul Claudel, Paul Valéry, and Marcel Jouhandeau. "I'll find an expression that sounds strange, and because I like it I'll consult the *Dictionnaire des difficultés du français*. So, I can see that it's an expression that has fallen out of use. And there are mysteries that interest me a lot—it's a foreigner who sees these things—like how, all of a sudden, does an error get introduced into the spoken language and everyone says it?"[13]

Octavio Paz has observed that Bianciotti's use of the language is "natural, elegant, without archaism or liberties, free of expressionism and affectation, a French that does not belong to any one region but rather to literary tradition."[14] His first guide was Valéry, whom he discovered in 1945, in a supplement of *La Nación* devoted to the poet, who had just died. Bianciotti was then studying at the seminary, where he had gone to get an education as the first step in his escape from the pampas, but already he knew he had no vocation. "One kind of theology was being replaced by another," he writes. He soon obtained the original French versions of the translations, along with a bilingual dictionary. "That was how I entered the delicate labyrinth of the French language."[15] Indeed, by the time he himself took to writing in French, it was with the devotion of a convert.

If he has often kept his distance from being too easily identified as a Latin American, his work bears the constant and unmistakable perspective of a foreigner. Most of his characters come from elsewhere, and many are Argentine, reflecting variations on his own experience, transposed. So the protagonist of *Sans la miséricorde du Christ*, Adélaïde Marèse, is a woman from the lonely pampa, the daughter of Piedmontese immigrants, educated in a convent, who precariously made her way to Paris. So the narrator in his first story written in French, "La barca en el Néckar" (The boat on the Neckar), is an older man in Paris, reflecting on his youth as a poet back in Tubingen, Germany, and how his native tongue has irretrievably slipped away from him. As a literary critic, Bianciotti has occupied a comparable position: mostly treating the work of foreigners. He tends to steer away from Latin Americans, yet has made exceptions—Severo Sarduy, Julio Cortázar, Juan Carlos Onetti before he was known in France, Silvina Ocampo, Silvia Baron Supervielle. And in his capacity as a reader for editorial committees, he has also been supportive of Latin Americans behind the scenes: he encouraged the publication of Nivaria Tejera's novelistic memoir of Cuba, though Gallimard turned it down; he convinced his subsequent publisher, Grasset, to hire Alicia Dujovne Ortiz to write her biography of Eva Perón.

At any rate, as an Argentine who wanted out of Argentina—typical enough for his generation—he might well be accused of an exaggerated reverence for Europe. Long after their encounters in the early 1960s, in a text on Witold Gombrowicz, who had warned that Argentines should be careful of importing European culture at the risk of not having their own, Bianciotti commented, perhaps playing to his audience a bit, "I think there is never enough of European culture in Latin America or elsewhere."[16] He had become fascinated with France early on through his reading of Rubén Darío, from the time he first entered the seminary, and later through the influence of Victoria Ocampo and her activities with *Sur*. When he moved to Paris, his enthusiasm gained by comparison with Madrid, where life had been difficult for him and the swaggering Castillian character not to his liking. "Why," as Alice Kaplan has reflected, "do people want to adopt another culture? Because there's something in their own they don't like, that doesn't *name them*."[17] Bianciotti discovered French to be "an intimate language," more akin to his sensibility; in addition, France had a quality unique among its neighbors, "the perpetual sense of the critique." After all, he says, France "is the country that invented the art of conversation in the seventeenth century. That is, the history of the reply. The reply that puts you on the alert: you have to listen, you have to try to respond."[18] And yet, although he flourishes in such an environment, he certainly recognizes the advantages of his origins, where writers have been ultimately self-taught: "What I like about Latin America is that there is no cultural system. Since we have no past, we take from everywhere. The most extreme case, when they say Borges is a European writer, it's just the opposite. In Europe it's inconceivable, that way of making a sort of sauce with everything. A European belongs to a closed culture—he's French, English, German, Italian."[19]

But not only does he people his books with outsiders; within the very mechanism of the narratives he employs strategies of distancing. In the early novels, their textures reminiscent of Nathalie Sarraute and other writers of the *nouveau roman*, the attention to *mise-en-scène* and the lush descriptions of décor serve to offset the interchange between characters, who may be seen almost in function of their placements and displacements. With *La busca del jardín* and the more thoroughly autobiographical later novels that he describes as "autofictions," *What the Night Tells the Day* (1992) and *Le Pas si lent de l'amour* (How Slow the Pace of Love, 1995), memory itself is repeatedly put in question as the means by which fragments of the past are retrieved: memory turns out to be a language of its own, and utterly subjective in its connections. By contrast, in his first novels written in French, *Sans la miséricorde du Christ* and *Seules les larmes seront comptées* (Only the Tears Will Be Counted, 1989), the narrators keep to the side, not quite self-effacing, playing a significant though minor role in their story, as if mere servants of destiny. By underlining the process of narrative in these ways, Bianciotti seeks less to focus on stagecraft than to inquire into concepts of the self. This, of course, is directly bound up with not just language, but also the voyage and becoming a foreigner—as if to say, the more borders crossed, the more a secure notion of identity is cast in doubt.

On its simplest level, the passage may be the result of time, the curve of years traversed, a distance from oneself. Near the end of *What the Night Tells the Day*, which follows the writer's life from childhood until his departure from Argentina, he discovers his old passport from that period, some four decades prior to the writing. "I stare in disbelief at my passport photo, spellbound in contemplation: How I would love to be that stranger who knows nothing of me, so sure of his chances, on his own, mysteriously sleek. . . . Perhaps he did not know his own face any more than I can recognize myself in it."[20] What *is* recognized is difference, all the more so when in contrast with what was left behind. In *La busca del jardín*, precisely the chapter called "Yo" (me), when the protagonist crosses the ocean for a return visit home to bid a last farewell to his now-aged parents, he is terrified to think what would have become of him had he not left. Out of courtesy he forces himself to suppress the gestures, words, and tastes, that would signal his difference, "to try to be who he would have been" had he stayed. He is surprised, therefore, by the absolute certainty with which his sister, who lives at home, utters the word "me," the full mass of her body condensed into that affirmation, as if she never thought to wonder what it meant.[21] And yet, in an earlier chapter about that visit, "Structura," he suddenly understands, noticing the similar principle by which they tell stories, "that he was but a biological repetition, distant in time," of his father, whom he had never really loved, a pragmatic man who offered no tenderness.[22]

In comparing these two books, which treat many of the same experiences in Argentina, one finds in the later work another aspect of difference more openly portrayed: the author's homosexuality. It may be that no longer writing in Spanish had freed him somewhat in treating the subject, even if this was already his third book in French; perhaps too, the project of a novelistic memoir was motivated in part by the need to speak at last more directly, or else the project required he do so. In any event, it would be reductive to propose his sexual affinities as the real reason he went to Paris, like other Argentine artists "fleeing the twin homophobias of machismo and Peronism," as Doug Ireland describes the situation in reviewing the book.[23] While homosexuality had been depicted in several of his books, and his own sexuality is more than suggested in the earlier novel, including a scene of tenderness and caresses between the boy and a young soldier visiting the farm, *What the Night Tells the Day* shows him entering into awareness of both his body and mind, and the effects of a series of attractions and identifications that are not limited to gay issues. Neither here nor in the later book, *Le Pas si lent de l'amour*, which covers his time in Italy and Spain, where he nearly starved, and his first years in Paris, does a gay identity, as it were, take shape.

On the contrary, for Bianciotti, identity is far more than a sum of desires and cultural factors; it is by nature elusive, refusing to be fixed. That's why it baffles him how, as soon as "one changes country, customs, even language, the first thing people worry about is the loss of identity. Our identity is precisely what we keep inventing, the circumstances of our own life, the evolution of our thought."[24] In this sense, identity could be seen as not just what is manifest but also what may be imminent and unsuspected. Thus, to set off on a voyage becomes a hopeful act, as though to enter "the space of that virtual life . . . where we might have fulfilled our true destiny," in a time that is "at the margin of all causality, where the enigmatic hold that absent things have on us would cease finally." At least for a while, "the voyage makes me what I am not."[25]

Indeed, his work is riddled with absence, the absence that determines a life. At the center of his first novel, *Los desiertos dorados*, is a son who vanished, presumed dead, and whose possible return remains a constant source of speculation for his mother, sister, and teenage son, although they each deny their obsession. On her island a hundred kilometers off the coast of Baja California, a vague zone, Consuelo Perth invites her farflung friends every summer to her mansion. Like the hostess and her name, like the multiple styles of the architecture and its furnishings, the guests each seem to come from not one specific place but many; inherently they are all hybrids, identified simply by their varied names (O'Brian, De Cid, Rawicz) and accents (Clara's Andalusian elisions). And like Bianciotti himself after a decade abroad, the island stands at a distance from the Spanish-speaking continent, the characters referring sooner to California coastal cities and points further. A kind of chamber play unfolding over three days, few events mark the story. By his reigning absence, her son Raúl is the real outsider. The landscape, the house, even the shadows, are fraught with intangible signs of his return, beginning with the discovery of an unfamiliar sailboat anchored in the bay. Worse for Consuelo, one guest keeps nervously speaking of premonitions. But after the culminating masquerade party where each costume might pose a surprise, the expected occurrence turns out to be the cook's heart attack, who must be rushed to a hospital on the coast, while the son remains more absent than ever.

In a prologue to Bianciotti's third novel, *Ritual* (1972), Sarduy speaks of the "polyphony of discourses" in the book, where one that is "always absent organizes the others" and draws them beyond itself; "its legible mark is silence."[26] A similar dynamic may be found in Bianciotti's relationship to the two languages he worked in during his first decades as a writer, where French and French literary style inform the Spanish of his novels. As for *Ritual*, the text offers not just one but rather gradations of absence that exert such influence, depending on the shifting focus of the narrative: the wife who died young and the old gentleman enduring without her, who plays host now in his isolated mansion near Nice, deciding in the end he will sell the house and go back to his lands in Argentina; the man's dying cat that no longer cares to eat; la Morandi and her past glory; Saulnier, the unwritten book he keeps planning, and the love he once briefly experienced; the palace on the opposite hill, unoccupied since the war, where Adrian the gentleman first met his wife. For him it seems hardly more than a diversion, the "complex calculus of encounters he has intended to provoke" by inviting them, yet his guests—all foreigners to the place—each stand on the precipice of the present, between an irretrievable past and a future whose changes also demand some reconciliation with the past.[27]

The generative absence in Bianciotti's first books, which he fills with his profusions of language—the elaborate approach onto the island that begins *Los desiertos dorados*, as though out of an adventure story, the long sinuous sentences and finesse of details, and then reaching the house, the ornate descriptions of the rooms, the incrusted fragments of a history, until suddenly the characters appear, their entrance no longer postponed—brings him close to Sarduy's notion of the baroque as a superabundance of signifying around an empty center, though his own practice is more subdued. In a way like Sarduy's concern with surface, with the text as object, the foundational emptiness at the heart of Bianciotti's novels of this period may be seen as "more than metaphysical or psychoanalytical," as Graciana Vázquez Villanueva insists in her deconstructivist reading of the work; for her that void is ultimately "literary or textual."[28] Bianciotti himself has said that such writing was a kind of refuge from the native realm that had motivated his escape. Nevertheless, this too, the inclination to see its essential reality as text, ends up a reductive assessment of the work. He has made it clear, by the manner and frequency of his statements, just how real the emptiness of the pampa was for him. And in light of his most recent book, the social grouping in these earlier novels reflects the particular milieu he kept finding himself in, first in Spain and then during his first decade in Paris: a *grande dame*, maybe a little past her prime, and her more or less willing entourage. For the first eight years in Paris, during which he wrote two novels, he lived as part of the in-house group around the painter Leonor Fini, who had invited him to Paris as her assistant after his work executing her designs for a Madrid production of *A Doll's House*; at home they spoke Italian, and there he met a stimulating crowd of artists and intellectuals, including venerable figures like Jouhandeau and Jacques Audiberti.[29]

Like the pampa but in reverse, the imperial and stylish women characters at or near the center of his first three books—his second novel, *Detrás del rostro que nos mira* (Behind the Face that Looks at Us, 1969), features an older woman writer as the protagonist, and in the third, la Morandi's influence is crucial—signaled an absence as well. These recall that elegant woman in the magazine photo seen by the boy on the pampa, that drew him toward a life he did not yet know. But there is a further turn provoked by such a figure precisely in the contrast which that woman, that image, offers alongside the women on the pampa, whose own reality might be described as a sort of inhabited absence. To varying degrees, in his next three books Bianciotti seeks to explore and render a difficult measure of presence to the women figures he knew in his childhood, to rescue them from the anonymity of their existence. This was part of the return he accomplished in writing of the land he left behind, precisely by trying to understand women like his mother—peasant women who served a collective function, even more than the men, and who seemed to have no chance of escaping nor hardly a foothold even to dream of such a journey as his.

In *La busca del jardín*, aside from the maiden aunts who flutter about in their indistinguishable roles to help in house and farm, there is one, Marta Podio, widowed before her time, who does at least seek an opening beyond. It is her subscription to the monthly women's magazine that grants the others some grounds for fantasy, and those magazines the father destroys in a bonfire after she commits suicide—to the boy's bitter regret and the illiterate women's delight. Suicide is her means of escape, but the resourcefulness with which she manages the feat leaves a lasting impression in the family: her arms too short to aim the rifle at her chest and pull the trigger, she rigs it up with a string by way of the bolt in the door.[30] The grandmother does not have it any better, installing herself at one son's house, then another's, bringing with her few effects but which seem magical to the boy: her peacock with its tail, her phonograph and records. Having crossed the eternity of ocean, she longs for the hills of her native Piedmont, conjuring quite a different reality than the endless plains. As for the dutiful mother, she lacks even these scant glimmers of light. Bianciotti will later remember his mother, in *What the Night Tells the Day*, as never laughing, her eyes that "never let themselves betray terror or sorrow in front of her children."[31] In the earlier novel, when the other women with the boy spontaneously dress the mother in her old bridal gown and improvise a whole procession out around the house, she suddenly stops, tears it all off, and marches back inside, prisoner to her fate.

Such women, emigrants who left for America to create an agriculture in those virgin lands, invented the homeland, says Bianciotti. "But no one celebrates their memory, there are no poets to sing of this anonymous gesture."[32] To that end, in effect, he came to see his role as a "public writer," to register the dissatisfactions and thwarted desires of those who are silent, and to speak by way of the personal for the collective.[33] In *El amor no es amado*, half of the stories return to the Argentine pampa, though often it is to portray the harshness and cruelty of the life. "La escalera del cielo" (The stairway of heaven) begins with the brutish old woman Podio whipping the pregnant Marietta for resting in the shade of an ombú tree. She had been sent to gather up the wheat left in the fields by the harvesting machine. The young woman goes into labor on the spot, Podio delivers the child, and within days Marietta dies of an untreated fever. Having no use for the baby because it is a girl, Podio hands her over to an old gaucho who works there and has no family. He raises the girl, teaches her to read and to ride a horse, until the day he finds Podio beating the girl and kills the old woman. "What, who died with her?" the story asks. "The mean, murderous, wicked woman. But also an immigrant girl and, with her, the images of that almost infinite, hopeful crossing" that began in the Piedmont hills and the long struggle since in trying to cultivate that land.[34] The book begins, however, in a more reflective mode, with "Las iniciales" (The initials), where the writer considers his own mother, born on the pampa and married young, "a girl who grew up, got old, and died without ever seeing the sea."[35] He tries to read her life of work and raising children, and to question the process of memory, the scant details by which he might recuperate her image. Looking back across his own departure and her recent death, he addresses her directly in the end, admitting he often failed to show his love, wanting now "to raise to you, in my way, an altar of words." But even there he falls short, asking "how to say what is loved," unable to really separate her portrait from himself.[36]

Sans la miséricorde du Christ, Bianciotti's first novel in French, was also the first he set in Paris. In fact, the narrator, who is a foreigner from a northern land, and the protagonist, Adélaïde Marèse, are neighbors in the same building the author himself has lived in for years; the story takes place mostly in their neighborhood, the upper part of the 3rd arrondissement. The local café they frequent, the Mercury, serves as the dramatic center of the narrative, a place whose clientele reflects the district, predominantly a vast array of working-class foreigners in addition to the local prostitutes, thus a terrain sympathetic to outsiders. The hardworking owner, along with his parents, who come to help out in the bar, seem typical of *la France profonde*, keeping a close eye on the accounts. His wife, though, is a figure in transition, and he is often at war with her, for she is a former prostitute. Their daughter Rosette, in a way like Adélaïde at the opposite end of life who for a time looks after her, is a girl at the edge of innocence, an innocence that is compromised, tainted by the conditions around her. On the night of her tenth birthday, early in the story, when the waiter gets carried away playing with her in the back of the bar in what becomes an erotic game, the owner brutally beats up the young man, who dies. So begins, during the month of August—the empty month when most Parisians are away on vacation—the slow dissolution of the café, the family, but also of Adélaïde's frail hopes. By the end, after disappointment in her budding friendship with a gentleman friend—the only one actually from the district—and then Rosette's delinquency and accidental death, Adélaïde as well dies, from heart failure.

The narrator, who hesitates to take on the responsibility of telling her story, remarks that the French version of her name—she preferred they avoid speaking in her native tongue—better suits her fragility and shy grace.[37] Throughout, language will be inextricably bound up with her destiny. He himself admits that his feelings vary according to the words he uses: "I can be desperate in one language and barely sad in another. Each language makes us lie, excludes a part of the facts, of ourselves." For Adélaïde, learning to live in French, she began to walk another way, to stand differently. "Everything became more reserved, more discreet," she notes. "To say *soledad* is to say something that's vast, universal . . . *solitude*, by contrast, is yours alone."[38] After the first event at the bar, she regrets not having better protected the girl, and this recalls her own childhood on the Argentine pampa: the women and mothers, uncelebrated in their labors, and her father the dreamer, humiliated and beaten the one time they caught him loafing. He took his revenge by setting fire to the wheat fields, and then hanged himself in despair; at his funeral, she realized she had only herself to protect now and that her departure was urgent. She had "to destroy her world in order to enter into the world."[39] The long journey since turned out to be an apprenticeship in "the reconquest of the memory buried in her veins."[40] Thirty years it took, after coming to Europe, before she visited the native village of her father in the Piedmont hills, and there, hearing the dialect again, she found the secret connection to her past: she recognized "a sound, just one note, a vowel," like the French letter *u* in *solitude*, an intimate sound that also belonged "to the forbidden language of childhood."[41]

The experience, of course, was Bianciotti's own at the time of writing the novel. The most constant theme in his work, especially since he began to write of the pampa, is the sense that the past is always with us, embedded in our present, forming what we are. A recurring phrase in the narratives, "the center of my life," speaks of the effort to read the past, to understand "that moment when . . . my destiny was revealed to me."[42] For the narrator of *Seules les larmes seront comptées*, whose concern is mostly with characters other than himself, the moment came as a young man when he witnessed, in a hospital amphitheater, his dying mother exhibited for the sake of a prominent doctor's lesson to a group of medical students. Thirty years later, as administrator of that same Paris hospital, his secret mission will be accomplished as he oversees the demolition of the old amphitheater, and through all the detours of his narrative he at last comes to inhabit the memory of his mother in her final days.

But memory, too, is a voyage, "which prefers echoes and affinities to chronology."[43] If Bianciotti describes his latest novels as "autofictions," in spite of their close relation to his own experience, it is because in the economy of fiction, imagination takes precedence over autobiography. "Something very important that lasted for years can end up reduced to a few moments. So, you describe a character who was crucial for you, but at the same time you linger because there's the light that counts, the wind that blows.... When one has developed a taste for words, for cadences, for the phrase, there's nothing to be done, one lies. One lies."[44] And yet, regardless of the turns of memory or imagination, his intermittent analyses of a situation go right to the heart of the matter, with a sober compassion even for himself, for that distant stranger figuring out the way to go. Describing the decline in his fortunes during his first months in Italy, in *Le Pas si lent de l'amour*, he admits: since "I left the farm for the seminary, I have never felt at home anywhere; I feel myself an intruder who must earn the right to be there where he is."[45] Less than two years after writing these lines he was elected a member of the Académie Française. Despite his success, surrounded by friends at the ceremony who knew the circuitous path of his life, he insisted that the idea of "arriving" had always been absent from his ambitions—and perhaps that was really how he ended up there.[46]

Conclusion
The Lights of Home

Certainly, Latin America's relationship with Paris has changed through the twentieth century, as its culture grew ever more complex. For the writers treated here, coming from the periphery of the West turned out to be an element of strength, a means by which they might establish a fruitful distance, an ironic distance, from the very city where they chose to live. Indeed, if there remain any centers now, of a colonial or cultural influence, such places have been quite transformed and rejuvenated by the practice of artists from outside. For Latin American writers, Paris has begun to shift imperceptibly from the capital of the past to a locus—one of many, foreign and domestic—for the future.

Has the history of the last two centuries therefore run its course? The myth of Paris faded years ago, yet something familiar still remains: a scent, an attitude, a cultural memory. If Latin American literature no longer benefits as much from its fashionable status of the 1960s and 1970s in France, that is because the novelty—and the political urgency—have worn off. The simplified view that French readers may have had of the work has matured, grown more nuanced. The writers who came to Paris were not alone in pursuing their various enterprises; the receptive environment made it possible for them to stay and grow and gain recognition according to individual merits, not as tokens or representatives of their native lands.

All the same, inescapably, Latin American writers do not have to be reminded—numerous as they may be, and regardless of longevity or the extent of assimilation there—that they are still foreigners in France, even if that is now home. As the French philosopher Gaston Bachelard might have said, to perceive the lights of home you have to stand outside. The Latin American writers in Paris could thus gaze in both directions, across the Atlantic and back, as they reflected upon two places at the same time, two experiences of home that coexisted in a curious suspension.

As for any exile or voyager, the question is bound to come up: what about the return? Earlier in the century, most of the writers who went off to Paris had to go back where they started if they were to maintain and build upon a sense of who they were as Latin Americans. After mid-century, thanks to the writers and artists above all, the collective identity was more or less consolidated. Against that background, writers like those in this study could appreciate the inherent complications of such an elusive issue as identity, especially in the Americas, which has been one long unending story of hybridity and confused trails. But it was not a matter of choosing loyalties: those who stayed in Paris, no matter how many times they crossed the ocean in body or spirit, knew they would always be returning back to their American home, returning to depart once again.

Notes

All translations throughout the text are by the author except where indicated.

Introduction

1. Luis Harss and Barbara Dohmann, *Into the Mainstream* (New York: Harper, 1967), 40.
2. José Donoso, *The Boom in Spanish American Literature: A Personal History*, trans. Gregory Kolovakos (New York: Columbia UP, 1977), 21.
3. The situation may have been worse in the Caribbean. Kamau Brathwaite relates that it was still not possible, in the 1960s, to phone or send a message directly from an English-speaking island to a French-speaking island, although they could literally see each other across the water. Instead, the communication had to be routed first through England or France.
4. Domingo F. Sarmiento, *Facundo: or, Civilization and Barbarism*, trans. Mary Mann (1845; 1868. New York: Penguin, 1998), 11.
5. Leopoldo Zea, *The Latin-American Mind*, trans. James H. Abbott and Lowell Dunham (1949. Norman: U of Oklahoma P, 1963), 45–49, 83–87.
6. "France, in the nineteenth century, came to represent the equilibrium we needed in our stormy tug-of-war between allegiance to Spain and allegiance to the United States. Paris gave us culture without strings and a sense, furthermore, of elegance, disinterestedness, wholeness, aristocracy, and links to the culture of the classics, sorely lacking in the vagabond, unrooted, homogenizing pioneer culture of the United States or in the monastic, far-too-rooted, isolated culture of Spain." Carlos Fuentes, prologue to José Enrique Rodó, *Ariel* (Austin: U of Texas P, 1988), 16–17.
7. José Enrique Rodó, *Ariel*, trans. Margaret Sayers Peden (1900. Austin: U of Texas P, 1988), 61.
8. Rodó, 98–99.
9. Leopoldo Zea, *Latin America and the World*, trans. Frances K. Hendricks and Beatrice Berler (1960. Norman: U of Oklahoma P, 1969), 15, 76, 82.
10. David Viñas, *De Sarmiento a Cortázar* (Buenos Aires: Siglo Veinte, 1974), 144–145, 150, 164–167.
11. Viñas, 168–171.
12. Jason Weiss, interview with Julio Ramón Ribeyro, *Hispamérica* 68 (1994): 52.
13. Laurence Hallewell, "The Impact of the Spanish Civil War on Latin American Publishing," *Intellectual Migrations: Transcultural Contributions of European and Latin American Emigrés*, ed. Iliana L. Sonntag (Madison: SALALM, 1987), 139.
14. Viñas, 183–186.

15. Carlos Fuentes draws on this history of familial ties between France and Latin America in his novel *Distant Relations* (New York: Farrar Straus Giroux, 1982), which traces the mysterious relationship between two families named Heredia— one Mexican, the other French—where the key to their common origin proves ever elusive.
16. Emir Rodríguez Monegal, "The Boom: A Retrospective," *Review* 33 (1984): 31. In his interview with Alfred Mac Adam, Rodríguez Monegal says specifically, "Paris is really the international capital of Latin America even today."
17. Pedro Henríquez Ureña, *Literary Currents in Hispanic America* (Cambridge: Harvard UP, 1949), 117.
18. Henríquez Ureña, 121.
19. Pedro Henríquez Ureña cites Martí, Jean Franco cites Darío, as the first poet of *modernismo*. These poets, of course, were later known as the national poets of Cuba and Nicaragua, respectively.
20. Sylvia Molloy, *La diffusion de la littérature hispano-américaine en France au XXe siècle* (Paris: PUF, 1972), 18. She quotes Pedro Salinas in speaking of the "Paris complex."
21. Henríquez Ureña, 168.
22. Molloy, 18–19.
23. Molloy, 19. Remy de Gourmont, who was friendly with a number of these writers, initiated the column "Lettres latino-américaines" in 1897 with the Venezuelan critic Pedro Emilio Coll as editor. Francisco Contreras took over the job in 1910 (23–24).
24. Molloy, 19. For *Hispania* and *La Revue de l'Amérique latine*, see: 72.
25. Gwen Kirkpatrick, *The Dissonant Legacy of Modernismo* (Berkeley: U of California P, 1989), 23.
26. Molloy, 30–31. Gómez Carrillo and Ventura García Calderón continued to write in Paris, especially on the tragedies of the war. The poet José García Calderón died at Verdun and the Colombian poet Hernando de Bengoechea, who wrote in French, also died in battle.
27. Jean Franco, *The Modern Culture of Latin America* (Harmondsworth: Penguin, 1970), 82.
28. Molloy, 107.

1. The Voyage Out

1. Rubén Darío, *Autobiografía, Obras Completas*, vol. 1 (Madrid: Afrodisio Aguado, 1950), 102. The autobiography was written in 1912.
2. Darío, *Autobiografía*, 102.
3. Darío, *Autobiografía*, 103–104.
4. Rubén Darío, "En París," *Peregrinaciones, Obras completas*, vol. 3 (Madrid: Afrodisio Aguado, 1950), 381–382.
5. Darío, *Autobiografía*, 149–150.
6. Darío, "París y los escritores extranjeros," *Letras, Obras Completas*, vol. 1, 463–464.

7. From a letter to Federico Gamboa, 7 May 1911. Quoted in Molloy, 48.
8. Darío, "De la necesidad de París," *Todo al vuelo, Obras completas*, vol. 2 (Madrid: Afrodisio Aguado, 1950), 535.
9. Octavio Paz, "El caracol y la sirena," *Cuadrivio* (Mexico: Joaquín Mortiz, 1965), 47.
10. For an index of articles and authors in *Mundial Magazine*, see Ana María Hernández de López, El Mundial Magazine *de Rubén Darío* (Madrid: Beramar, 1988), 305–324.
11. From an unpublished plan of work by Güiraldes, written at the age of twenty-four. Quoted in Giovanni Previtali, *Ricardo Güiraldes and* Don Segundo Sombra (New York: Hispanic Institute, 1963), 31. Translation by Previtali.
12. Previtali, 30–31.
13. Güiraldes, *Obras Completas*, 36.
14. Güiraldes, "Un libro," *Obras Completas*, 610.
15. Molloy, 144–145.
16. Güiraldes, *Obras completas*, 798.
17. Alfonso Reyes and Pedro Henríquez Ureña, *Correspondencia*, vol. 1: 1907–1914 (Mexico: FCE, 1986), 195–202.
18. By the middle of 1914, seeing that he might soon be out of a job with the advance of Venustiano Carranza in Mexico, Reyes had arranged for possibile work as a translator with Veuve Bouret and Garnier, though they paid poorly. When the war broke out, however, both houses shut down their operations. Paulette Patout, *Alfonso Reyes et la France* (Paris: Klincksieck, 1978), 106.
19. Octavio Paz, "El jinete del aire," *Puertas al campo* (Barcelona: Seix Barral, 1972), 51–53.
20. Valery Larbaud and Alfonso Reyes, *Correspondance, 1923–1952*, ed. Paulette Patout (Paris: Marcel Didier, 1972), 123–125.
21. Larbaud and Reyes, *Correspondance*, 118–119 (Patout's notes).
22. Quoted in Patout, *Alfonso Reyes et la France*, 297.
23. Patout, *Alfonso Reyes et la France*, 294–295. Earlier, Patout raises the intriguing speculation, proposed by friends of Reyes, that one of his essays from *Cartones de Madrid* (1917)—based on notes taken in Paris in 1914—may have inspired a famous passage in Marcel Proust's *La Prisonnière* (1923). The similarity concerns their descriptions of the richness of Paris street sounds, with the calls of its merchants, and how these bear the essence of the entire city, its flavor and characters. The intermediary, suggests Patout, may well have been the young French-Mexican writer Ramon Fernandez, whom Reyes met in Madrid in 1917 and who subsequently became friendly with Proust in Paris. See: 289–291.
24. Rosario Hiriart, *Más cerca de Teresa de la Parra* (diálogos con Lydia Cabrera) (Caracas: Monte Avila, 1980), 51–52. Many of the biographical details here are gathered from this book.
25. Rosario Hiriart, *Lydia Cabrera: Vida hecha arte* (New York: Torres, 1978), 148–149.
26. Hiriart, *Lydia Cabrera: Vida hecha arte*, 144–145.

240 • Notes

27. Hiriart, *Lydia Cabrera: Vida hecha arte*, 144–145.
28. Hiriart, *Más cerca de Teresa de la Parra*, 123–124.
29. Hiriart, *Más cerca de Teresa de la Parra*, 111.
30. Doris Meyer, *Victoria Ocampo* (New York: Braziller, 1979), 15–16. Most of the biographical details in this section, except where noted, are drawn from Meyer's biography.
31. Victoria Ocampo, *El Imperio Insular*, Autobiografía 2 (Buenos Aires: Sur, 1980), 115–120, 124–130. Much of the preceding two paragraphs was drawn from these pages, which were letters from Ocampo to her friend Delfina Bunge in Buenos Aires.
32. Ocampo, "Ravel," *Testimonios*, 2, 401–403.
33. Quoted in Meyer, *Victoria Ocampo*, 106.
34. Ocampo, "Carta a Ricardo Güiraldes," *Testimonios*, 5 (Buenos Aires: Sur, 1957), 60.
35. These figures are from the Peruvian critic Jorge Puccinelli, who meticulously gathered all those articles. César Vallejo, *Desde Europa*, ed. Jorge Puccinelli (Lima: Fuente de Cultura Peruana, 1987).
36. Vallejo, "Cooperación," *Desde Europa*, 15–16.
37. Vallejo, "El verano en Deauville," *Desde Europa*, 59–63.
38. Vallejo, "La conquista de París por los negros," *Desde Europa*, 76.
39. Vallejo, "La visita de los reyes de España a París," *Desde Europa*, 132.
40. In two letters to Gerardo Diego, in 1931 and 1932, he describes some of these frustrations in Madrid. César Vallejo, *Epistolario general* (Valencia: Pre-Textos, 1982), 234, 243.
41. Vallejo, "El crepúsculo de las águilas," *Desde Europa*, 168–169.
42. Vallejo, "Una gran reunión latinoamericana," *Desde Europa*, 191–193.
43. Vallejo, "Oriente y Occidente," *Desde Europa*, 210.
44. Vallejo, "Sociedades coloniales," *Desde Europa*, 273–275.
45. Vallejo, "La juventud de América en Europa," *Desde Europa*, 324–325.
46. Vallejo, "Los artistas ante la política," *Desde Europa*, 253–255.
47. Quoted in René de Costa, *Vicente Huidobro: The Careers of a Poet* (Oxford: Clarendon-Oxford UP, 1984), 43. Much of the information presented in this section has been drawn from this study.
48. Efraín Szmulewicz, *Vicente Huidobro: Biografía emotiva* (Santiago: Universitaria, 1978), 65–66.
49. Luis López Alvarez, *Conversaciones con Miguel Angel Asturias* (Madrid: Magisterio Español, 1974), 75. These interviews took place in Paris, mostly in the summer of 1973.
50. Rita Guibert, *Seven Voices*, trans. Frances Partridge (New York: Vintage, 1972), 132.
51. López Alvarez, 79.
52. Carpentier, *Entrevistas* (Havana: Letras Cubanas, 1985), 283.
53. Carpentier, *Entrevistas*, 139.
54. Alejo Carpentier, *Crónicas*, vol. 1 (Mexico: Siglo Veintiuno, 1985), 316.
55. Carpentier, *Crónicas*, 1:295–299.

56. Carpentier, *Crónicas*, 1:305–310.
57. Carpentier, *Crónicas*, 2:187–193.
58. Carpentier, *Entrevistas*, 82–84. Of the series "Le coq-à-l'âne," Carpentier said in this interview, from 1963: "Generally they took off from a word. They arrived without preconceived ideas; thus for example, Prévert would say, 'So, what happened with that whale?' They started talking about that whale, they spent fifteen minutes talking of an imaginary whale" (83).
59. Carpentier, *Entrevistas*, 459.

The French Reception

1. Odile Felgine, *Roger Caillois* (Paris: Stock, 1994), 269. Much of the initial discussion of Caillois's activities, though the details are commonly available, has been derived from this biography.
2. Claude Fell, "'La Croix du Sud,' tremplin de la littérature latino-américaine en France," *Río de la Plata* 13–14 (1992): 177.
3. Molloy, 183.
4. Fell, 177.
5. Jason Weiss, interview with Julio Ramón Ribeyro, 59.
6. Jason Weiss, unpublished interview with Annie Morvan, 27 June 1994.
7. Fell, 181.
8. Jean-Claude Villegas, "Aux seuils d'une collection," *Río de la Plata* 13–14 (1992): 198–199.
9. Elvira Orphée, "Visita a Roger Caillois," *Mundo Nuevo* 2 (1966): 57.
10. Fell, 186–187.
11. Molloy, 183–184.

2. Writers' Beginnings

1. Gabriel García Márquez and Plinio Apuleyo Mendoza, *El olor de la guayaba* (Bogotá: La Oveja Negra, 1982), 69.
2. Raymond L. Williams, *Gabriel García Márquez* (Boston: Twayne, 1984), 41.
3. Mendoza, 68.
4. Karine Berriot, *Julio Cortázar, l'enchanteur* (Paris: Presses de la Renaissance, 1988), 17–18. Her account is drawn from García Márquez's memorial article, "El argentino que se hizo querer de todos," *El País* [Madrid] 19 February 1984.
5. Gabriel García Márquez, "Meeting Hemingway," *International Herald Tribune* [Paris] 15–16 August 1981: 5W.
6. Jacques Gilard, prologue, *Obra periodística, vol. 4: De Europa y América (1955–60)*, by Gabriel García Márquez (Barcelona: Bruguera, 1983), 30–47.
7. Gilard, 14–20.
8. Mario Vargas Llosa, *A Fish in the Water*, trans. Helen Lane (New York: Farrar Straus Giroux, 1994), 108–109, 384, 458.
9. Mario Vargas Llosa, *... sobre la vida y la política* (Buenos Aires: InterMundo, 1989), 31. This is drawn from the first part of the book, an extended interview with

Ricardo A. Setti, from 1986.
10. Mario Vargas Llosa, *The Perpetual Orgy*, trans. Helen Lane (New York: Farrar Straus Giroux, 1986), 9.
11. Mario Vargas Llosa, *Contra viento y marea*, 1 (Barcelona: Seix Barral, 1986): "Homenaje a Javier Heraud" (42–43), "Toma de posición" (91–92), "En un pueblo normando, recordando a Paúl Escobar" (101–104).
12. Gerald Martin, "Mario Vargas Llosa: Errant Knight of the Liberal Imagination," *On Modern Latin American Fiction*, ed. John King (London: Faber, 1987), 214.
13. Mario Vargas Llosa, "The Mandarin," *Making Waves*, trans. John King (London: Faber, 1996), 132–136.
14. Mario Vargas Llosa, "Albert Camus and the Morality of Limits," *Making Waves*, 114–115.
15. Vargas Llosa, ... *sobre la vida y la política*, 94–95.
16. Mario Vargas Llosa, "Sebastián Salazar Bondy and the Vocation of the Writer in Peru," *Making Waves*, 61–65.
17. Vargas Llosa, *A Fish in the Water*, 457.
18. Alfredo Bryce Echenique, "No uno sino varios Nobel," *Crónicas personales* (Barcelona: Anagrama, 1988), 115–116.
19. Alfredo Bryce Echenique, *Permiso para vivir (antimemorias)* (Barcelona: Anagrama, 1993), 128–131.
20. Bryce Echenique, *Permiso para vivir*, 110–116.
21. Bryce Echenique, *Permiso para vivir*, 52–56.
22. Alfredo Bryce Echenique, "Confesiones sobre el arte de vivir y escribir novelas," *Los mundos de Alfredo Bryce Echenique*, eds. César Ferreira and Ismael P. Márquez (Lima: Fondo Editorial, 1994), 29–30. This text was given as a talk in Austin, Texas, in November 1982.
23. Bryce Echenique, *Permiso para vivir*, 20.
24. César Ferreira, "Los cuentos de Alfredo Bryce Echenique," *Los mundos de Alfredo Bryce Echenique*, 89.
25. Bryce Echenique, "Confesiones sobre el arte de vivir y escribir novelas," *Los mundos de Alfredo Bryce Echenique*, 35–36.

3. Clarifying Sojourns

1. "The first time I met Camus," Paz stated in a 1979 interview, "was in an homage to Antonio Machado in Paris. Jean Cassou and I were the speakers; María Casares recited some poems. ... We saw each other various times after that." He goes on to recount how he warned Camus, after reading *L'homme révolté* (1951), that the chapter on Lautréamont would provoke Breton's displeasure and that Sartre would attack the book as a kind of heresy; to Camus's surprise, according to Paz, both reactions did indeed come to pass. Octavio Paz, *Pasión crítica* (Barcelona: Seix Barral, 1985), 197–199.
2. Enrico Mario Santí, *El acto de las palabras* (Mexico: FCE, 1997), 196–200. This is reflected, moreover, by the various references in Paz's book to the sphere of writ-

ers connected to or bearing an influence on the Collège de Sociologie. Earlier in his essay on the book (124), Santí links the French moralist tradition to other Latin American books of the mid-twentieth century that dealt with themes of national identity as well: Ezequiel Martínez Estrada's *Radiografía de la pampa* (1933), Gilberto Freyre's *Casa grande e senzala* (1933), José Lezama Lima's *La expresión americana* (1957).
3. Octavio Paz, *The Labyrinth of Solitude*, trans. Lysander Kemp (New York: Grove, 1961), 18. He remarks on this connection in a footnote.
4. Paz, *The Labyrinth of Solitude*, 170.
5. Octavio Paz, *Itinerario* (Barcelona: Seix Barral, 1994), 25.
6. Santí, 36–37. The quote is from a statement by Paz.
7. Jason Wilson, *Octavio Paz* (Boston: Twayne, 1986), 40, 56.
8. Guibert, 240.
9. Santí, 275–278.
10. Paz, *Itinerario*, 96–98. In light of this chronology, it is interesting to consider that in the spring of 1951, Luis Buñuel asked Paz to present *Los Olvidados* at the Cannes Film Festival; Paz enthusiastically mounted a campaign to support the film when it was shown, enlisting Marc Chagall and Jacques Prévert, among others, despite the disapproval of the official Mexican delegates to the festival, who felt that Buñuel had denigrated Mexico.
11. Guibert, 229–231.
12. Ivonne Bordelois, *Correspondencia Pizarnik* (Buenos Aires: Seix Barral, 1998), 43–44. Letter to Rubén Vela, who then had a diplomatic post in Valencia.
13. Bordelois, 49–50. Letter to León Ostrov.
14. Bordelois, 15. Bordelois, who was taking classes at the Sorbonne, often visited Pizarnik in this apartment in 1961.
15. Bordelois, 58. Letter to Antonio Beneyto, probably in 1961.
16. Alejandra Pizarnik, *Obras completas* (Buenos Aires: Corregidor, 1993), 367. These comments are from a short text Pizarnik wrote in December 1962, "El poeta y su poema."
17. Bordelois, 68–69. Undated letter to Antonio Requeni.
18. Bordelois, 52–54. Bordelois points out that Cortázar and Héctor Murena were both contributors to *Cuadernos*, and that relatives of Pizarnik's Jewish family in Poland had suffered under the Nazis and the communists, thus dashing any political sympathies she might have had.
19. Bordelois, 288. Letter to Ivonne Bordelois, from Buenos Aires, 16 July 1969.
20. Frank Graziano, ed., trans. Maria Rosa Fort and Frank Graziano, *Alejandra Pizarnik: A Profile* (Durango: Logbridge-Rhodes, 1987), 111. From Pizarnik's journal entry, February 27, 1961: "I imagine horrible situations to oblige myself to act. Thus the vision of the *clochards* to drive myself to frantically work in the office without thinking about the improbability of reaching their state since at any moment I can return to Buenos Aires—my bourgeois home."
21. Bordelois, 90. Letter to her parents.

4. Diplomatic Pastures

1. Guibert, 334.
2. Guibert, 166–167.
3. Quoted in Donoso, 56–57.
4. Guibert, 174–176.
5. Miguel Angel Asturias, "Telefonemas teatrales," *Viajes, ensayos y fantasías* (Buenos Aires: Losada, 1981), 20–21. This collection also includes some pieces written earlier in his life.
6. Volodia Teitelboim, *Neruda*, trans. Beverly J. DeLong-Tonelli (Austin: U of Texas P, 1991), 426–432.
7. Jorge Edwards, *Adiós, Poeta* (Barcelona: Tusquets, 1990), 249–265.
8. Edwards, 146–151.
9. Edwards, 228–235.
10. Carpentier, *Entrevistas*, 479. The interview where these statements were found was published in late April 1980, around the time of his death.
11. Carpentier, *Entrevistas*, 169.
12. Carpentier, *Entrevistas*, 169–170.
13. Carpentier, *Entrevistas*, 190, 261. The interviews where these statements are found date from 1970 and 1975.
14. Edwin Williamson, "Coming to Terms with Modernity: Magical Realism and the Historical Process in the Novels of Alejo Carpentier," *On Modern Latin American Fiction*, ed. John King, 100.
15. Roberto González Echevarría, *Alejo Carpentier: The Pilgrim at Home* (Austin: U of Texas P, 1990), 22.
16. González Echevarría, 283.

Tradition of Pilgrimage

1. Jason Weiss, interview with Julio Ramón Ribeyro, 52–53.
2. Alfredo Bryce Echenique, "Confesiones sobre el arte de vivir y escribir novelas," *Los mundos de Alfredo Bryce Echenique*, eds. César Ferreira and Ismael P. Márquez, 27.
3. Angel Flores, *Spanish American Authors: The Twentieth Century* (New York: Wilson, 1992), 793.
4. Bryce Echenique, 35.
5. Plinio Mendoza, *Años de fuga* (Barcelona: Plaza & Janes, 1979), 316.

5. Interstitial Spaces

1. Julio Cortázar, *Entretiens avec Omar Prego*, trans. Françoise Rosset (Paris: Gallimard, 1986), 57–58. Cocteau's book, in translation, was prefaced by the Spanish writer Ramón Gómez de la Serna.
2. Julio Cortázar, "Surrealism," trans. Alfred Mac Adam, *Review* 51 (1995): 38–39. This is an excerpt from his 1947 essay, *Teoría del Túnel: notas sobre la situación del surrealismo y existencialismo* (Madrid: Alfaguara, 1994).

3. Evelyn Picon Garfield, "'The Exquisite Cadaver of Surrealism,'" *Review* 7 (1972): 18–21.
4. Julio Cortázar, "The Death of Antonin Artaud," trans. Alfred Mac Adam, *Review* 51 (1995): 40–41. The text first appeared in *Sur* 163 (1948).
5. The first story he published, "House Taken Over," in a magazine edited by Borges in 1946, had come to him entirely in a dream.
6. María Esther Vázquez, "La Maga, Cortázar, el azar, un barco, un vagón de subterráneo," *La Maga* 5 (special issue, "Homenaje a Cortázar") (1994): 6. In 1952, they discovered the axolotls in the small zoo within the Jardin des Plantes, which became the obsession of his story "Axolotl."
7. Julio Cortázar, "Acerca de la situación del intelectual latinoamericano," *Ultimo Round* 2 (Mexico: Siglo XXI, 1969), 272. This was a long public letter sent to Roberto Fernández Retamar and first published in the Revista de la Casa de las Américas in Havana, 1967.
8. Ernesto González Bermejo, *Conversaciones con Cortázar* (Barcelona: Edhasa, 1978), 12–13.
9. Julio Cortázar, *Hopscotch*, trans. Gregory Rabassa (New York: Random House, 1966), 436.
10. Julio Cortázar, "Del sentimiento de no estar del todo," *La vuelta al día en ochenta mundos* 1 (Mexico: Siglo XXI, 1967), 32, 37. See also his essay on the composition of his novel *62: A Model Kit* in "La muñeca rota," *Ultimo Round* 1, where he states: "The mystery . . . is always *in between*, interstitially" (261).
11. Berriot, 142.
12. Cortázar, *Entretiens avec Omar Prego*, 72–73.
13. González Bermejo, 42–44.
14. Saúl Yurkievich, "Conjugar poesía y revolución, Marx y Rimbaud, en eso creía" (interview by Paula Rodríguez), *La Maga* 5 (1994): 7.
15. The titles here used in translation are taken from their title stories as published in English. Curiously, both the French (1963) and American (1967) translations of his stories offered only selections from these three books in a single volume. Gallimard, his main publisher in Paris, brought out another selection from the same books in 1968, and then published the French translation of his collected stories in 1997.
16. Julio Cortázar, "Axolotl," *Blow-Up and Other Stories*, trans. Paul Blackburn (New York: Collier, 1968), 4, 7.
17. Julio Cortázar, "A Yellow Flower," *Blow-Up and Other Stories*, 50.
18. Julio Cortázar, "The Night Face Up," *Blow-Up and Other Stories*, 66.
19. González Bermejo, 61–63.
20. Julio Cortázar, "The Pursuer," *Blow-Up and Other Stories*, 164, 169–172.
21. Julio Cortázar, "The Other Heaven," *All Fires the Fire*, trans. Suzanne Jill Levine (New York: Pantheon, 1973), 129.
22. Alejandra Pizarnik, "Nota sobre un cuento de Julio Cortázar: 'El otro cielo,'" *El deseo de la palabra* (Barcelona: Ocnos, 1975), 218.
23. Emir Rodríguez Monegal, "Le Fantôme de Lautréamont," trans. Suzanne Jill Levine, *Review* 7 (1972): 29.

24. Julio Cortázar, "The Southern Thruway," *All Fires the Fire*, 23.
25. Julio Cortázar, "Manuscript Found in a Pocket," *A Change of Light*, trans. Gregory Rabassa (New York: Knopf, 1980), 110.
26. Julio Cortázar, "Graffiti," *We Love Glenda So Much*, trans. Gregory Rabassa (New York: Knopf, 1983), 35.
27. Saúl Yurkievich, "Salir a lo abierto," *Julio Cortázar: al calor de tu sombra* (Buenos Aires: Legasa, 1987), 59–61. Yurkievich draws on Cortázar's own concept of the short story as a self-sufficient and spherical form, in "Del cuento breve y sus alrededores," *Ultimo Round* 1.
28. Julio Cortázar, "Del sentimiento de no estar del todo," *La vuelta al día en ochenta mundos* 1, 41.
29. González Bermejo, 66–69.
30. Berriot, 191.
31. Cortázar, *Hopscotch*, 32.
32. These comments are drawn from several statements by Cortázar: on the rhythms of modern painting available in Europe, González Bermejo, 110–112; on the notion of swing in writing, Cortázar, *Entretiens avec Omar Prego*, 222–223; on the example of jazz as a means of liberation toward a more open vision and the permeability of a sponge, Cortázar, "Así se empieza," *La vuelta al día en ochenta mundos* 1, 7.
33. Yurkievich, "Julio Cortázar: al calor de tu sombra," *Julio Cortázar: al calor de tu sombra*, 197.
34. Cortázar, "La muñeca rota," *Ultimo Round* 1, 248–249.
35. Cortázar, *Hopscotch*, 373–374.
36. Curious coincidence?? Midway through his essay on "The 'Uncanny,'" Freud speaks of the involuntary repetition that renders uncanny and seemingly inescapable what might otherwise look like innocent chance, using as an example the number 62 recurring close together on addresses, hotel rooms, railway compartments, and how a person will be "tempted to ascribe a secret meaning to this obstinate recurrence." A comparable atmosphere might be said to pervade Cortázar's novel, yet he never made such reference in any of his statements about the book. Sigmund Freud, "The 'Uncanny,'" trans. Alix Strachey, *Studies in Parapsychology* (New York: Collier, 1963), 43.

    On Cortázar's globe-trotting experience as a translator, see his essay, accompanied by details from Paul Delvaux's eerie nocturnal cityscapes, "Noches en los ministerios de Europa," *La vuelta al día en ochenta mundos* 1, 113–119.
37. Julio Cortázar, *62: A Model Kit*, trans. Gregory Rabassa (New York: Avon, 1973), 8.
38. Cortázar, *62: A Model Kit*, 9–10.
39. Cortázar, *62: A Model Kit*, 63.
40. González Bermejo, 94–95.
41. Cortázar, "Acerca de la situación del intelectual latinoamericano," *Ultimo Round* 2, 268–270.
42. Julio Cortázar, "Novel Revolution," trans. John Incledon, *Review* 24 (1979): 81, 84.
43. Mario Szichman, "Entrevista: David Viñas," *Hispamérica* 1 (1972): 66. See also Viñas, *De Sarmiento a Cortázar*, 189–190.

44. Julio Cortázar, "Respuesta," *Hispamérica* 2 (1972): 56.
45. Julio Cortázar, *A Manual for Manuel*, trans. Gregory Rabassa (New York: Pantheon, 1978), 21–22.
46. Cortázar, *A Manual for Manuel*, 3–4.
47. Julio Cortázar, "The Fellowship of Exile," trans. John Incledon, *Review* 30 (1981): 14–16.
48. Carol Dunlop and Julio Cortázar, *Los autonautas de la cosmopista* (Mexico: Nueva Imagen, 1984), 43.

6. Transgressive Gestures

1. Jorge Edwards, "Una vida cubana," *El whisky de los poetas* (Santiago: Universitaria, 1994), 210. Edwards recounts that García Márquez intervened with Fidel Castro to allow Sarduy's visit, who "returned (to Paris) without saying anything or almost anything." This is the only reference I have found to Sarduy's brief return.
2. Severo Sarduy, "Exilado de sí mismo," *Cuadernos Hispanoamericanos* 563 (1997): 9–10. *A-islado* might also be translated as *un-islanded* or even *non-islander*: at any rate, the exact play of the word cannot be fully carried over, since *aislado* means isolated, *isla* is island, and *islar* or *islado* do not exist as such. His meaning might really suggest that he is an isolated case in not living on his island anymore. I have chosen to play instead on the implication of *exile* in his being an *ex-islander*.
3. Roberto González Echevarría, *La ruta de Severo Sarduy* (Hanover: Ediciones del Norte, 1987), 36.
4. González Echevarría (47–50) offers two reasons for the Cuban government's attacks on Sarduy, in the hands of Roberto Fernández Retamar and other writers, starting in the late 1960s: his near-assimilation into the French intellectual fold and his involvement with the journal *Mundo Nuevo*, which by then had ceased publishing its first series, in part due to criticism for receiving funds indirectly from the Congress for Cultural Freedom, a front for the CIA; *Mundo Nuevo* was also considered by the Cubans as a competitor to its own Casa de las Américas journal as a leading voice for the new Latin American literature. Other reasons might also be added: Sarduy's homosexuality, which often figured in his writings; the fact that his own literary aesthetic couldn't be further from the Cuban government's preference for socialist realism; and as editor at Le Seuil, he helped publish famous Cuban dissidents Heberto Padilla and Reinaldo Arenas.
5. González Echevarría, 36–37.
6. Severo Sarduy, *Written on a Body*, trans. Carol Maier (New York: Lumen, 1989), 41.
7. Jean-Michel Fossey, "From Boom to Big Bang," *Review* 13 (1974): 11.
8. González Echevarría, 24.
9. Sarduy, *Written on a Body*, 65.
10. González Echevarría, 41.
11. Sarduy, *Written on a Body*, 82. The brief essay, "Cubes," takes as its occasion Larry Bell's minimalist sculptures.

12. González Echevarría, 46.
13. González Echevarría, 51. This is a citation from Sarduy's interview with Alicia Dujovne-Ortiz, "Cuba sí, Cuba no," *Les Nouvelles Littéraires*, 13 November 1980: 38.
14. González Echevarría, 47.
15. Severo Sarduy, *Cobra* and *Maitreya*, trans. Suzanne Jill Levine (1975, 1987; Normal: Dalkey Archive, 1995), 36.
16. Fossey, 12.
17. Sarduy, "Dispersion (False Notes/Homage to Lezama)," *Written on a Body*, 56–57.
18. According to González Echevarría (67–68), both novels were ultimately critiques of previous interpretations of Cuban culture: *Gestos* as a take on Carpentier's *The Chase*, and *From Cuba with a Song* responding to Lezama Lima by way of his disciple Cinto Vitier's *Lo cubano en la poesía*. These two masters, in sum, sought each in their way to achieve a totalizing vision of Cuban culture, an impossible project in Sarduy's view. He wanted to preserve the irreducible heterogeneity.
19. George Lamming, *The Castle of My Skin* (1953; New York: Schocken, 1983), x. Lamming's introduction was written for the Schocken edition.
20. Severo Sarduy, "Chronology," *Review* 6 (1972): 26.
21. Marie-Anne Macé, *Severo Sarduy* (Paris: L'Harmattan, 1992), 22.
22. Severo Sarduy, *Gestos* (Barcelona: Seix Barral, 1963), 62.
23. Antonio Benítez-Rojo, *The Repeating Island*, trans. James Maraniss (Durham: Duke UP, 1992), 22–23. The author dwells on these qualities throughout his book.
24. Severo Sarduy, "La Playa," *Para la voz* (Madrid: Fundamentos, 1978), 52.
25. Sarduy, *Para la voz*, 15–16.
26. Severo Sarduy, "Páginas en blanco (Cuadros de Franz Kline)," *Big Bang* (Barcelona: Tusquets, 1974), 102.
27. Severo Sarduy, *From Cuba with a Song*, trans. Suzanne Jill Levine (1972; Los Angeles: Sun & Moon, 1994), 140–141.
28. Sarduy, *Cobra*, ix. From the "Translator's Preface," in which Suzanne Jill Levine quotes Sarduy in an interview with Rodríguez Monegal.
29. Roberto González Echevarría, "In Search of the Lost Center," *Review* 6 (1972): 29–30.
30. Roland Barthes, "The Baroque Face," trans. Susan Homar, *Review* 6 (1972): 32. This text first appeared in *La Quinzaine littéraire* when Sarduy's novel came out in French, in 1967, just before its publication in Spanish. *Mundo Nuevo* published the Spanish version of Barthes' essay that same year.
31. Roland Barthes, *Le plaisir du texte* (Paris: Seuil, 1973), 17. Richard Miller's translation of these passages was taken not from the American edition of Barthes' book, but from the flyleaf of the Dalkey edition of Sarduy's novel.
32. Macé, 44.
33. Severo Sarduy, *Barroco* (Buenos Aires: Sudamericana, 1974), 17–18.
34. Sarduy, *Barroco*, 99.
35. Sarduy, *Barroco*, 103.

36. Emir Rodríguez Monegal, "Metamorphoses of the Text," trans. Enrique Sacerio Garí, *Review* 13 (1974): 16–17.
37. Sarduy, "Copy/Simulacrum," *Written on a Body*, 93–94.
38. Julián Ríos, "Conversación con Severo Sarduy: Maitreya o la entrada de Buda en La Habana," *Quimera* 20 (1982): 21.
39. Ríos, 20.
40. Suzanne Jill Levine, *The Subversive Scribe* (Saint Paul: Graywolf, 1991), 177–178.
41. Severo Sarduy, "Deterritorialization," *The Review of Contemporary Fiction* 4.2 (1984): 104–107. The essay first appeared in Spanish in 1975. Among his examples of "history inverted," he cites the perspective of both William Burroughs and Jean Genet.
42. Ríos, 23.
43. González Echevarría, 213–214.
44. Severo Sarduy, *Christ on the Rue Jacob*, trans. Suzanne Jill Levine and Carol Maier (San Francisco: Mercury House, 1995), 101–103.
45. Sarduy, *Christ on the Rue Jacob*, 34.
46. Severo Sarduy, *Cocuyo* (Barcelona: Tusquets, 1990), 208.
47. François Wahl, trans. Blas Matamoro, "La escritura a orillas del estanque," *Cuadernos Hispanoamericanos* 563 (May 1997): 23.
48. Severo Sarduy, *Pájaros de la playa* (Barcelona: Tusquets, 1993), 21–28.
49. Sarduy, *Pájaros de la playa*, 109, 131, 162, 133.
50. Severo Sarduy, *Epitafios* (Miami: Universal, 1994), 22. Of the seven epitaphs, this is from the second.
51. Despite his relative success, most of Copi's books are out of print in France a decade after his death.
52. Copi interview by Michel Cressole, "Un mauvais comédien, mais fidèle à l'auteur," *Libération* [Paris], 15 December 1987: 36. This is reprinted from the published edition of his play, *Le Frigo* (Paris: Persona, 1983).

    Raúl Damonte Taborda was his father, Georgina Botana his mother, Natalio Botana his grandfather, and Salvadora Onrubias was his grandmother.
53. For one of several such instances in the French press, giving this source for his name, see Mathieu Lindon and Marion Scali's memorial article, "Copi: On a perdu l'original," *Libération*, 15 December 1987: 35. Jorge Damonte's derivation is from his unpublished chronology, "Quelques dates dans la vie de Copi." The connection to his paleness was made by his friend José Tcherkaski in preface to the 1981 interview conducted with Copi, "No tengo estilo," *Radar* 5 (1990): 20.
54. Copi, preface to his unpublished novel, *Río de la Plata*, from 1984, in *Copi*, ed. Jorge Damonte (Paris: Bourgois, 1990), 84–86. Copi notes that the Uruguayan president at the time, Luis Battle Berres, tended to give out such titles to exiles from Latin American military dictatorships.
55. Copi, preface to unpublished novel, *Copi*, 86–87.
56. Lise Bloch-Morhange and David Alper, *Artiste et métèque à Paris* (Paris: Buchet/Castel, 1980), 201–204. In their interview with Jorge Lavelli, who arrived in Paris in 1960 and first triumphed in 1963 directing Witold Gombrowicz's play "Le

250 • Notes

Mariage," he speaks at length about this period of Argentine theater and its innovative force (when Gombrowicz, as well, was living in Buenos Aires).

57. Cressole, "Un mauvais comédien, mais fidèle à l'auteur," 36.
58. César Aira, Copi (Rosario: Viterbo, 1991), 101. Aira emphasizes Copi's affection for this aunt.
59. Copi, Les poulets n'ont pas de chaises (Paris: Denoël, 1966), 20–21, 22–23, 48–51. Alfredo Arias directed a theatrical adaptation in 1984 based on the comic strips of la Femme assise.
60. The titles of those plays translated into English are given by their published titles. These are available in two books: Copi, Plays Volume 1, trans. Anni Lee Taylor (London: Calder, 1976) and the anthology Gay Plays (New York: Ubu, 1989). The full title of the play The Homosexual or the Difficulty of Sexpressing Oneself makes use of its theme of gender confusions to render the French s'exprimer accordingly.
61. Copi, Théâtre, I (Paris: UGE–10/18, 1986), 70.
62. Copi, Théâtre, I, 72.
63. Copi, 13. Alfredo Arias, the original director, recounts here in rather comic terms the night of the attack.
64. Jean-Pierre Thibaudat, "Eva Perón, parfaitement pas atroce," Libération, 8 June 1993: 36. In the revival, Evita's mother was played by Monique Mélinand, who had toured South America in the early 1940s with Louis Jouvet's company: Thibaudat offers the provocative hypothesis that Evita, as an aspiring actress, may have even seen Mélinand perform in Buenos Aires in 1942.
65. Aira, 107.
66. Tcherkaski, "No tengo estilo," 21.
67. Bloch-Morhange and Alper, 27–28. Arrabal, in the interview, speaks of Panic as a reaction specifically against Breton, but by extension other movements as well. He does not name Copi as pertaining to that lineage, but there are certain affinities; Topor even illustrated the cover to Copi's first novel, L'Uruguayen.
68. His other two one-man performances were: Le Frigo (1983), in which he played several characters and the sole prop was a refrigerator that never opened, and Les Escaliers du Sacré–Coeur (1984), written for six characters but which he performed solo; it was given a full production only in 1990. The latter was modeled after gaucho verse style, though written in French.
69. Aira, 55, 117–119.
70. Aira, 19–20. The inherent irony of Copi's tale, according to Aira, is that Uruguay has long served as the locus of Argentine realism.
71. Copi, L'Uruguayen (Paris: Bourgois, 1973), 23. Specifically, the single block of prose is used in his first four novels, but not in his last two. Except for the first novel, where the block is uninterrupted, the other blocks are divided into chapters, each a single block in itself.
72. Aira, 29.
73. Copi, Le bal des folles (Paris: Bourgois–10/18, 1977), 118. Christian Bourgois was

the publisher for nearly all of Copi's plays, but this was the last of Copi's novels he brought out.
74. Aira, 44.
75. Colette Godard, "Copi le voyageur," *Copi*, ed. Jorge Damonte, 39.
76. Copi, *La Cité des Rats* (Paris: Belfond, 1979), 21. Late in the book, Gouri is horrified to look in the mirror and find himself momentarily changed, with a disturbing resemblance to Mickey or a human (119).
77. Damonte, "Quelques dates dans la vie de Copi," 2.
78. Copi, preface to unpublished novel, *Copi*, 81.
79. Copi, *Cachafaz* (Arles: Actes Sud-Papiers, 1993), 5. Copi had reserved for himself the role of the transvestite la Raulito, which Lavelli was going to direct; Cachafaz was to be played by Facundo Bo, who had played Evita. But it was only produced posthumously, in its French translation, directed by Alfredo Arias.
80. Graciela Montaldo, "Un argumento contraborgiano en la literatura argentina de los años '80," *Hispamérica* 55 (1990): 111. Montaldo discusses novels by three writers: Copi, Alberto Laiseca, and César Aira, with some references to Osvaldo Lamborghini, as well.
81. Copi, *La vie est un Tango* (Paris: Libres-Hallier, 1979), 107–109.
82. *La guerre des pédés*, like *La Cité des Rats* a few years previously, was first published serially in the journal *Hara-Kiri*.
83. Copi interview with José Tcherkaski, "No tengo estilo," 20. Despite such responses, Tcherkaski still apparently intended to title his unpublished book of conversations, *Copi: Homosexualidad y creación*.
84. Copi, *La guerre des pédés* (Paris: Albin Michel, 1982). The local gay militants decline to turn them in to the police, aware that these represent the same exotic pleasures they have always sought in traveling to Third World countries (28). Soon after, they learn that most of the transvestites had escaped as well from Brazilian concentration camps for homosexuals (35).

As for Conceição, written with an *i*, her name specifically implies immaculate conception (and the explanation of her birth in an Amazon tribe is hardly conclusive); written with a *p*, the word would mean simply conception.
85. Copi, *La guerre des pédés*, 75–77. Other figures killed in this passage include theater people—Sylvia Monfort, Coluche, Marcel Marceau—as well as the cartoonists Wolinski and Roland Topor.
86. Gustavo Tambascio, "Una herencia inoportuna: El teatro de Copi, a diez años de su muerte," *Cuadernos Hispanoamericanos* 563 (1997): 108–109.
87. Osvaldo Pellettieri, "Copi: un argentino y sus 'comedias de muerte' europeas," in Copi, *Una visita inoportuna* (Buenos Aires: TMGSM, 1993), 7–8. In the early 1990s, *The Four Twins* was also produced in Buenos Aires, as was Copi's final play.
88. Maria Casares and Copi had a point in common as well: the role of Madame in Genet's play *The Maids*. He played it in an Italian production in 1980, and she played it in a production for French television that aired early in 1985.
89. Copi, *La Nuit de Madame Lucienne*, in *L'avant-Scène Théâtre* 773 (1985): 34.

Outside Looking In

1. Jean-Baptiste Marongiu, "Paris, ville ouverte," review of *Le Paris des étrangers depuis 1945*, eds. Antoine Marès and Pierre Milza, *Libération*, 20 April 1995: xi. Many of the details in this paragraph are taken from this review.
2. For decades the Polish bookstore in Paris has been located on a prime block of the Boulevard Saint-Germain.
3. In particular, I recall a piece in the *Los Angeles Times* and a column by Edmund White in *Vogue*. The journals in 1984–85 were *Moving Letters, Frank, Sphinx, Paris Exiles*, plus another edited by a professor at the American College; also, the English-language city magazine *Passion*, mostly a Canadian venture, had a monthly fiction page at that time.
4. J. Gerald Kennedy, *Imagining Paris* (New Haven: Yale UP, 1993), 28.
5. For an extensive discussion of this period, see Christopher Sawyer-Lauçanno, *The Continual Pilgrimage* (New York: Grove, 1992), which treats specifically American writers in Paris, between 1944 and 1960, and James Campbell's *Exiled in Paris* (New York: Scribner, 1995), which places many of the Americans in a more international context that also includes Jean Genet, Samuel Beckett, and J. P. Donleavy, as well.
6. Michel Fabre, *From Harlem to Paris* (Urbana: U of Illinois P, 1991).
7. Albrecht Betz, *Exil et engagement*, trans. Pierre Rusch (Paris: Gallimard, 1991), 81, 109, 153–154, 168–170.
8. Ana Vasquez and Ana Maria Araujo, *Exils latino-américains: La malédiction d'Ulysse* (Paris: L'Harmattan, 1988), 13–14.
9. Vasquez and Araujo, 34.
10. One of the main areas of Vasquez and Araujo's research was the children of these exiles who came at a young age and struggled to adapt, often rebelling against a past they barely knew—and their parents' continued illusions about it—in an effort to rid themselves of its burden.
11. Vasquez and Araujo, 209. On this idea of living more than once, of the sense of reincarnation made possible by exile, they proceed to quote at length here from Uruguayan writer and longtime Paris resident Fernando Aínsa's *De Aquí y de Allá* (1987. Montevideo: Mirador, 1991), his citation of a character from Uruguayan writer Julieta Campos who says, "I devote my life to exploring what I have never lived." Aínsa concludes, "We could say that is almost the exile's vocation."
12. The prize was challenged on the grounds that the novel was not unpublished as required—Les Lettres Nouvelles had brought it out in French in 1970—but it had not appeared in the original Spanish.
13. The French editions of her work are: *Le Ravin* (1958. Actes Sud, 1986), *Somnambule du soleil* (Denoël/Les Lettres Nouvelles, 1970), *Fuir la spirale* (Actes Sud, 1987), *J'attends la nuit pour te rêver, Révolution* (L'Harmattan, 1997). She has also published several small editions of poetry.

    Her first novel was published in Cuba in 1959, after the revolution, and reissued in the Canary Islands in 1982. It has recently been published in England, translated by Carol Maier, as *The Ravine* (Middlesex: Middlesex UP, 2002). For a discussion of this work, along with Spanish writer Ana María Matute's *A School of the Sun*, see Joseph Schraibman, "Two Spanish Civil War Novels: A Woman's Perspective," in *The Spanish Civil War in Literature*, eds. Janet Pérez and Wendell Aycock (Lubbock: Texas Tech UP, 1990), 149–159.

14. Jason Weiss, unpublished interview with Luis Mizón, 7 July 1997. He informed me that a year before the coup, as a professor of legal history during Salvador Allende's Popular Unity government, he had rather frivolously joined the Communist Party, not out of great conviction. After the coup, he was dismissed precisely because of his membership in the party. A year later, unable to find work, he left the country.

   Mizón's first book in France was *Poème du Sud et autres poèmes*, trans. Roger Caillois and Claude Couffon (Paris: Gallimard, 1982). Caillois, who translated the long title poem, died in 1978. Couffon has translated well over 100 books, including Tejera's first novel back in the 1950s.

15. Jason Weiss, interview with Milagros Palma, 11 July 1997. "Entrevista en París con Milagros Palma," *Linden Lane Magazine* XVII: 2, 3, 4 (summer/fall/winter, 1998): 10–12. Her second and third novels in particular, *Desencanto al amanecer* (Disillusionment at Dawn, 1995), and *El Pacto* (The Pact, 1996), are set in fictional Central American countries during revolutionary times.

   Both publishing companies, which include distribution, bring out books in French. Indigo mostly offers translations, as well as some books in Spanish.

16. Guibert, 299–300. Pablo Neruda, for his part, weighed in on both sides in the dispute, in his piece "With Cortázar and with Arguedas," *Passions and Impressions*, trans. Margaret Sayers Peden (New York: Farrar Straus, 1983), 231–233. "It has always been my position," says Neruda, "that a writer in our forgotten countries should live in those lands and defend them." He then goes on to defend the American authenticity of Cortázar, Vargas Llosa, Fuentes, and García Márquez.

17. Roland Forgues, *Bajo el Puente Mirabeau corre el Rímac* (Grenoble: Edicious det Tignahus, 1987), 68.

18. Forgues, 222–223.

19. Forgues, 107.

7. The Privileged Eye

1. Julio Ramón Ribeyro, *La Tentación del Fracaso, 2: Diario Personal 1960–1974* (Lima: Campodónico, 1993), 123.

2. When Ribeyro got the job in the spring of 1961, his friends and fellow Peruvian writers Luis Loayza and Mario Vargas Llosa were also working at France Presse. At present, writers there include Julio Olaciregui, from Colombia, and Luisa Futoransky, from Argentina.

3. Julio Ramón Ribeyro, *La Tentación del Fracaso, 1: Diario Personal 1950–1960* (Lima: Campodónico, 1992), 33. His diary entry, dated 10 August 1953, was motivated by a visit to the Old Navy, the popular café frequented by Latin Americans on the boulevard Saint-Germain.

4. Julio Ramón Ribeyro, "Carta a Juan Antonio," *Asedios a Julio Ramón Ribeyro*, eds. Ismael P. Márquez and César Ferreira (Lima: Fondo Editorial de la Pontificia Universidad Católica del Perú, 1996), 65. Letter from Paris dated 28 January 1954.
5. Ribeyro, "Carta a Juan Antonio," *Asedios a Julio Ramón Ribeyro*, 69–70.
6. Ribeyro, *La Tentación del Fracaso*, 1, 52. Diary entry dated 11 October 1954. He had been living in Europe for two years by then, and published two stories and two articles during that time; Madrid was his first stop, from November 1952 to July 1953, when he went on to Paris.
7. Ribeyro, *La Tentación del Fracaso*, 1, 70. Diary entry, from Madrid, dated 28 February 1955. During his year and a half in Paris, 1953–54, Ribeyro wrote his first book of stories, *Los gallinazos sin plumas* (1955). In Madrid through the first half of 1955, he began to work on his first novel, *Crónica de San Gabriel* (1960).
8. Weiss, interview with Julio Ramón Ribeyro, 56.
9. Ribeyro, *La Tentación del Fracaso*, 2, 169. Diary entry dated 23 April 1972.
10. Ribeyro, *La Tentación del Fracaso*, 2, 190–192. Diary entries dated 28 and 30 December 1973.
11. Weiss, 57.
12. Susana Reisz, "La hora de Ribeyro," *Asedios a Julio Ramón Ribeyro*, 89. Her text was originally read when Ribeyro was awarded the Juan Rulfo prize in Guadalajara, Mexico, in 1994.
13. Washington Delgado, "Fantasía y realidad en la obra de Ribeyro," *La palabra del mudo*, 1, by Julio Ramón Ribeyro (Lima: Milla Batres, 1973), xii.
14. Julio Ramón Ribeyro, "The Banquet," *Marginal Voices*, trans. Dianne Douglas (Austin: U of Texas P, 1993), 54.
15. Alfredo Bryce Echenique, "El arte genuino de Ribeyro," *Cuentos completos*, by Julio Ramón Ribeyro (Madrid: Alfaguara, 1994), 11.
16. Ribeyro, *La palabra del mudo*, ix. Letter to the publisher dated 15 February 1973. Ribeyro's stories had a curious publishing history: the two volumes under this title presented the first twenty years of his stories, or six collections; the last two of these, written between 1964 and 1973, had never appeared as separate books. A third volume of the collected stories, comprising a single book, appeared in 1977, and a fourth, two more books, in 1992. Of these, only one book from the last volume had appeared separately, though many stories were published in mostly Peruvian newspapers and journals. Moreover, the single volume of collected stories published by Alfaguara in Spain, in 1994, contained several new stories inserted into the older collections according to their themes.
17. Julio Ortega, "Peru Today, But Above All, Peru Tomorrow," *Review* 57 (1998), 9.
18. Ribeyro, *La Tentación del Fracaso*, 1, 49–51. Diary entries from August to October 1954. As he notes, other Peruvians staying in the hotel then, at 15 Rue de la Harpe, included the poet Blanca Varela and the painter Benjamín "Morros" Moncloa.
19. Ribeyro, *La Tentación del Fracaso*, 1, 54. Diary entry dated 8 November 1954. On 21 December, he reflects on his book of stories as a whole, pleased that they at least maintain a certain unity, a vision that he admits is "a bit miserable, but exact and credible." His other concern in these stories "has been for psychological accu-

racy," and "the pressure of events on people. My stories could be defined, with some exceptions, as 'the psychological history of a human decision.'" (59–60)
20. Weiss, 55.
21. Ribeyro, *La Tentación del Fracaso*, 2, 29. Diary entry dated 26 July 1961. Specifically, this statement referred to a manifesto he was drawing up at Vargas Llosa's suggestion on the role that intellectuals should play in Peru.
22. Ribeyro, *La Tentación del Fracaso*, 2, 95. Diary entry dated 11 March 1965.
23. Ribeyro, "Of Modest Color," *Marginal Voices*, 28.
24. James Higgins, *Cambio social y constantes humanas: La narrativa corta de Ribeyro* (Lima: Fondo Editorial de la Pontificia Universidad Católica del Perú, 1991), 43.
25. Ribeyro, "Alienation," *Marginal Voices*, 57.
26. Higgins, 113.
27. Ribeyro, "Sobre las olas," *Cuentos completos*, 507.
28. Julio Ramón Ribeyro, "Silvio in the Rose Garden," *Silvio in the Rose Garden*, trans. Maria Rosa Fort and Frank Graziano (Gettysburg: Logbridge-Rhodes, 1989), 101. The story was written in 1976. I have slightly retranslated the final phrase.
29. Julio Ramón Ribeyro, *Prosas apátridas*, 3rd ed. (Barcelona: Tusquets, 1986), 179–180. Fragment number 199 out of 200. Some of these pieces he took from his diaries.
30. Although several stories in *Los cautivos* were written as late as 1971 or 1972, and "La juventud en la otra ribera" is from 1969, Ribeyro included it in the later collection. Regardless of other reasons he may have had for grouping it with *Silvio en El Rosedal*, I am suggesting that it is more consistent thematically that way.
31. Ribeyro, "Las cosas andan mal, Carmelo Rosa," *Cuentos completos*, 329.
32. Weiss, 54–55.
33. Jorge Coaguila, *Ribeyro, la palabra inmortal* (Lima: Campodónico, 1995), 64. This book is a series of interviews from the early 1990s.
34. Ribeyro, *La Tentación del Fracaso*, 2, 219–220. Diary entry dated 26 September 1974; in another entry that day, he tells of separate visits the previous day that lasted for hours with two Peruvian friends living in Paris then, the poet-novelist Manuel Scorza and the poet Rodolfo Hinostroza.
35. Ribeyro, *La Tentación del Fracaso*, 1, 210. Diary entry dated 9 August 1958.
36. Ribeyro, "El ropero, los viejos y la muerte," *Cuentos completos*, 402–406.
37. Ribeyro, "El polvo del saber," *Cuentos completos*, 421. This story, as it happens, was included in *Silvio en El Rosedal*, the book of displacements.
38. Ribeyro, "Mayo 1940," *Cuentos completos*, 685. These stories, though undated, were probably written during the 1980s. They comprised the first collection within the fourth volume of *La palabra del mudo* (1992), but in the complete edition of his stories two years later they were placed at the very end, perhaps because they marked precisely a sort of return to his beginnings.
39. Ribeyro, "Los otros," *Cuentos completos*, 749. In this final paragraph about the present, he places the year as 1980, but there is no indication as to the dates of the other stories in the collection.
40. Ribeyro, *Prosas apátridas*, 158–159. Fragment number 165.

41. A portion of this book was published in 1987, but two stories included in the complete edition were written later.
42. Weiss, 53.
43. Ribeyro, "La casa en la playa," *Cuentos completos*, 676–677.
44. Jason Weiss, unpublished interview with Juan José Saer, 2 July 1997.
45. Ricardo Piglia/Juan José Saer, *Diálogo* (Santa Fe: Universidad Nacional del Litoral, 1995), 37–38.
46. Weiss, unpublished interview with Juan José Saer. The theme he proposed for his grant was on the *nouveau roman* and French cinema's *nouvelle vague*.
47. Piglia/Saer, *Diálogo*, 66–67.
48. In my interview with him, he spoke of working on a new book of stories, *Lugar* (place), set in the present, which would take place all over the world, with two or three in Santa Fe. It would be like his other books, he said, only "the space has been extended a little."
49. Ana Basualdo, "El desierto retórico: entrevista con Juan José Saer," *Quimera* 76 (1988): 14.
50. Weiss, unpublished interview with Juan José Saer.
51. Juan José Saer, *Juan José Saer* (Buenos Aires: Celtia, 1986), 12.
52. Piglia/Saer, *Diálogo*, 78–79.
53. Juan José Saer, *La mayor* (1976; Buenos Aires: Centro Editor de América Latina, 1982), 137–139.
54. Mirta E. Stern, "Juan José Saer: Construcción y teoría de la ficción narrativa," *Hispamérica* 37 (1984): 17–18. Saer as well, on various occasions, has commented on this de-emphasis of the event. Silvia Larrañaga-Machalski, in her entry on Saer in *Histoire de la littèrature hispano-américaine de 1940 à nos jours*, eds. Claude Cymerman and Claude Fell (Paris: Nathan, 1997), sees a new importance given to anecdote and event in his later work (149), but I think these remain subordinate to the problematic of the telling. In *La pesquisa*, for instance, his most recent novel, the detective story comprising the main part of the narrative is often interrupted by the circumstances of the telling, which, in turn, place the detective story in doubt as to its veracity, to the point of offering an alternate ending.
55. Piglia/Saer, *Diálogo*, 38.
56. Stern, 19–20.
57. Juan José Saer, *Cicatrices* (1969; Buenos Aires, Centro Editor de América Latina, 1983), 287.
58. Juan José Saer, *Une littérature sans qualités* (Cognac: Arcane 17, 1985), 51.
59. Juan José Saer, *El limonero real* (1974; Buenos Aires: Centro Editor de América Latina, 1983), vi–viii. Mirta Stern, in her prologue, elaborates on the cyclical nature of the narrative and its classical dimensions, echoing not only *Genesis*, but the *Odyssey*, as well, in Wenceslao's voyage out and back again. Further, she shows how Saer recycles elements from his own earliest stories, in the general setting and also the sacrifice of the lamb.
60. Saer began writing *El limonero real* while still in Argentina and finished it in Paris, though this biographical detail has no particular bearing on the book.

61. Saer, *La mayor*, 44.
62. Saer, *La mayor*, 49.
63. Saer, *La mayor*, 77.
64. María Teresa Gramuglio, "El lugar de Saer," in Saer, *Juan José Saer*, 274.
65. Gramuglio, 263.
66. Basualdo, 14.
67. Juan José Saer, *El concepto de ficción* (Buenos Aires: Ariel, 1997), 16–17.
68. Saer, "La forêt épaisse du réel," *Une littérature sans qualités*, 14. As he has on various occasions, in another essay in this volume, "Borges romancier," he describes the life of the novel as a genre as extending from the *Quixote* to Flaubert's *Bouvard et Pécuchet*. After came something else. (43) In this respect, he agrees with Nathalie Sarraute's view of the nineteenth-century novel as an outmoded form, and yet he, like others, for lack of a better term, continues to refer to the novel in more modern usage.
69. Juan José Saer, *Nobody Nothing Never*, trans. Helen Lane (New York: Serpent's Tail, 1993), 196.
70. Saer, *Nobody Nothing Never*, 93. The illusion of continuity even extends to the reigning feeling of nothingness in that half of the book's fifteen chapters open with the sentence, "In the beginning, there is nothing." Despite all that subsequently transpires each time, the question seems to remain (and a refrain in other works as well): did it really happen, and in what world?
71. Raquel Linenberg-Fressard, "Entrevista con Juan José Saer," *Río de la Plata* 7 (1988): 156–157.
72. The narrator's dilemma, on returning to Europe, echoes this account of a return in the opposite direction, as told by an Uruguayan woman in Vasquez and Araujo's *Exils latino-américains: La malédiction d'Ulysse*: "I felt a stranger in my own country. I was lost. I no longer recognized myself. It was like being dispossessed of my past, of a part of myself. What was I going to do with all that I had lived in Europe? How was I to give some continuity to my life? How was I to communicate?" (212)
73. Juan José Saer, *The Witness*, trans. Margaret Jull Costa (London: Serpent's Tail, 1990), 35.
74. Saer, *The Witness*, 31.
75. Saer, *The Witness*, 65, 69.
76. Although the novel bears some traits common to New World captivity narratives, the narrator neither rejoices at his return to "civilization" nor seeks to identify with his captors. Rather, as an exile comparing two societies, he regards the Indians as the only men worthy of the term (109).
77. Juan José Saer, *The Event*, trans. Helen Lane (New York: Serpent's Tail, 1995), 24–25.
78. Saer, *The Event*, 182.
79. He was awarded Spain's prestigious Premio Nadal for the novel. Later, another mostly linear novel, his crime story *La pesquisa*, became a modest best-seller in Argentina. Since the mid-1970s most of his books have been translated into

258 • Notes

French; these include one book of poetry, a collection of some twenty years' work, *El arte de narrar* (The Art of Narrating)—an indication not only of his sense of irony, but of his desire to blur the borders between genres.
80. Juan José Saer, *Glosa* (Barcelona: Destino, 1988), 26. Each time he runs into another friend through the novel, he offers a similar list of European cities, with a different order of details (63, 118, 220).
81. Juan José Saer, *Lo imborrable* (Buenos Aires: Alianza, 1993), 15.
82. Saer, *Lo imborrable*, 145. Saer further discusses the contemporary self in crisis and the verbal convention of the I, largely in relation to this novel, in Claudio Canaparo's interview with him in *Journal of Latin American Cultural Studies* 4.1 (1995): 78.
83. Saer, *Lo imborrable*, 187.
84. Juan José Saer, *La pesquisa* (Buenos Aires: Seix Barral, 1994), 22. This novel is now available in English as *The Investigation*, trans. Helen Lane (New York: Serpent's Tail, 1999).
85. Saer, *La pesquisa*, 128.
86. At this point in the novel (71–72), Pichón compares that stretch of the river he used to know so well with the Seine. Many Latin American writers have made such comparisons—Silvia Baron Supervielle and Silvina Ocampo, with the Río de la Plata, or the Peruvian poets with the Rímac, as presented in Roland Forgues' *Bajo el Puente Mirabeau corre el Rímac*.
87. Saer, *La pesquisa*, 78.

8. Tsuris of the Margins

1. Her first two novels, written in the 1980s and sharing the same protagonist, both use these terms more or less in their back cover texts. *Son cuentos chinos* (1983), the first, asks: "Can there be in this world a greater misfortune than being a woman, fortyish, alone, not at all thin, Jewish, South American, and rather voluble in her passions?"
   In Argentina she grew up at the periphery as well, in a suburb of Buenos Aires with the unlikely name of Santos Lugares (Holy Places).
2. Ethel Krauze, "De Vacas y de Bestsellers," *Excelsior* 24 May 1989: 16. In her column, Mexican writer Krauze laments that at this late date, except for the big names, the different countries of Latin America still do not know each other's literature. Aside from local writers, she contends, publishers prefer to translate new European authors sooner than offer the work of writers from other parts of Latin America. It remains the case, therefore, that it is more often on the occasion of international literary conferences that writers exchange their books and become known to each other, and that is how, "at a congress on the other side of the world," she chanced upon Futoransky's first novel—which at that date would have been the Spanish edition (1983), since the Argentine edition didn't come out until 1991.
3. Luisa Futoransky, "Egeo," *Lo regado por lo seco* (Buenos Aires: Noé, 1972), 22–23.
4. Futoransky, "Feudo de Lot," *Lo regado por lo seco*, 32.

5. Luisa Futoransky, "Vitraux de exilio," *Partir, digo* (Valencia: Prometeo, 1982), 13. The translation was published in Luisa Futoransky, *The Duration of the Voyage*, trans. Jason Weiss (San Diego: Junction, 1997), 19.
6. Elia Espinosa, "Entre albas y crepúsculos," *Plural* 161 (1985): 52.
7. Futoransky, *The Duration of the Voyage*, 33.
8. Literally, the title translates as "They're Chinese stories," the sense being in the manner of tall tales. The title of the French translation of the novel could only approximate this as well: *Chinois chinoiseries*. In this way, her title invokes China at the same time as it suggests something lost or else dreamed up in the translation.
9. Luisa Futoransky, *Son cuentos chinos* (1983; Buenos Aires: Planeta, 1991), 21.
10. Francine Masiello, "Bodies in Transit: Travel, Translation, and Gender," *Voice-Overs: Latin American Translation Theory*, eds. Daniel Balderston and Marcy Schwarz (forthcoming). The quotes are taken from a manuscript copy of the essay, used with permission. The writer also credits Julia Kushigian's work on contemporary orientalism in Latin American literature.
11. Graciela Speranza, "Luisa Futoransky," *Primer plano*, 32 January 1993: 7. Interview.
12. Masiello.
13. Luisa Futoransky, "De donde son las palabras." Unpublished essay, 1997. Used with permission. The closing paragraphs of this essay, including the last phrase here quoted, provide the poet's introductory remarks to the recent mass-market anthology of her poetry, Luisa Futoransky, *De donde son las palabras* (Barcelona: Plaza & Janés, 1998), 5.
14. Saúl Sosnowski, *La orilla inminente* (Buenos Aires: Legasa, 1987), 17–18.
15. Rosa Sarabia, *Poetas de la palabra hablada* (London: Tamesis, 1997), 108.
16. Futoransky, *The Duration of the Voyage*, 39.
17. Futoransky, "She, The Fisherwoman," *The Duration of the Voyage*, 43.
18. Futoransky, *The Duration of the Voyage*, 35.
19. Luisa Futoransky, *De Pe a Pa* (Barcelona: Anagrama, 1986), 13.
20. Futoransky, *De Pe a Pa*, 45.
21. Futoransky, *De Pe a Pa*, 105–106. "When oh when will I be able to understand Who is Who here by the way they fold their newspaper in the métro . . . ?" As examples of her absurd misreadings, she offers: her continued puzzlement at what the Jeu de Paume museum had to do with apple juice (*jus de pomme*); how religious the French must have been when the métro was constructed since so many lines end with stations named for Mary (Marie), which she mistakes for *Mairie* (town hall); not getting the joke, hearing *c'est marron* (that's brown) when people were really saying *c'est marrant* (that's funny).
22. Jason Weiss, interview with Luisa Futoransky, 27 June 1994. *Linden Lane Magazine* 18: 1, 2 (spring, summer, 1999): 4–5.
23. Speranza, 7. Her books published in Argentina, after *Lo regado por lo seco* (1972), include: in poetry, *Antología* (1985), and *La Parca, enfrente* (1995), and the novels *Son cuentos chinos* (1991, for the Argentine edition), and *Urracas* (1992).
24. Futoransky, *The Duration of the Voyage*, 51.

25. Futoransky, "Fleeting Fragile Love, Deep Disturbance of the Pulse," *The Duration of the Voyage*, 51.
26. Futoransky, *The Duration of the Voyage*, 63.
27. Luisa Futoransky, *La sanguina* (Barcelona: Taifa, 1987), 72.
28. Guillermo Sucre, *La máscara, la transparencia* (Mexico: FCE, 1985), 343.
29. Jorge Rodríguez Padrón, "Voces desde la periferia: dos notas," *RevistAtlántica de Poesía* 3 (1991): 143.
30. Luisa Futoransky, *Lunas de miel* (Barcelona: Editorial Juventud, 1996), 55–59.
31. The French edition of *Urracas* came out in 1990 under the title *Julia*. Futoransky has had five books published in French, all with notable translators: her collection of poems, *Partir, digo*, her first and third novels, and her two nonfiction books.
32. *Speranza*, 7.
33. Futoransky, *The Duration of the Voyage*, 67.
34. Futoransky, *The Duration of the Voyage*, 85.
35. Futoransky, *The Duration of the Voyage*, 87–95.

Living in Another Language

1. Gilles Deleuze and Félix Guattari, *Kafka: Toward a Minor Literature*, trans. Dana Polan (Minneapolis: U of Minnesota P, 1986), 17.
2. Ngũg- wa Thiong'o, *Moving the Centre* (London: James Currey; Portsmouth: Heinemann, 1993), 106–108. For more on these issues, see Ngũg- wa Thiong'o, *Decolonising the Mind* (London: James Currey; Portsmouth: Heinemann, 1986), especially "The Language of African Literature."
3. Jason Weiss, *Writing at Risk: Interviews in Paris with Uncommon Writers* (Iowa City: U of Iowa P, 1991), 178–180. The interview with Jabès took place in 1982.
4. Weiss, 187. This new path in his writing attracted readers from many directions besides poetry—philosophy, ethics, religion, linguistics—and even those who didn't normally read literature.
5. Weiss, 12–13. The interview with Cioran is from 1983.
6. Julio Ortega, *Antología de la poesía hispanoamericana actual* (Mexico: Siglo Veintiuno, 1987), 15.
7. Jason Weiss, interview with Alicia Dujovne Ortiz, 15 August 1997. *Hispamérica* XXVIII: 82 (1999): 45–58.
8. Weiss, interview with Alicia Dujovne Ortiz.

9. The Translated Self

1. Jonathan Rosenbaum, "Ambiguous Evidence: Cozarinsky's 'Cinema Indirect'," *Film Comment* (September–October 1995): 42.
2. Jason Weiss, unpublished interview with Edgardo Cozarinsky, 19 April 1995.
3. Jacques Leenhardt and Pierre Kalfon, *Les Amériques latines en France* (Paris: Gallimard, 1992), 142. In the final pages of the book, an introductory panorama of the subject, Cozarinsky is quoted to this effect.

4. Edgardo Cozarinsky, "The Sentimental Journey," trans. Ronald Christ and the author, *Urban Voodoo* (1985; New York: Lumen, 1990), 12.
5. Cozarinsky, 14.
6. Cozarinsky, 26–29.
7. Cozarinsky, 30.
8. Jason Weiss, unpublished interview with Rubén Bareiro Saguier, 9 July 1997. Resisting such distortions of nostalgia impelled him "to recuperate many of [his] experiences" growing up in a Paraguayan village that went into his first book of stories, *Ojo por diente* (An Eye for a Tooth). This book, in turn, caused him to be thrown into jail on a visit to Paraguay, after it won Cuba's Casa de las Américas prize in 1971; released after an international outcry, he was not able to return there until the dictator Alfredo Stroessner was deposed in 1989.
9. Kip Hanrahan, liner notes, Juan José Mosalini, *One Man's Tango*, CD, Shanachie, 1998. In this respect, Hanrahan draws a parallel between Mosalini's art and that of Julio Cortázar.
10. Weiss, unpublished interview with Edgardo Cozarinsky.
11. Cozarinsky, 127.
12. Cozarinsky, 47–49.
13. Cozarinsky, 121–23.
14. Cozarinsky, 103.
15. Cozarinsky, 127.
16. Cozarinsky, 33.
17. Cozarinsky, 35–37.
18. Cozarinsky, 79–83.
19. Edgardo Cozarinsky, *Borges in/and/on Film* (New York: Lumen, 1988), 12. A version of this book, only half of which comprises Borges' early film criticism, was first published in Spanish in 1974; each subsequent edition, including the French and Italian, has been revised with added material.
20. Edgardo Cozarinsky, *Boulevards du crépuscule* (Sunset Boulevards), film script, Les Films d'Ici, 1992.
21. Anton Tchekhov/Benjamin Fleischmann/Edgardo Cozarinsky, *Le violon de Rothschild* (Arles: Actes Sud, 1996), 81. The book includes the short story, the film script and, embedded within it, the libretto, besides Cozarinsky's notes and other materials.
22. Tchekhov/Fleischmann/Cozarinsky, 79.

10. New World Transplants

1. To distinguish himself from his father—a former politician and director of a newspaper—who had the same name, he shortened his name from Eduardo González-Manet.
2. Jason Weiss, interview with Eduardo Manet, 5 October 1996. *Sites* 2:2 (fall 1998): 261–267 (abridged); *Linden Lane Magazine* XX:1 (spring 2001): 13–15.

3. Phyllis Zatlin, *The Novels and Plays of Eduardo Manet: An Adventure in Multiculturalism* (University Park: Pennsylvania State UP, 2000), 75.
4. Zatlin, 105.
5. Weiss, interview with Eduardo Manet. Among the writers who joined him, at a 1979 meeting in support of Cuban exiles in Paris, were Eugène Ionesco, Fernando Arrabal, Bernard Henri-Lévy, Philippe Sollers, and Nathalie Sarraute.

    At the Biarritz Film Festival in 1994, Manet states in the interview, the Colombian writer Alvaro Mutis made a defense similar to Beckett's before an audience: "Listen, all writers are exiles. I was born in Colombia, I've been living for many years in Mexico. That's not the problem. Eduardo writes in French. He can write in Chinese, but he will be a Cuban or a Latin American writer."
6. Roger Blin, *Souvenirs et propos* (Paris: Gallimard, 1986), 242–243.
7. Zatlin, 126.
8. Zatlin, 139. She refers to Diana Taylor's book, *Theatre of Crisis: Drama and Politics in Latin America* (1991).
9. Zatlin, 148–149.
10. Eduardo Manet, *Un balcon sur les Andes; Mendoza, en Argentine . . . ; Ma'Déa* (Paris: Gallimard, 1985), 72–73.
11. Manet, *Un balcon sur les Andes*, 214, 250. Both her mother first, and her aunt later, are made to speak through Ma'Déa's voice.
12. Manet, *Un balcon sur les Andes*, 252–254.
13. Eduardo Manet, *Monsieur Lovestar et son voisin de palier* (Arles: Actes Sud, 1995), 39. Though written in 1987, according to Zatlin, it did not premiere until 1995.
14. Weiss, interview with Eduardo Manet.
15. Alan Riding, "Neocolonialists Seize French Language," *New York Times*, 8 October 1997: E1. In discussing foreigners who write in French, Riding clearly misapplies the word 'neocolonialist.'
16. Weiss, interview with Eduardo Manet.
17. Eduardo Manet, *La Mauresque* (Paris: Gallimard, 1982), 130–131. On these pages, just past halfway through the novel, mother and son are taking a long bus ride in moving to Havana and stop in the city of Camagüey: the main plaza suddenly stirs up memories for his mother of her childhood in Córdoba, recalling her more distant relatives in Tangier, Beirut, Damascus—places where the Jews of Spain settled in the centuries after their exodus.
18. Weiss, interview with Eduardo Manet.
19. Eduardo Manet, *Zone interdite* (Paris: Gallimard, 1984), 69–70.
20. Eduardo Manet, *L'île du lézard vert* (Paris: Flammarion, 1992), 402.
21. Manet, *L'île du lézard vert*, 232.
22. Eduardo Manet, *Habanera* (Paris: Flammarion, 1994), 188.
23. Eduardo Manet, *Rhapsodie cubaine* (Paris: Grasset, 1996), 25.
24. Silvia Baron Supervielle, "El Cambio de lengua para un escritor," *El Cambio de lengua para un escritor* (Buenos Aires: Corregidor, 1998), 11.
25. Silvia Baron Supervielle, "El País de las Afueras," *El Cambio de lengua para un escritor*, 85.

26. Jason Weiss, interview with Silvia Baron Supervielle, 26 June 1997. *Quimera* 178 (March 1999): 46–52.
27. Weiss, interview with Silvia Baron Supervielle.
28. Baron Supervielle, "El País de las Afueras," 86.
29. Weiss, interview with Silvia Baron Supervielle.
30. Baron Supervielle, "El Cambio de lengua para un escritor," 10.
31. Weiss, interview with Silvia Baron Supervielle.
32. Weiss, interview with Silvia Baron Supervielle.
33. Baron Supervielle, "El Cambio de lengua para un escritor," 11.
34. Baron Supervielle, "El Cambio de lengua para un escritor," 22.
35. Baron Supervielle, "El Cambio de lengua para un escritor," 15.
36. Hector Bianciotti, "La cueillette des vestiges," *Le Nouvel Observateur*, 24 February 1984: 76.
37. Silvia Baron Supervielle, *Lectures du vent* (Paris: José Corti, 1988), 19.
38. Baron Supervielle, *Lectures du vent*, 25.
39. Baron Supervielle, *Lectures du vent*, 34.
40. Baron Supervielle, *Lectures du vent*, 46.
41. Baron Supervielle, *Lectures du vent*, 55.
42. Silvia Baron Supervielle, "Le profil muet," *Elles: A Bilingual Anthology of Modern French Poetry by Women*, ed. and trans. Martin Sorrell (Exeter: U of Exeter P, 1995), 199–200. In this paragraph from the essay, I have modified his translation.
43. Baron Supervielle, *Lectures du vent*, 62.
44. Silvia Baron Supervielle, *L'eau étrangère* (Paris: José Corti, 1993), 35.
45. Baron Supervielle, *L'eau étrangère*, 12.
46. Baron Supervielle, *L'eau étrangère*, 23.
47. Baron Supervielle, *L'eau étrangère*, 38.
48. Baron Supervielle, *L'eau étrangère*, 67.
49. Baron Supervielle, *L'eau étrangère*, 68.
50. Baron Supervielle, *L'eau étrangère*, 98.
51. Silvia Baron Supervielle, *Après le pas* (Paris: Arfuyen, 1997), 7.
52. Baron Supervielle, *Après le pas*, 23.
53. Baron Supervielle, *Après le pas*, 39.
54. Baron Supervielle, *Après le pas*, 36.
55. Baron Supervielle, *Après le pas*, 48.
56. Baron Supervielle, *Après le pas*, 52.
57. Baron Supervielle, *Après le pas*, 54.
58. Weiss, interview with Silvia Baron Supervielle.
59. Baron Supervielle, "El Cambio de lengua para un escritor," 16–18.
60. Silvia Baron Supervielle, *L'or de l'incertitude* (Paris: José Corti, 1990), 130.
61. Baron Supervielle, *L'or de l'incertitude*, 49.
62. Baron Supervielle, *L'or de l'incertitude*, 165–166.
63. Baron Supervielle, *L'or de l'incertitude*, 167.
64. Baron Supervielle, *L'or de l'incertitude*, 264.
65. Baron Supervielle, *L'or de l'incertitude*, 227.

66. Silvia Baron Supervielle, *Le Livre du retour* (Paris: José Corti, 1993), 203–204.
67. Baron Supervielle, *Le Livre du retour*, 10. That accompanying absence would include her father, to whom she dedicated the book, still living in Buenos Aires. *L'or de l'incertitude* was dedicated to her mother, "whose silence was a word of beauty."
68. Baron Supervielle, *Le Livre du retour*, 26–27.
69. Baron Supervielle, *Le Livre du retour*, 68.
70. Hector Bianciotti, "Le langage du silence," *Le Monde*, 16 April 1993: 33.
71. Baron Supervielle, *Le Livre du retour*, 238.
72. Baron Supervielle, *Le Livre du retour*, 215.
73. Weiss, interview with Silvia Baron Supervielle.
74. Patrick Kéchichian, "L'étrangère des deux rives," *Le Monde*, 29 September 1995: 17.
75. Silvia Baron Supervielle, *Nouvelles Cantates* (Paris: José Corti, 1995), 5–6.
76. Silvia Baron Supervielle, *La Frontière* (Paris: José Corti, 1995), 7–8.
77. Baron Supervielle, *La Frontière*, 21–23.
78. Weiss, interview with Silvia Baron Supervielle.
79. Baron Supervielle, *La Frontière*, 59, 63.
80. Baron Supervielle, *La Frontière*, 124.
81. Baron Supervielle, *La Frontière*, 46.
82. Baron Supervielle, *La Frontière*, 113.
83. Baron Supervielle, *La Frontière*, 148.
84. Baron Supervielle, *Après le pas*, 53.

11. *Académicien*

1. Hector Bianciotti, *La busca del jardín* (Barcelona: Tusquets, 1978), 23–24. As with Bianciotti's other books written in Spanish, this novel was first published in French translation, by Françoise-Marie Rosset. In each case, I will refer to the date of that first edition. (His very first novel was published shortly before the French version, in the same year: he had sent it to Sudamericana in Buenos Aires, and then—without a response—one day he received a copy. They rejected his next book.)
2. Bianciotti, 11–17.
3. Jason Weiss, interview with Hector Bianciotti, 23 June 1994. *Voice Literary Supplement* (May 1995): 19 (abridged); *Hopscotch* 1:4 (1999): 105–111.
4. Hector Bianciotti, *Discours de réception de Hector Bianciotti à l'Académie française* (Paris: Grasset, 1997), 88.
5. Rafael Humberto Moreno-Duran, "Entrevista con Héctor Bianciotti: La travesía nocturna de la escritura," *Quimera* 3 (1981): 27.
6. Bianciotti, *La busca del jardín*, 90–91.
7. One could even draw a line, starting with this novel, to say that he had entered the "season" of French literary prizes. *Le traité des saisons* earned him the Prix Médicis for best foreign book in 1977, which was awarded earlier in the decade to both Sarduy and Cortázar. Among subsequent honors, his first novel in French, *Sans la miséricorde du Christ*, also won an important prize, the Prix Fémina, in 1985.

8. Moreno-Duran, 26. The phrase is Bianciotti's, describing his method in the interview.
9. Hector Bianciotti, "Changer de langue changer de façon d'être," *La Quinzaine littéraire* 436 (16–31 March 1985): 10.
10. Weiss, interview with Hector Bianciotti.
11. Bianciotti, "Changer de langue changer de façon d'être," 10.
12. José Luis Reina, "La isla íntima: entrevista con Héctor Bianciotti," *Quimera* 74 (1988): 56.
13. Weiss, interview with Hector Bianciotti.
14. Octavio Paz, "Hector Bianciotti, la liberté et la forme," trans. Jean-Claude Masson, *Le Monde du Vendredi*, 7 February 1992: 23.
15. Hector Bianciotti, *What the Night Tells the Day*, trans. Linda Coverdale (New York: The New Press, 1995), 163.
16. Hector Bianciotti, untitled text, *Gombrowicz en Europe*, ed. Rita Gombrowicz (Paris: Denoël, 1988), 123. The text dates from 1984.
17. Alice Kaplan, *French Lessons* (Chicago: U of Chicago P, 1993), 209.
18. Weiss, interview with Hector Bianciotti.
19. Weiss, interview with Hector Bianciotti.
20. Bianciotti, *What the Night Tells the Day*, 253.
21. Bianciotti, *La busca del jardín*, 151–154.
22. Bianciotti, *La busca del jardín*, 130.
23. Doug Ireland, "Day for Night," *Voice Literary Supplement* (May 1995): 18. On the other hand, it might not be reductive to see the homosexual angle as decisive for The New Press in choosing to translate and publish *What the Night Tells the Day*, the first and so far only work by the author available in English. Ireland does not spend his entire article on Bianciotti's being gay, but most of it; reviews of the book in the French press, by contrast, including Paz's article, do not dwell much on his sexuality.
24. Monique Nemer, "Les flash-back d'Hector," *Le Monde Aujourd'hui*, 24–25 November 1985: xii.
25. Hector Bianciotti, "Le retour à Ithaque," *Le Monde*, 9 August 1985: 12.
26. Severo Sarduy, "Tapiz," *Ritual*, by Hector Bianciotti (Barcelona: Tusquets, 1973), 10.
27. Hector Bianciotti, *Ritual*, 53.
28. Graciana Vázquez Villanueva, *Travesía de una escritura* (Buenos Aires: Corregidor, 1989), 52.
29. Weiss, interview with Hector Bianciotti. Also living there was the Polish critic Kot Jelenski, who first gave him Gombrowicz's address in Buenos Aires when Bianciotti went back for a visit in 1961; Gombrowicz subsequently saw him in Paris several times. The figure of Fini was transformed in *La busca del jardín*, in the chapter "Busca" (quest), into the Lady in Red with her extravagant salon; in *Le Pas si lent de l'amour*, he changed her name to Domenica.
30. Bianciotti, *La busca del jardín*, 36.
31. Bianciotti, *What the Night Tells the Day*, 252.

32. Reina, 60.
33. Nemer, xii. Bianciotti uses the term "public writer" in this interview from 1985, but also as recently as 1997 in his speech on the occasion of being inducted into the Académie Française.
34. Hector Bianciotti, *El amor no es amado* (Barcelona: Tusquets, 1983), 122.
35. Bianciotti, *El amor no es amado*, 12.
36. Bianciotti, *El amor no es amado*, 27.
37. Hector Bianciotti, *Sans la miséricorde du Christ* (Paris: Gallimard, 1985), 12.
38. Bianciotti, *Sans la miséricorde du Christ*, 42–43.
39. Bianciotti, *Sans la miséricorde du Christ*, 103.
40. Bianciotti, *Sans la miséricorde du Christ*, 137.
41. Bianciotti, *Sans la miséricorde du Christ*, 312.
42. Hector Bianciotti, *Seules les larmes seront comptées* (Paris: Gallimard, 1988), 344.
43. Hector Bianciotti, *Le Pas si lent de l'amour* (Paris: Grasset, 1995), 159.
44. Weiss, interview with Hector Bianciotti.
45. Bianciotti, *Le Pas si lent de l'amour*, 47.
46. Bianciotti, *Discours de réception de Hector Bianciotti à l'Académie française*, 82–83.

Bibliography

Primary Sources

Asturias, Miguel Angel. *París 1924–1933: Periodismo y creación literaria.* Nanterre, France: ALLCA XXe. Université Paris X. Centre de Recherches Latino-Américaines, 1988.

———. *The President.* Trans. Frances Partridge. Prospect Heights, IL: Waveland, 1997.

Baron Supervielle, Silvia. *Lectures du vent.* Paris: José Corti, 1988.

———. *L'or de l'incertitude.* Paris: José Corti, 1990.

———. *L'eau étrangère.* Paris: José Corti, 1993.

———. *Le Livre du retour.* Paris: José Corti, 1993.

———. *Nouvelles Cantates.* Paris: José Corti, 1995.

———. *La Frontière.* Paris: José Corti, 1995.

———. *Après le pas.* Paris: Arfuyen, 1997.

———. *El cambio de lengua para un escritor.* Buenos Aires: Corregidor, 1998.

———. *La ligne et l'ombre.* Paris: Seuil, 1999.

———. *Essais pour un espace.* Paris: Arfuyen, 2001.

———. *La rive orientale.* Paris: Seuil, 2001.

Bianciotti, Hector. *Ritual.* Barcelona: Tusquets, 1973.

———. *Los desiertos dorados.* Barcelona: Tusquets, 1975.

———. *La busca del jardín.* Barcelona: Tusquets, 1978.

———. *El amor no es amado.* Barcelona: Tusquets, 1983.

———. "La cueillette des vestiges." *Le Nouvel Observateur* (24 February 1984): 76.

———. "Changer de langue changer de façon d'être." *La Quinzaine littéraire* 436 (16–31 March 1985): 10.

———. "Le retour à Ithaque." *Le Monde* (9 August 1985): 12.

———. *Sans la miséricorde du Christ.* Paris: Gallimard, 1985.

———. *Seules les larmes seront comptées.* Paris: Gallimard, 1988.

———. "Le langage du silence." *Le Monde* (16 April 1993): 33.

———. *What the Night Tells the Day.* Trans. Linda Coverdale. New York: New Press, 1995.

———. *Le Pas si lent de l'amour.* Paris: Grasset, 1995.

———. *Discours de réception de Hector Bianciotti à l'Académie française.* Paris: Grasset, 1997.

———. *Comme la trace de l'oiseau dans l'air.* Paris: Grasset, 1999.

———. *Une passion en toutes Lettres.* Paris: Gallimard, 2001.

Bryce Echenique, Alfredo. *La vida exagerada de Martín Romaña*. Bogotá: Oveja Negra, 1985.

———. "Confesiones sobre el arte de vivir y escribir novelas." *Los mundos de Alfredo Bryce Echenique*. Eds. César Ferreira and Ismael P. Márquez. Lima: Fondo Editorial, 1994. 25–41.

Cabrera, Lydia. *Cuentos Negros de Cuba*. Miami: Universal, 1993.

Carpentier, Alejo. *Reasons of State*. Trans. Francis Partridge. London: Writers and Readers, 1977.

———. *Crónicas*. 2 vols. Mexico: Siglo Veintiuno, 1985–1986.

———. *Entrevistas*. Havana: Letras Cubanas, 1985.

———. *Explosion in a Cathedral*. Trans. Harriet de Onís. New York: Noonday, 1989.

Copi. *Les poulets n'ont pas de chaises*. Paris: Denoël, 1966.

———. *L'Uruguayen*. Paris: Bourgois, 1973.

———. *Plays Volume 1*. Trans. Anni Lee Taylor. London: Calder, 1976.

———. *Le bal des folles*. Paris: Bourgois–10/18, 1977.

———. *La Cité des Rats*. Paris: Belfond, 1979.

———. *La vie est un tango*. Paris: Hallier, 1979.

———. *La guerre des pédés*. Paris: Albin Michel, 1982.

———. *La Nuit de Madame Lucienne*. *L'Avant-Scène Théâtre* 773 (1985).

———. *Théâtre*, I. Paris: UGE–10/18, 1986.

———. *Cachafaz*. Arles: Actes Sud, 1993.

———. *Una visita inoportuna*. Buenos Aires: TMGSM, 1993.

Cortázar, Julio. *Hopscotch*. Trans. Gregory Rabassa. New York: Random House, 1966.

———. *La vuelta al día en ochenta mundos*. 2 vols. Mexico: Siglo XXI, 1967.

———. *Blow-Up and Other Stories*. Trans. Paul Blackburn. New York: Collier, 1968.

———. *Ultimo Round*. 2 vols. Mexico: Siglo XXI, 1969.

———. "Respuesta." *Hispamérica* 2 (1972): 55–58.

———. *All Fires the Fire*. Trans. Suzanne Jill Levine. New York: Pantheon, 1973.

———. *62: A Model Kit*. Trans. Gregory Rabassa. New York: Avon, 1973.

———. *A Manual for Manuel*. Trans. Gregory Rabassa. New York: Pantheon, 1978.

———. "Novel Revolution." Trans. John Incledon. *Review* 24 (1979): 81–84.

———. *A Change of Light*. Trans. Gregory Rabassa. New York: Knopf, 1980.

———. "The Fellowship of Exile." Trans. John Incledon. *Review* 30 (1981): 14–16.

———. *We Love Glenda So Much*. Trans. Gregory Rabassa. New York: Knopf, 1983.

———. *Entretiens avec Omar Prego*. Trans. Françoise Rosset. Paris: Gallimard, 1986.

———. "The Death of Antonin Artaud." Trans. Alfred Mac Adam. *Review* 51 (1995): 40–41.

———. "Surrealism." Trans. Alfred Mac Adam. *Review* 51 (1995): 37–39.

———. *Unreasonable Hours*. Trans. Alberto Manguel. Toronto: Coach House, 1995.

Cozarinsky, Edgardo. *Vudú urbano*. Barcelona: Anagrama, 1985.

———. *Borges in/and/on Film*. Trans. Gloria Waldman and Ronald Christ. New York: Lumen, 1988.

———. *Urban Voodoo*. New York: Lumen, 1990.

———. *Boulevards du crépuscule*. Film script. Les Films d'Ici. 1992.

———. *La novia de Odessa*. Buenos Aires: Emecé, 2001.
———. *El pase del testigo*. Buenos Aires: Sudamericana, 2001.
Damonte, Jorge, ed. *Copi*. Paris: Bourgois, 1990.
Darío, Rubén. *Obras Completas*. 4 vols. Madrid: Afrodisio Aguado, 1950.
———. *Selected Poems*. Trans. Lysander Kemp. Austin: U of Texas P, 1965.
Dunlop, Carol, and Julio Cortázar. *Los autonautas de la cosmopista*. Mexico: Nueva Imagen, 1984.
Fuentes, Carlos. *Distant Relations*. Trans. Margaret Sayers Peden. New York: Farrar Strauss Giroux, 1982.
Futoransky, Luisa. *Lo regado por lo seco*. Buenos Aires: Noé, 1972.
———. *Partir, digo*. Valencia: Prometeo, 1982.
———. *Son cuentos chinos*. 1983. Buenos Aires: Planeta, 1991.
———. *De Pe a Pa*. Barcelona: Anagrama, 1986.
———. *La sanguina*. Barcelona: Taifa, 1987.
———. *Urracas*. Buenos Aires: Planeta, 1992.
———. *La parca, enfrente*. Buenos Aires: Tierra Firme, 1995.
———. *Lunas de miel*. Barcelona: Juventud, 1996.
———. *Cortezas y fulgores*. Albacete: Barcarola, 1997.
———. *The Duration of the Voyage: Selected Poems*. Trans. Jason Weiss. San Diego: Junction, 1997.
———. *De donde son las palabras*. Barcelona: Plaza & Janés, 1998.
González Bermejo, Ernesto. *Conversaciones con Cortázar*. Barcelona: Edhasa, 1978.
Guibert, Rita. *Seven Voices*. Trans. Frances Partridge. New York: Vintage, 1972.
Güiraldes, Ricardo. *Don Segundo Sombra*. Trans. Harriet de Onís. 1935. New York: Signet, 1966.
———. *Obras Completas*. Buenos Aires: Emecé, 1962.
Huidobro, Vicente. *The Selected Poetry of Vicente Huidobro*. Ed. David M. Guss. New York: New Directions, 1981.
Leenhardt, Jacques, and Pierre Kalfon. *Les Amériques latines en France*. Paris: Gallimard, 1992.
López Alvarez, Luis. *Conversaciones con Miguel Angel Asturias*. Madrid: Magisterio Español, 1974.
Manet, Eduardo. *The Nuns*. Trans. Robert Baldick. London: Calder and Boyars, 1970.
———. *Eux ou La prise du pouvoir*. Paris: Gallimard, 1971.
———. *Holocaustum ou le Borgne*. Paris: Gallimard, 1972.
———. *La Mauresque*. Paris: Gallimard, 1982.
———. *Zone interdite*. Paris: Gallimard, 1984.
———. *Un balcon sur les Andes; Mendoza, en Argentine . . . ; Ma'Déa*. Paris: Gallimard, 1985.
———. *L'île du lézard vert*. Paris: Flammarion, 1992.
———. *Habanera*. Paris: Flammarion, 1994.
———. *Monsieur Lovestar et son voisin de palier*. Arles: Actes Sud, 1995.
———. *Rhapsodie cubaine*. Paris: Grasset, 1996.
———. *D'amour et d'éxil*. Paris: Grasset, 1999.

———. *Song of the Errant Heart.* Trans. Robert Davies. Montreal: French Millennium Library, 2001.
———. *La sagesse du singe.* Paris: Grasset, 2001.
Mendoza, Plinio. *Años de fuga.* Barcelona: Plaza & Janes, 1979.
Ocampo, Victoria. *Testimonios.* 10 vols. Buenos Aires: Sur, 1941-78.
———. *El imperio insular.* Buenos Aires: Sur, 1982.
Parra, Teresa de la. *Mama Blanca's Memoirs.* Trans. Harriet de Onís. Pittsburgh: U of Pittsburgh P, 1993.
Paz, Octavio. *Libertad bajo palabra [1935–1957].* 1957. Madrid: Cátedra, 1990.
———. *The Labyrinth of Solitude.* Trans. Lysander Kemp. New York: Grove, 1961.
———. *Cuadrivio.* Mexico: Joaquín Mortiz, 1965.
———. *Puertas al campo.* Barcelona: Seix Barral, 1972.
———. *Itinerario.* Barcelona: Seix Barral, 1994.
Piglia, Ricardo, and Juan José Saer. *Diálogo.* Santa Fe: Universidad Nacional del Litoral, 1995.
Reyes, Alfonso. *Obras Completas.* Vol. 3. Mexico: FCE, 1956.
Reyes, Alfonso, and Victoria Ocampo. *Cartas echadas.* Mexico: UAM, 1983.
Reyes, Alfonso, and Pedro Henríquez Ureña. *Correspondencia.* Vol. 1. Mexico: FCE, 1986.
Ribeyro, Julio Ramón. *La palabra del mudo, I.* Lima: Milla Batres, 1973.
———. *Prosas apátridas.* 3rd ed. Barcelona: Tusquets, 1986.
———. *Silvio In The Rose Garden.* Trans. Maria Rosa Fort and Frank Graziano. Gettysburg: Logbridge-Rhodes, 1989.
———. *La Tentación del Fracaso, I: Diario Personal 1950–1960.* Lima: Campodónico, 1992.
———. *La Tentación del Fracaso, II: Diario Personal 1960–1974.* Lima: Campodónico, 1993.
———. *Marginal Voices.* Trans. Dianne Douglas. Austin: U of Texas P, 1993.
———. *Cuentos completos.* Madrid: Alfaguara, 1994.
Saer, Juan José. *Cicatrices.* 1969. Buenos Aires: Centro Editor de América Latina, 1983.
———. *El limonero real.* 1974. Buenos Aires: CEAL, 1983.
———. *La mayor.* 1976. Buenos Aires: CEAL, 1982.
———. *Une littérature sans qualités.* Cognac: Arcane 17, 1985.
———. *Juan José Saer.* Buenos Aires: Celtia, 1986.
———. *Glosa.* Barcelona: Destino, 1988.
———. *The Witness.* Trans. Margaret Jull Costa. London: Serpent's Tail, 1990.
———. *Nobody Nothing Never.* Trans. Helen Lane. New York: Serpent's Tail, 1993.
———. *Lo imborrable.* Buenos Aires: Alianza, 1993.
———. *La pesquisa.* Buenos Aires: Seix Barral, 1994.
———. *The Event.* Trans. Helen Lane. New York: Serpent's Tail, 1995.
———. *El concepto de ficción.* Buenos Aires: Ariel, 1997.
Sarduy, Severo. *Gestos.* Barcelona: Seix Barral, 1963.
———. *From Cuba with a Song.* Trans. Suzanne Jill Levine. 1972. Los Angeles: Sun & Moon, 1994.

———. *Barroco*. Buenos Aires: Sudamericana, 1974.
———. *Big Bang*. Barcelona: Tusquets, 1974.
———. *Para la voz*. Madrid: Fundamentos, 1978.
———. "Deterritorialization." Trans. Naomi Lindstrom. *The Review of Contemporary Fiction* 4.2 (1984): 104–109.
———. *Colibrí*. Bogata: Oveja Negra, 1985.
———. *Written on a Body*. Trans. Carol Maier. New York: Lumen, 1989.
———. *Cocuyo*. Barcelona: Tusquets, 1990.
———. *Pájaros de la playa*. Barcelona: Tusquets, 1993.
———. *Epitafios*. Miami: Universal, 1994.
———. *Cobra* and *Maitreya*. Trans. Suzanne Jill Levine. 1975, 1987. Normal: Dalkey Archive, 1995.
———. *Christ on the Rue Jacob*. Trans. Suzanne Jill Levine and Carol Maier. San Francisco: Mercury House, 1995.
———. "Exilado de sí mismo." *Cuadernos Hispanoamericanos* 563 (1997): 8–11.
Tchekhov, Anton, Benjamin Fleischmann, and Edgardo Cozarinsky. *Le violon de Rothschild*. Arles: Actes Sud, 1996.
Vallejo, César. *The Complete Posthumous Poetry*. Trans. Clayton Eshleman and José Rubia Barcia. Berkeley: U of California P, 1978.
———. *Obras completas*. 9 vols. Barcelona: Laia, 1976–79.
———. *Epistolario general*. Valencia, Spain: Pre-Textos, 1982.
———. *Desde Europa*. Lima: Fuente de Cultura Peruana, 1987.

Secondary Sources

Aira, César. *Copi*. Rosario: Viterbo, 1991.
Ayerza de Castilho, Laura, and Odile Felgine. *Victoria Ocampo*. Paris: Criterion, 1991.
Berriot, Karine. *Julio Cortázar, l'enchanteur*. Paris: Presses de la Renaissance, 1988.
Bloch-Morhange, Lise, and David Alper. *Artiste et métèque à Paris*. Paris: Buchet/Castel, 1980.
Coaguila, Jorge. *Ribeyro, la palabra inmortal*. Lima: Campodónico, 1995.
Costa, René de. *Vicente Huidobro: The Careers of a Poet*. Oxford: Oxford UP, 1984.
Cymerman, Claude, and Claude Fell, eds. *Histoire de la littérature hispano-américaine de 1940 à nos jours*. Paris: Nathan, 1997.
Deleuze, Gilles, and Félix Guattari, *Kafka: Toward a Minor Literature*. Trans. Dana Polan. Minneapolis: U of Minnesota P, 1986.
Donoso, José. *The Boom in Spanish American Literature: A Personal History*. Trans. Gregory Kolovakos. New York: Columbia UP, 1977.
Forgues, Roland. *Bajo el Puente Mirabeau corre el Rímac*. Grenoble: Edicious det Tignahus, 1987.
Franco, Jean. *The Modern Culture of Latin America*. Harmondsworth: Penguin, 1970.
González Echevarría, Roberto. *La ruta de Severo Sarduy*. Hanover: Ediciones del Norte, 1987.

———. *Alejo Carpentier: The Pilgrim at Home*. Austin: U of Texas P, 1990.
Henríquez Ureña, Pedro. *Literary Currents in Hispanic America*. Cambridge: Harvard UP, 1949.
Henríquez Ureña, Pedro, and Alfonso Reyes. *Epistolario íntimo*. Vol. 3. Santo Domingo: UNPHU, 1983.
Hiriart, Rosario, ed. *Cartas a Lydia Cabrera* (Correspondencia inédita de Gabriela Mistral y Teresa de la Parra). Madrid: Torremozas, 1988.
Hiriart, Rosario. *Lydia Cabrera: Vida hecha arte*. New York: Torres, 1978.
———. *Más cerca de Teresa de la Parra* (Diálogos con Lydia Cabrera). Caracas: Monte Avila, 1980.
Jones, Julie. *A Common Place: The Representation of Paris in Spanish American Fiction*. Lewisburg: Bucknell UP, 1998.
Kaplan, Alice. *French Lessons*. Chicago: U of Chicago P, 1993.
Larbaud, Valery, and Alfonso Reyes. *Correspondance, 1923–1952*. Ed. Paulette Patout. Paris: Marcel Didier, 1972.
Macé, Marie-Anne. *Severo Sarduy*. Paris: L'Harmattan, 1992.
Meyer, Doris. *Victoria Ocampo*. New York: Braziller, 1979.
Molloy, Sylvia. *La diffusion de la littérature hispano-américaine en France au XXe siècle*. Paris: PUF, 1972.
Patout, Paulette. *Alfonso Reyes et la France*. Paris: Klincksieck, 1978.
Rodó, José Enrique. *Ariel*. Trans. Margaret Sayers Peden. Austin: U of Texas P, 1988.
Sarmiento, Domingo F. *Facundo*. Trans. Mary Mann. 1868. New York: Penguin, 1998.
Sosnowski, Saúl. *La orilla inminente*. Buenos Aires: Legasa, 1987.
Szichman, Mario. "Entrevista: David Viñas." *Hispamérica* 1 (1972): 62–67.
Vasquez, Ana, and Ana Maria Araujo. *Exils latino-américains: La malédiction d'Ulysse*. Paris: L'Harmattan, 1988.
Viñas, David. *De Sarmiento a Cortázar*. Buenos Aires: Siglo Veinte, 1974.
Wahl, François. "La escritura a orillas del estanque." Trans. Blas Matamoro. *Cuadernos Hispanoamericanos* 563 (1997): 19-25.
Weiss, Jason. *Writing at Risk: Interviews in Paris with Uncommon Writers*. Iowa City: U of Iowa P, 1991.
Yurkievich, Saúl. *Julio Cortázar: al calor de tu sombra*. Buenos Aires: Legasa, 1987.
Zatlin, Phyllis. *The Novels and Plays of Eduardo Manet: An Adventure in Multiculturalism*. University Park: Pennsylvania State UP, 2000.
Zea, Leopoldo. *The Latin-American Mind*. Trans. James H. Abbott and Lowell Dunham. Norman: U of Oklahoma P, 1963.
———. *Latin America and the World*. Trans. Frances K. Hendricks and Beatrice Berler. Norman: U of Oklahoma P, 1969.

Index

Agence France Presse, 51, 137, 164, 253n2
Aira, César, 111, 113–16
Ainsa, Fernando, 252n11
Alberdi, Juan Bautista, 3–5
Altaforte, 127
Amado, Jorge, ix, 43
Apollinaire, Guillaume, 17, 21, 32–33, 62
Arguedas, José María, 43, 126
Arrabal, Fernando, 96, 109, 112
Artaud, Antonin, 40, 82, 107
Asturias, Miguel Angel, 10, 12, 24–25, 34–37, 43–46, 51, 68–70
   as ambassador to France, 68–69
   critique of the Boom writers, 69
   and Gabriel García Márquez, 68–69
   and Georges Raynaud, 35
   and Guatemala, 34–37, 68–69
   and indigenist perspective, 35–37, 69
   Leyendas de Guatemala, 24–25, 35, 37, 43, 69
   and Mayan culture, 35, 68–69
   and politics, 34–37, 68–69
   El Señor Presidente, 37

Bareiro Saguier, Rubén, 47, 56, 68, 182, 185, 261n8

Baron Supervielle, Silvia, 203–19
   Après le pas, 209–12
   on Argentine identity, 204
   on changing language, 205, 216
   L'eau étrangère, 207–9
   and "enigmatic language," 204–5
   La Frontière, 217–19
   Lectures du vent, 206–7
   Le Livre du retour, 214–17
   Nouvelles Cantates, 217
   L'or de l'incertitude, 212–14
   on Paris as catalyst, 204–5
   as "total exile," 204–5
   as translator, 217
Barthes, Roland, 97–98, 102, 106
Bataille, Georges, 38, 41, 60, 107
Beckett, Samuel, 42, 179, 192–93
Berriot, Karine, 88
Betz, Albrecht, 123
Bianciotti, Hector, 96, 205–6, 216, 221–33
   and the Académie Française, 224, 233
   El amor no es amado, 223–24, 230–31
   La busca del jardín, 221–23, 226–27, 230
   changing language, 223–24
   generative absence in, 227–29

and homosexuality, 227
and identity, questions of, 226–27
and life on the pampa, 221, 223, 229–32
as literary critic, 222, 225
Le Pas si lent de l'amour, 226–27, 233
as "public writer," 230
Sans la miséricorde du Christ, 224–26, 231–32
Seules les larmes seront comptés, 226, 232–33
and tension between languages, 222–24, 232
What the Night Tells the Day, 226–27, 230
and women characters, 229–32
and writing in French, 222, 224–25
Biblioteca Breve prize, 50, 125
bilingualism, 180, 182
Blin, Roger, 192–93
Boom in Spanish-American literature, the, 12, 50, 78, 99
Bordelois, Ivonne, 63
Borges, Jorge Luis, 19, 42–43, 51
Breton, André, 41, 59–60
Bryce Echenique, Alfredo, 54–57, 75, 77, 140
Huerto cerrado, 55–56
on orality and Peru, 55–56
and politics, 55–57
La vida exagerada de Martín Romaña, 56–57, 77
A World for Julius, 55

Cabrera, Lydia, 10, 23–26
Cuentos Negros, 23–26
and "discovery" of Cuba, 25
as painter, 23–25
on Paris, 25
Cabrera Infante, Guillermo, 43, 96, 180
Caillois, Roger, 11, 41–45, 60, 101, 125
La Croix du Sud collection, 42–44
in Latin America, 41–42
See also Ocampo
Calveyra, Arnaldo, 64, 181
Camus, Albert, 49, 51–52
See also Paz
Carpentier, Alejo, 10, 12, 35, 37–40, 43, 51, 59, 72–74

artistic collaborations, 39–40
and Cuban identity, 37–39
and Cuban music, 38
and Cuban Revolution, 72–74
Explosion in a Cathedral, 73–74
on literature and politics, 72–74
the "marvelous real," 38
radio work, 40, 241n58
Reasons of State, 74
and Robert Desnos, 37–40
Spanish Civil War, 40
changing languages, 13, 28, 32, 96, 117, 179–81
See also Manet; Baron Supervielle; Bianciotti
Cioran, E. M., 60, 179–80
Colección Archivos, 45–46
Collazos, Oscar, 91
Copi, 95–96, 108–20
as actor, 111, 250n68, 251n88
and Argentina, 109, 112, 116–19
Le bal des folles, 114–15
La Cité des Rats, 116
as cartoonist, 108–10
on death, 120
Eva Perón, 111–12
and exile, 108–12, 115–18
la Femme assise, 109–11, 250n59
gender confusions in, 112–13, 115, 118–19
La guerre des pédés, 118–19
and homosexuality, 112–15, 118–19
La Nuit de Madame Lucienne, 119–20
self-parody, 108, 114–15, 118–19
L'Uruguayen, 113–14
writing as provocation, 108, 111–15, 117–18
Cortázar, Julio, 43–44, 64, 81–93
and alternate systems of reality, 86–87, 89–93
and Argentine identity, 83, 88, 91
Los autonautas de la cosmopista, 93
and Buenos Aires, 81, 86
and Cuban Revolution, 91
and exile, 87, 93, 126
and the fantastic, 83–85, 87–88, 90
Hopscotch, 77, 82–83, 85, 88–89, 92

humanistic concerns, 82–83, 85–90, 92–93
and jazz, 85, 89
A Manual for Manuel, 91–93, 102
on Paris as catalyst, 82–84, 89, 92
and permeability, 89–90
political concerns, 83, 85, 87–88, 90–92
62: A Model Kit, 89–92
and surrealism, 82–83, 93
as translator, 82–83, 90
Couffon, Claude, 125, 253n14
Cozarinsky, Edgardo, 183–90, 197
on Borges, 188
and dangers of nostalgia, 184–86
and film, 183, 188–90
Rothschild's Violin, 189–90
Sunset Boulevards, 189
Urban Voodoo, 184–88
La Croix du Sud collection, 11, 99
See also Caillois
Cuadernos, 64, 243n18
Cuban Revolution, 12, 52, 71, 96–97, 124–25, 247n4
See also Carpentier; Cortázar; Manet

Darío, Rubén, 8–9, 15–18, 22
disappointments with Paris, 16–17
enthusiasm for Paris, 15–16
and *Mundial Magazine*, 17
Debray, Régis, 77, 92
Deleuze, Gilles, and Félix Guattari, 177
Delgado, Washington, 140
Desnos, Robert, 35, 59
See also Carpentier
distance and creative freedom, 53, 60, 141, 151
Donoso, José, 2, 78, 99
Drieu La Rochelle, Pierre, 27–28
Dujovne Ortiz, Alicia, 181–82, 225

Echeverría, Esteban, 3, 7
Edwards, Jorge, 67, 70–71, 247n1
Espinosa, Elia, 166
exile
and community, 121–22, 177–79, 181
and cultural displacement, 184, 186–89

identity in, 56–57, 122–24
and Spanish-American literature, 2, 11–12, 124–27
See also Cortázar; Sarduy; Copi; Saer; Futoransky; Baron Supervielle
explorers' narratives, 93, 113–14, 157–58, 212–14

Fell, Claude, 43–44
Fernández Retamar, Roberto, 4, 91, 247n4
Ferreira, César, 56
Forgues, Roland, 126
Fossey, Jean-Michel, 97, 99
Frank, Waldo, 28, 36
French Revolution, influence on Latin America, 1, 73–74
Freund, Gisèle, 27, 29
Fuentes, Carlos, 44, 51, 67, 70, 78, 180, 237n6, 238n15
Futoransky, Luisa, 163–76
and the "absent language," 169, 172
and Buenos Aires, 168
De Pe a Pa, 170–72
exile, theme of, 165–68, 170–73, 175–76
and Jewish experience, 164, 175–76
and opera, 163, 68
Partir, digo, 165–66
La sanguina, 172–73
Son cuentos chinos, 166–68
Urracas, 173–75

Gallimard (publisher), 11, 26, 42–44, 99, 222, 225
García Calderón, Ventura, 8–9, 17, 21, 24
García Márquez, Gabriel, 47–50, 54, 78
art and politics, 48–50
and Ernest Hemingway, 49
and Julio Cortázar, 49
No One Writes to the Colonel, 48–49
One Hundred Years of Solitude, 48, 71, 99
See also Asturias
Garro, Elena, 61
Gilard, Jacques, 49–50
Godard, Colette, 116
Gombrowicz, Witold, 105, 122, 225, 249–50n56

Gómez Carrillo, Enrique, 8–9, 11, 15, 17, 21
González Echevarría, Roberto, 73–74, 96–98, 102, 105, 247n4
Gramuglio, María Teresa, 154
Gris, Juan, 10, 30, 32–33
Güiraldes, Ricardo, 10, 18–20, 28
   Don Segundo Sombra, 19–20, 43
   and Valery Larbaud, 18–20

Hanrahan, Kip, 185–86
Harss, Luis, and Barbara Dohmann, 2, 43
Hemingway, Ernest, 54–56, 76;
   See also García Márquez
Henríquez Ureña, Pedro, 7–8, 20
Higgins, James, 142–43
Huidobro, Vicente, 10, 30, 32–35, 59
   Altazor, 34
   and Creationism, 32–33
   and film, 33–34
   interdisciplinary collaborations, 32–33
   and politics, 33–34

Institut des Hautes Etudes de l'Amérique Latine, 45
International Congress of Antifascist Writers (also, International Congress of Writers in Defense of Culture), 32, 40, 59
Ireland, Doug, 227

Jabès, Edmond, 178–79
James, Henry, 56, 75, 184

Kaplan, Alice, 225
Kennedy, J. Gerald, 122
Keyserling, Count Hermann, 27–28
Kirkpatrick, Gwen, 9
Krauze, Ethel, 258n2

Lamming, George, 4, 100
language and foreignness, 169–72, 186, 205, 216
Larbaud, Valery, 10–11, 21–22, 41
   See also Güiraldes
Larreta, Enrique, 8–9, 21
Lautréamont, comte de (Isidore Ducasse), 6, 82, 86

Lavelli, Jorge, 109
Les Lettres Nouvelles, 64, 205
Levine, Suzanne Jill, 104
Libre, 78
La Licorne, 42
Lugones, Leopoldo, 9, 20–21

Maison de l'Amérique Latine, 45
Manet, Eduardo, 96, 125, 191–203
   Un balcon sur les Andes, 195–96
   and Cuban Revolution, 192–93, 202–3
   and cultural context, 193, 195–97
   as cultural intermediary, 198, 201
   Habanera, 201–2
   L'île du lézard vert, 200–1
   and Jewish identity, 198, 201
   Lady Strass, 194–95
   La Mauresque, 198–99
   Monsieur Lovestar et son voisin de palier, 197
   The Nuns, 192–94
   Rhapsodie cubaine, 202–3
   theatre and revolution, 192–96
   on writing in French, 191–93, 197–98
   Zone interdite, 199–200
Martin, Gerald, 52
Masiello, Francine, 168–69
Mendoza, Plinio Apuleyo, 48–50, 78–79
   Años de fuga, 78–79
mestizaje, 2–3, 5, 36–37, 39, 200, 203
Michaux, Henri, 20, 60–61, 166
Miomandre, Francis de, 19, 22, 24–26, 41
Mistral, Gabriela, 10, 29, 42
Mizón, Luis, 125, 253n14
modernismo, 7–9
Molloy, Sylvia, 9, 19, 43, 45
Monnier, Adrienne, 19, 21–22, 27
Moro, César, 51, 180–81
Morvan, Annie, 44
Mundo nuevo, 78, 98, 247n4

Nadeau, Maurice, 64, 124, 205, 222
Neruda, Pablo, 42, 59, 69–72, 253n16
   as ambassador to France, 70–72
   cancer, 70, 72
   and Chilean politics, 70–71
   and Cuba, 71
   and Spanish Civil War, 70

Ngūg- wa Thiong'o, 178
Noailles, Anna de, 9, 28
Nobel prize, 10, 33, 43, 68, 71
Nord-Sud, 10, 32–33
nostalgia, and imagination, 25, 53, 73, 105, 184–86, 223
nouveau roman, 100, 150, 226
Nouvelle Revue Française, 19, 42, 64

Ocampo, Victoria, 10, 26–29
  and Argentine critics, 28
  on belonging to America, 28
  and Roger Caillois, 28–29, 41–42
  and *Sur*, 27–28
Ortega, Julio, 140, 180–81
Ortega y Gasset, José, 27–28

Padilla, Heberto, 71, 99
Palma, Milagros, 125–26
Paris
  as catalyst, 50, 63–64; *See also* Cortázar; Baron Supervielle
  and exiled writers, 121–27;
  as myth, 6, 47, 56–57, 75–77, 126–27;
  North American writers in, 75–76, 122–23;
  as refuge, 77–79, 123–24;
  as return voyage, 3, 164, 213–14, 223, 232
Parra, Teresa de la, 10, 23–26
  and Caracas, 23–24
  Ifigenia, 23–24
  Mama Blanca's Memoirs, 23–24
  in sanatorium, 25–26
Paz, Octavio, 17, 21, 42, 59–64, 224
  and Albert Camus, 60, 242n1
  and break with the left, 61
  The Labyrinth of Solitude, 60–62
  Libertad bajo palabra, 60–62
  on the Marquis de Sade, 61–62
  on Mexico, 60–61
  Salamandra, 62, 64
  on Sor Juana Inés de la Cruz, 61
  and surrealists, 59–61
Picasso, Pablo, 30, 33, 40
Picon Garfield, Evelyn, 82
Pigafetta, Antonio, 212–14
Piglia, Ricardo, 78, 150, 152

Pillement, Georges, 37, 41
Pizarnik, Alejandra, 62–65, 86
Arbol de Diana, 64
Poe, Edgar Allan, 82–83
Prensa Latina, 36–38
Prévert, Jacques, 38, 40, 241n58
Prix Médicis, 102, 264n7

ramassage, 48, 76, 138
Raynaud, Georges, *see* Asturias
Reisz, Susana, 140
Reverdy, Pierre, 10, 32–33
Reyes, Alfonso, 10, 20–23
  and Marcel Proust, 22, 239n23
Ribeyro, Julio Ramón, 6, 43–44, 52, 56, 68, 75, 137–49
  Los cautivos, 145–46
  on encounter with Europe, 145–46, 148
  Los gallinazos sin plumas, 140–41
  and Lima, 137, 141, 146–48
  and the margins, 137–40, 142
  and Paris, 137–42, 149;
  and Peru, 138, 148–49
  on race relations, 142–43
  Relatos santacrucinos, 147–48
  theme of displacements, 143–45
Rodó, José Enrique, 4, 17
Rodríguez Monegal, Emir, 78, 86, 103
Rodríguez Padrón, Jorge, 173
Rojas, Armando, 126–27
romanticism, 7
Rosenbaum, Jonathan, 183
Rousset, David, 61

Sábato, Ernesto, 43, 47
Saer, Juan José, 149–62
  and circular narratives, 151, 156–57, 159–60
  The Event, 158–59
  exile, narratives of, 157–59, 161–62
  fiction, concept of, 155–56
  Glosa, 159–60
  Lo imborrable, 160–61
  El limonero real, 152–53
  La mayor, 151, 153–54
  and memory, nature of, 151, 153–54, 157–58, 160–61
  narratives as ensemble, 154–55

Nobody Nothing Never, 156–57
La pesquisa, 161–62
political resonances, 156–57, 160–61
Santa Fe as mythical locus, 149–51, 155
The Witness, 157–58
Salazar Bondy, Sebastián, 53, 76–77
   Pobre gente de París, 76–77
Santí, Enrico Mario, 60–61
Sarabia, Rosa, 169
Sarduy, Severo, 78, 95–108, 216–17
   as art critic, 95–98
   and the baroque, 98, 103
   and the body, 97–98, 106–7
   Cobra, 99, 102–5
   Cocuyo, 106–7
   Colibrí, 105
   and Cuban identity, 97–99, 101
   on death, 106–8
   and exile, 95–96, 104–6
   From Cuba with a Song, 97, 99, 101–2
   Gestos, 97, 99–100
   Maitreya, 104–5
   Pájaros de la playa, 97, 107
   representations of Cuba in, 99–101, 104–6
   and signifying absence, 96, 98, 102, 104, 106
   and surface of text, 95, 97–98, 103
   transvestism in writing, 97, 101, 103–4
   writing as disruption, 97, 99, 101–3, 105
Sarmiento, Domingo F., 3
Sartre, Jean-Paul, 51–52, 60–61
Scorza, Manuel, 126
Le Seuil (publisher), 45, 99
Spain, rejection of, 1, 3
Spanish Civil War, 34
   See also Vallejo; Carpentier; Neruda
Stern, Mirta, 152, 256n59
Sucre, Guillermo, 173
Supervielle, Jules, 6, 20–22, 28–29, 204
Sur, 42, 61
   See also Ocampo
surrealists, 10, 38, 41
   See also Paz

Tambascio, Gustavo, 119
Tejera, Nivaria, 96, 124–25, 181, 225

Tel Quel, 97–99, 101, 105
Tzara, Tristan, 33, 35

UNESCO, 42, 45, 61, 68, 83, 139

Valéry, Paul, 21, 27, 41
Vallejo, César, 10, 12, 29–32, 35, 40, 59
   on art and politics, 31–32
   defense of Latin American cultures, 29, 31
   on Paris, 30–31
   Spanish Civil War, 32, 40
   on theater, 29–30
Varèse, Edgar, 33, 39
Vargas Llosa, Mario, 43–44, 50–55
   and Cuba, 52
   The Green House, 52
   and Julio Cortázar, 51
   on Paris, 53–54
   and Peru, 52–53
   on politics, 52–53
   The Time of the Hero, 50–52
Vásquez, Ana and Ana María Araujo, 124, 252n10, 257n72
Vázquez Villanueva, Graciana, 229
Verlaine, Paul, 15
Villegas, Jean-Claude, 44
Viñas, David
   on journey to Paris, 5–6
   critique of Cortázar, 92

Wahl, François, 97, 107
Williamson, Edwin, 73
Wilson, Jason, 61
writers as diplomats, 8–9, 15–17, 20–23, 59–62, 67–73, 139

Yurkievich, Saúl, 88–89

Zaldumbide, Gonzalo, 22, 24
Zatlin, Phyllis, 192, 194–95
Zea, Leopoldo, 5

Printed in Great Britain
by Amazon